C000145978

SLACK W.

Another Fishy Tale

Dedication

This book is dedicated to my family. Without the love and support of my wife, Dorothy and my parents Fred and Doris Normandale, not only would this book not have been written, the events recorded within would never have happened.

Psalm 107
V 23-24

They that go down to the sea in ships, that do business in great waters;
These shall see the works of the Lord and his wonders in the deep.

SLACK WATER

Another Fishy Tale

FRED NORMANDALE

ALSO BY THE SAME AUTHOR
FIRST OF THE FLOOD

Bottom End Publishing
Scarborough
PO Box 318

© Fred Normandale 2004

First published November 2004

All rights reserved. Reproduction of this book by photocopying or electronic means for non-commercial purposes is permitted. Otherwise, no part of this book may be reproduced, adapted, stored in a retrieval system or transmitted by any means, electronic, mechanical, photocopying, or otherwise without the prior written permission of Bottom End Publishing.

ISBN 0 9543686 1 4

Cover design by Barry Perks Design

Cover photographs (left to right): Bill 'Jitta' Sheader, Frank 'Rusty' Drydale, Bill Messruther, Tom Rowley Snr, Tom 'Denk' Mainprize, Colin 'Dilt' Jenkinson, Fred Normandale Snr, Bob Walker.

Prepared and printed by:
York Publishing Services Ltd
64 Hallfield Road
Layerthorpe
York YO31 7ZQ
Tel: 01904 431213; Website: www.yps-publishing.co.uk

CONTENTS

THANKS

Special thanks to my sister Jan Palmer for her dedication in proof reading, for her continuous attention to detail and helpful advice. Thanks also to my sisters Susan Wood and Christine Rhodes, Nancy Hines, Ian Forbes, Caroline Chapman, Gudrun Mode and Jilly Manser for their valuable reading and observations. To my Mum and Dad, Fred and Doris Normandale, Bill Messruther, Major Clark, Bob Walker, Colin 'Dilt' Jenkinson, Frank 'Rusty' Drydale, Brian Nicholson, Bobby Allen, Arthur Godfrey and Neil Mundy for their memories.

York Publishing Services have again maintained their very high standard in producing this book. Thanks to all at this Company for their friendly manner and professional attitude.

Author's Notes

The sea has always been a hard taskmaster. Men fought the hostile elements to catch fish long before Jesus took five fishermen to be disciples. In going to sea, there was an opportunity of wealth, not available to landsmen. Masters and crew, by risking their lives against the hostile elements, could reap great rewards from the bountiful ocean. With the advance of technology, the threat to mariners was greatly reduced, though by no means eradicated.

Sadly, the rewards from fishing now, seldom justify the hardship undertaken. Politicians must take a great deal of responsibility for the present dire state of the remaining UK industry.

This book relates to a time before enforced, unnecessary restrictions ruined this once wonderful, vibrant way of life. Men with tenacity and determination were able to reap a rich harvest by challenging the sea, though always respecting its power. They too were respected.

My earliest memories are of boats and of the wonderful characters around Scarborough's 'Old Town', known locally as the 'Bottom End'. The folk of this close-knit community lived a hand to mouth existence that was often made worse during winter months by prolonged bad weather. But what these people lacked in silver was more than compensated for by a quality of life that was unique and in which everyone had a place. The menfolk could find humour in the most trying of circumstances and were seldom lost for a cheery comment.

As a boy my playground was the beach, rocks, harbour, piers and the many different boats. My Dad and several uncles were fishermen and even before my teens I was able to sail on their boats for pleasure and frequently helped to land catches on their return from sea.

In the winter, when older, I gathered limpets from the rocks to help bait the miles of line the fishermen shot daily, or assisted with baiting the second batch of lines, prepared on shore while the boat was at sea. Even at this early age my burning desire was to be skipper of a fishing boat, though Dad wanted me to go to sea in the Merchant Navy.

On leaving school I joined the Merchant Navy, crossing the Atlantic to Canada, sailing to the Baltic, the Mediterranean, through the Suez Canal and visiting several ports in East and West Africa, before leaving to pursue my fishing ambition.

I'd been a crewman on several fishing boats, met and married Dotty and we had two lovely children, Paula and Danny. Now aged twenty-three, I'd left a safe, well-paid deck hand's job and in possession of a newly acquired skipper's (limited) certificate, had chartered the fishing vessel, *Pioneer* from its Grimsby owners. Now at last I was a skipper, but if I thought my troubles were over, I was wrong, they were just beginning.

MAP OF THE EAST COAST OF ENGLAND AND SCOTLAND

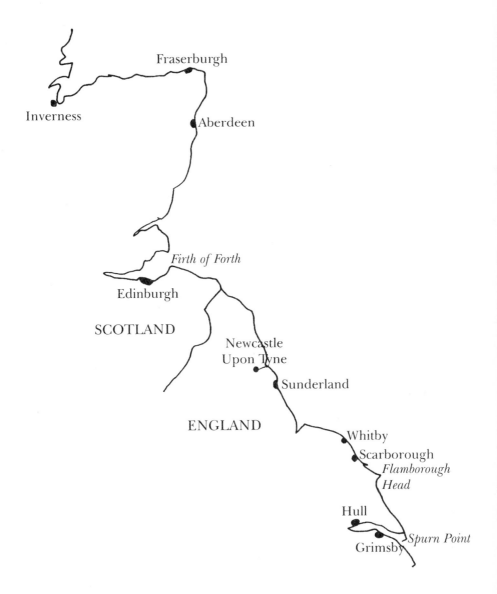

Fraserburgh

Inverness

Aberdeen

Firth of Forth

Edinburgh

SCOTLAND

Newcastle
Upon Tyne

Sunderland

ENGLAND

Whitby

Scarborough
*Flamborough
Head*

Hull

Spurn Point

Grimsby

CHAPTER 1

THE PIONEER

The *Pioneer* was berthed at the fish market and was the only vessel in port. A group of old men were standing on the quayside looking down at my new acquisition. Though I couldn't hear their conversation, I knew my vessel was the subject of scrutiny as various aspects of her were being studied and pointed at. Painted blue, she was fifty-four feet in length, had a six-cylinder, 180 horsepower 'Kelvin' engine and had recently been fitted out for trawling. A week earlier I'd brought the vessel to Scarborough from Grimsby, with the assistance of my Uncle Francis, universally known as 'Rusty', due to his hair colour. Two more crew had been enlisted and we were rigging the fishing gear in preparation for our first trip to sea. The trawl net, wires and other gear were strewn around the deck but were now taking some semblance of order.

The two other crewmembers, Raymond and Barney, though both fishermen, had been unemployed for some time. Raymond was a good hand at sea when he was sober, but was unreliable in port and occasionally needed calling in the early hours for sailing. Barney was an unknown quantity. He hadn't fished from Scarborough before, though he'd done many three-week voyages in the large trawlers from Hull. This was a tough life; fishing in extreme weather and in winter months, perpetual darkness.

On one of his trips to Icelandic waters, a huge wave had swamped the deck as the crew were shooting the trawl. Most of the men managed to hang on and survived with a wetting, but

Barney was thrown against the winch, breaking both legs. The crew, reluctant to move him, shouted to the skipper on the bridge, asking for advice. "Throw 'im behind the winch till we get the fuckin' net down," came back the reply.

On several occasions on board these deep sea vessels, men have been washed over the side by one wave, to be miraculously hurled back onto the ship by the next. It was a tough life indeed. I wondered how the contrast of inshore fishing would suit Barney.

By late afternoon we'd got our fishing gear assembled and ready to shoot, had taken on a hundred and fifty empty boxes, two tons of ice, eight hundred gallons of fuel and food for four days. We were fully ready for sea. I'd consulted the tide book, making sure there'd be plenty of water in the harbour before asking the crew to turn up at midnight. I went home pleased with the preparations and eagerly looking forward to getting to sea.

There were a few things on the boat I wasn't too happy with. The winch was a big, ungainly piece of machinery with a badly designed clutch and brake system, which clearly didn't work well. Also the deck bollards were not fixed to the deck solidly but were hinged on swivels. Only the base plate was bolted through the deck. The bollards would bang on the deck each time the net was hauled and would soon damage the deck planks. While these were important details, I felt it was essential that I caught some fish, to prove to the owners their faith in me was justified. Then maybe they'd consider some modifications.

As I walked from the pier I encountered a group of coblemen in deep discussion. Ernie 'Soapy' Williamson and Dickie Elliott from the coble *Who Cares* were grinning inanely to the displeasure of the *Constance's* crew, Bill Sheader and Bill Cammish.

I heard Ernie, a small, wiry man wearing an old, army battledress jacket say, "do yer want us t' give yer a hand," then added, "like we did last week." He and Dick laughed loudly.

I was intrigued and hovered close by to see what latest mischief this pair of comedians had been up to. The two men seldom took life seriously, hence the name of their boat.

It was as if a light had been turned on. 'Filey Bill' Cammish's eyes flashed and he said, "it was you two buggers, you've been playin' tricks on us, yer rotten sods," but then he laughed too.

"We'll shift that fleet tomorro'," said Bill Sheader, now also grinning, then he and his shipmate headed towards their boat, both talking at the same time.

Unable to contain my curiosity, I asked the remaining pair what they'd been up to. It appeared Ernie had bought a rubber, ghoulish hand, dripping with blood from the nearby joke shop. Having milked every ounce of humour from the prop, such as hanging the claw from his open zip, concealing it up his sleeve when buying tea in the tea-shack, he'd picked his nose, scratched his head with it and finally run out of ideas.

The rubber hand had been on board *Who Cares* when the two were hauling their pots the previous week. As Dick and Ernie tended their gear, they pulled up some pots belonging to the *Constance,* which had been accidentally shot over the top of their own. Before cutting their hauling line, allowing the offending gear to fall free so they could rejoin their rope, Ernie threw the hand into one of the other vessel's pots. It transpired that on the following day when this pot appeared at the *Constance's* side, 'Filey Bill', horrified at the sight, had insisted the fleet of pots was allowed to run back overboard.

On subsequent days, both Dick and Ernie found reason to ask both Bills in turn, "'ave yer hauled them pots near Scalby Ness yet?"

"Did yer get owt from them pots at Scalby Ness?"

Each time they were asked, the *Constance's* men would find a reason not to have hauled the gear containing the hand. Their replies were either, "we went to our off-shore gear," "we were runnin' short o' bait" or "we didn't have time."

I'd just witnessed the punch line, when the joke was revealed to the victims.

Dick and Ernie were two of the friendliest, likeable men around the harbour and they'd worked together for many years. They had a wonderful understanding of each other. They never argued but worked to each other's strengths.

Dick, a round-faced, bushy-haired man with eyebrows to match, had a strange bowel problem. If he had to go, he was given little notice and had a short span of control. Even if they were hauling pots or lines, Dick would say, "Ernie, I 'ave t' go!" Regardless of the weather, his oilskin top would come off, his waterproof trousers were round his ankles, followed by those underneath and he'd quickly have his bum over the lee side of the coble. Ernie would take the tiller and keep *Who Cares* in position to the wind and tide, while laughing at, and berating his buddy for his appalling timing.

When the occasion demanded, Dick could be serious. He had a great sense of the history of his wonderful old port and looked upon it as a legacy his generation would leave to the next. He'd often say, "I 'ope you young uns are gonna look after this 'arbour when us lot are gone." Profoundly he'd say, "we owe it to our sons an' successors t' leave this 'arbour, if not as good, then better than we in'erited it."

I was on board at a quarter to midnight with the engine running and lights lit, ready for sea. Rusty, carrying a small bag with a few clean clothes and a supply of baccy, arrived not long after. At midnight Barney arrived but it was ten past the hour before Raymond, bag in hand, staggered along the pier, clearly the worse for drink. He passed his bag to Rusty then descended the ladders to the boat with difficulty. As he reclaimed his carrier I clearly heard the clink of bottles. He wobbled his way aft to where I was standing. "Shorry ahm late shkipper, shlept in, but ah'll tek t' firsht watch t' make up for it."

I shuddered at the thought of Raymond with a supply of drink, in command of the boat while we slept below. "Go an' get turned in, I'll tek t' first watch, an' I'll tek care o' that for yer as well." I took the bag from his reluctant hands and he made his way aft to the cabin muttering that he wasn't as think as we drunk he was. I looked in the container to see six bottles of beer and a half bottle of rum. I dropped them in the harbour and made my way to the wheelhouse.

Entering the galley at the stern, passing the gas stove and small sink, I stepped up into the compact wheelhouse. The 'Decca Navigator' dials had stopped spinning and were now locked on to the signals from the shore based transmitters. The navigator's central clock was flashing a sequence of red, green and purple. Each of these colours related to lines on a chart. Our position at sea could be updated constantly by comparing the clock readings with the chart.

I called, "OK, chuck 'er off," to old George 'Puddin' Appleby, the hovering pierman, then as an afterthought, "thank yer Georgy." He released our head and stern ropes in turn, holding them high until the slack was taken in so the lines didn't get wet in the harbour. The ropes were coiled and stowed by my available crew.

Old George was coming up for retirement from his job with the Council, who operated port, but at almost sixty-five, he'd already started a new job as assistant to Johnny Clark, the harbour shipwright. George was known as Scarborough's oldest apprentice.

Still not fully confident of my charge, I carefully guided the *Pioneer* through the harbour mouth. Listening to the VHF radio, I was aware of other boats fishing and assessed them to be ten to fifteen miles to the north-east, so headed in that direction. The boat steered quite easily, assisted by two short rope strops, one each side of the wheel, which some previous helmsman had thoughtfully spliced. An eye in each, looped over the top spoke, held the helm steady. Minor adjustments to the course could be made, a spoke or two at a time by re-locating the strops, without having to constantly hold the wheel.

I'd reckoned that if we fished close to other vessels, I'd be able to assess how our gear was performing by comparing our catches with theirs, though not all skippers told the truth. It was also useful to compare the catches that boats landed with the hauls they'd reported. Some skippers exaggerated the size of their catches, others under-estimated.

An hour and a half's steaming brought us to a flat, rocky area where several boats could be seen fishing. Clouds of gulls, wheeling round two of them in the loom of the deck lights meant their crews were gutting a recent haul of fish. These birds never slept.

Even on the darkest night they could find the boats that were hauling their nets. I eased the throttle to neutral then gave a quick burst astern to take the way off the vessel. She was soon lying broadside to a gentle swell. A few minutes later Rusty and Barney arrived on deck to shoot the gear. Raymond could remain in his bunk until hauling time. I was annoyed with him for arriving drunk but he'd be sober soon and I'd have a crew of four. If I'd turned him away there would only have been three of us. It wasn't satisfactory but was another problem to address later.

Using the ungainly winch, which Barney had named 'Billy Smart' due to its comic performance, we lifted the heavy trawl doors outboard, suspending them from the gallows ready for deploying. The gallows, six-feet high, steel frames, one for'ard and one aft, allowed the wires to run overboard, clear of the boat's side. It was soon clear that Barney was unsure of what was expected of him, as he required constant instruction. Despite this, the cone-shaped net, its bottom part fastened to a necklace of iron and rubber ground rollers, or 'bobbins', was soon over the starboard side, ready for lowering. I returned to the wheelhouse, re-engaged the engine and with the wheel to starboard shouted, "pay away steady," through the dropped window to the men standing behind the contraption for'ard.

The *Pioneer* began to move in a tight clockwise circle but as soon as the net cleared the propeller I allowed the wheel to spin back to midships, though the weight of the gear still pulled our craft to starboard. The circle increased in diameter as the wire bridles attached to the top and bottom of the trawl, snaked across the deck. The swivel-mounted bollards were lifting and dropping on the deck as the brakes were applied to control the flow of cable. When the bridles were outboard and brakes applied, I eased the engine to dead slow and dashed out to the after gallow, shackling the trawl door to the wires. This would have been Raymond's job but I would do it for now.

Back in the wheelhouse, still turning to starboard and almost on course, I shouted "leggo" to the lads for'ard who released their brakes, allowing the matching steel doors to drop into the sea. As they sank, the doors quickly parted, acting as underwater kites, spreading the trawl. "Stop 'em at ninety," I yelled to the men at the winch as they paid out the shiny new wire warps. A ratio of approximately three to one was the benchmark and the depth was twenty-eight fathoms according to the echo sounder.

The wires, marked at ten-fathom intervals, continued to run out. Rusty kept a close eye on Barney as each held tension on the brakes, controlling the rate. As the required marks reached the stern, the brakes, now smoking with the friction, were applied. The two wires were drawn together making an angle of about thirty degrees at the stern of the boat, giving me manoeuvrability while towing the net. Now we were trawling I could concentrate on my fishing chart. There were several wrecks in the area, to be avoided at all costs.

Rusty passed me a welcome pot of coffee from the galley through the wheelhouse door then began to prepare breakfast. The smell of frying bacon and eggs wafting from the stove was wonderful. In no time at all a delicious fry-up was passed to me. The feast was devoured in less time than it had taken to cook, as I sat perched on an upturned fish box, my feet on the steering wheel, the plate on my knees. This was another temporary arrangement. When I was more confident I'd go below for meals, leaving someone else to steer. The other two men ate their breakfast leisurely at the cabin table below, close to where the still-unconscious Raymond lay snoring. On completion of the meal Rusty suggested to his shipmate that as he'd cooked the breakfast, Barney should do the washing up.

Minutes later, I looked out of the wheelhouse window to see Barney lowering a basket containing plates, mugs, pans and cutlery over the side with the intention of dragging them alongside until they were clean. "Don't do that," I called out in frustration, "you'll smash 'em or lose 'em."

He looked up to the window at my call, then scratched his head. "'Ow can I wash 'em then? Can yer put t' 'osepipe on fo' me?"

Rolling my eyes, not believing what I was hearing I said, "why don't yer use t' washing up bowl and some detergent?" It was as if I'd invented this method of cleaning. His eyes lit up at the suggestion. Untying the basket, he carried it into the galley. What had I let myself in for? It was going to be Rusty and me against the world. Ten minutes later the galley was quiet. Barney had washed the cutlery, drying it with a dubious looking cloth. He'd then stowed the frying pan, still thick with grease in the locker under the sink, before retreating to his bunk. Below he found Rusty lying in the berth on the opposite side of the cabin, reading.

I sat on the upturned box, surveying my surroundings, enjoying the first quiet moment I'd had since I'd brought the *Pioneer* to Scarborough. Had I done the right thing? Had I let my ambition overrule commonsense? I'd left one of the best jobs in the fleet, a position that was filled within an hour of my quitting, to be my own boss. Only time would tell.

We trawled for three and a half hours, pulling the net along the rocky seabed, occasionally altering course to avoid charted obstructions or other vessels. Early action was required when steering, as the drag from the trawl more than two hundred yards behind, severely hampered the manoeuvrability of the boat.

Daylight was heralded with a beautiful, gentle lightening of the sky to the east, which grew from a dark blue to green then glowing orange, long before the sun appeared. This was nature at her best and for the first time in ages I felt quite at peace with the world and quietly confident. It was impossible to be pessimistic in such surroundings. At the end of the trawl, with the strops on the wheel, I dropped into the galley, setting light to the gas under the already filled kettle. I was determined from the start to allow my crew a cup of tea or coffee, to ensure they were properly awake before going on deck to start work. Only if the trawl snagged an obstruction were all hands required on deck quickly. I could too clearly recall my time years earlier with skipper Tom Pashby in the *Whitby Rose*. He would shout, " 'aulin' time," down the cabin hatch and we were expected to be on deck within minutes, oilskin-clad, ready to haul the fishing gear. We'd be half asleep still when working the winch and handling heavy equipment. I was determined to avoid this dangerous practice if at all possible.

As soon as the kettle had a head of steam I descended into the darkened cabin to call the crew. Switching on the light I shouted, "away now me lucky lads, lets 'ave yer out, it's 'aulin' time. Show a leg."

The three men rolled from their bunks in various states of awareness. Raymond, bleary-eyed and hungover, was trying to find his jersey and smock but couldn't remember where he'd dropped them. They were discovered under the cabin table. Barney, after scratching his nether regions, a vacant expression on his face, was putting his seaboots on the wrong feet. Rusty, quiet but awake, sat on the seat locker with his baccy tin, rolling a cigarette. Normally I'd call out, then leave the cabin, but on this occasion I asked their preference of beverage. In future I'd make the drinks before calling out. Half an hour later the three men, at least awake, arrived on deck ready to haul the gear.

Rusty and Raymond made their way for'ard to the winch, leaving Barney at the stern to release the chain securing the wires. When funds allowed I would ask the owners to provide a towing post. This would make the vessel much easier to manoeuvre when trawling. I eased the engine throttle back and Rusty engaged the winch drive. The machine was propelled by a long, rotating shaft from the front of the engine, leading under the fishroom floor to a flywheel in the foremost compartment of the boat. A broad rubber drive belt connected the wheel to the winch on deck.

Barney released the chain and the winch began to heave, recovering the dripping, shiny wires, which were already losing their lustre after a four-hour immersion in salt water. We encountered quite a problem when the heavy steel boards broke the surface. Each time they were hauled to deck level and the winch unclutched, the boards dropped back into the water. The lever operating the winch, clearly a prototype, moved from clutch drive through neutral to brake. In neutral, the wires holding the weight of the gear were unrestrained and ran out again until the brake was applied.

We finally realised the boards had to be secured with a chain to prevent them from slipping back before the winch was unclutched. It was a dangerous practice passing a chain through the board's towing bracket while it was still under tension, but there was no alternative. 'Billy Smart' had a design flaw. *Pioneer* had been lying broadside to the wind for at least twenty minutes when eventually the wing ends of the trawl appeared at the boat's side. These didn't slip back too far as there was less strain on the winch now. I was on the deck assisting with the gear handling at this point, for, with the boat stopped in the water, I was no longer required in the wheelhouse.

Gulls were wheeling, screaming and diving into the water where the net was expected to emerge. They had more faith than me. I thought we must have lost most of the fish while messing about with the boards. Suddenly the codends rose to the surface, the fish floating due to the expanded gas in their bellies. It looked a reasonable haul. Rusty and I unfastened the two quarter ropes attached for'ard and aft on the net, taking them to the winch via a leading block on each gallow. Raymond, now sober, was standing at the winch waiting for my rope while Barney took the other. Hauling on these, the two men heaved the heavy ground gear from the water.

Raymond, showing signs of life now, enthused at the fish floating alongside. "Dun't look a bad 'aul skipper, t' gear must be fishin' OK." His observations echoed mine. It didn't look a bad haul and it sounded great to be called skipper and to have caught my first catch. At least it would be when it was on board.

I recalled more of Tom Pashby's words. "It's never ours 'til it's on t' deck me ol' kid."

As the bobbins dropped to the deck with a thud, I redoubled my efforts to get to the fish, pulling in the top part of the net. The combination rope and wire headline, with twenty-five reinforced, eight-inch, plastic balls attached, took some dragging in and I called to the men at the winch, "come on lads, give us a pull." Soon four of us were pulling at the net's sleeve leading down into the water, using the rolling motion of the boat to assist us.

With the fish tightly alongside in the heavy netting of the codend, I passed the 'gilson' hook through the rope strop, loosely encircling the net. Rusty, now at the winch, was holding the other end of the wire, which passed through a pulley block at the top of the lifting pole. I nodded and he took three turns of the wire around the revolving winch drum and began to heave. The strop tightened around the catch and the haul was hoisted, dripping, from the water. As it reached the edge of the boat's rail, Rusty paused, holding the bulky bag, finely balanced, waiting till the boat rolled gently to starboard. He then eased the sack of fish onto the deck. Even on a fine day it was a precise task. In bad weather, up to a ton of fish swinging wildly can cause damage to a vessel and injury to crew.

Waiting for the moment, he again hoisted the bag, allowing it to swing into the receiving pound in the centre of the deck. Raymond put a short strop through the quick release clip and tugged. At the same time I gave the metal clasp a gentle tap with the hammer. The sack of fish, mostly medium-sized cod burst open, almost sweeping us off our feet as they spilled from the net, leaping and thrashing. Raymond and I were up to our knees in fish in a second. Now exposed there were also whitings and a few haddock visible among the catch, plus several species of flatfish. I estimated the weight to be about six kit; sixty stone of quality fish. It was a good start.

As we paddled our way through the fish to the starboard side, a large catfish, at least four feet in length, grey with black spots marking its skin, wriggled to the surface from under the catch. The creature was heading in our direction, its gaping mouth encouraging our exit. Living solely on shellfish, its jaws could crush bone with little effort. Rusty promptly stunned it with the deck shovel, discouraging any further movement.

Once out of the fish pound I heard myself say, "come on lads, this is ours now, let's get it down quick an' get some more." I cringed inwardly and promised myself, unsuccessfully, not to use this phrase again. These were more words my old skipper used, much to my annoyance. Now I was saying them myself.

It was easier to shoot the gear the second time, now we were more familiar with the boat and had a full crew, so the trawl was back on the bottom without delay. The *Jann Denise*, a bonny craft with graceful lines, on which I'd recently been a deck hand, was passing close by as we completed the manoeuvre. Seeing the gulls following us, her skipper Bob Walker called on the radio, "*Pioneer*, you've just 'auled there Fred, did yer ger owt?"

"Might be four kit Bob," I replied glibly, "it's not bad stuff though, mostly green." Green was the term for any size of cod, large or small. I felt a little guilty understating our catch, but justified it to myself; if other boats were not doing so well, they'd all descend on this small area and soon clean it up.

I needn't to have worried. Bob replied, "there was six kit wi' us that go, maybe yer need a measure up."

I gave a chuckle to myself. This was a bit of micky taking, aimed at anyone underperforming or suspected of misreporting. He could read between the lines.

We continued without too many complications; catches remained fairly constant and apart from a little net damage, which was an occupational hazard and easily repaired, the day was pleasant and uneventful. If damage to a trawl was excessive and couldn't be mended quickly, a torn net could be removed from the bobbins and changed for a spare in less than an hour. We seemed to be competing with the other boats of similar engine power and I was now reporting our catches correctly. I was content and happily took the daytime watches. Rusty and Raymond each took a night watch.

During the next morning, while the crew were on deck gutting the latest catch, I looked to the south to see several vessels heading in our general direction. It was obvious by the configuration of masts and a single boom jutting from the starboard side, they were trawlers, newly out from Grimsby or Hull on the recent tide, sailing back to the Arctic. These vessels were a real hazard when outward bound, as there was no guarantee the watch-keepers would be sober. These men spent three weeks at sea then only two days on shore, before sailing again. They were known as two-day millionaires as they earned big money but had little opportunity to spend it. Many would be greeted at the dock by a taxi, which would be permanently engaged until the man sailed again. For most, their time ashore was a haze of wild parties, either in the local pubs or after closing time, at someone's home. Some men would hardly remember seeing their families.

One vessel in particular appeared to be heading straight for us, her sharp bow slicing cleanly through the sea, neat plumes of white water spouting to the sides. As she grew closer I began to worry. Was anyone on the bridge at all? I called to my crew saying, "this bugger isn't gonna miss us by much lads." They looked up from their work at the approaching ship, probably steaming in excess of ten knots. Grabbing the VHF microphone, I switched to channel sixteen, the international frequency all shipping is required to monitor and called urgently to the ship by name, which along with her Grimsby registration number, GY 121, was now clearly visible. There was no reply. I called again, to no avail.

As I hauled the wheel hard over to port, I noticed the trawler's stem veering slightly to port, showing a little of her starboard side, which reduced the risk of collision. I let the wheel fly back to midships, a little relieved, though there was still no sign of life on the bridge. I fervently hoped she'd maintain this new course and not head back towards us. Switching the VHF back to the local working frequency, I made a general call to all boats in the vicinity, saying we were about to encounter a close quarter situation with a Grimsby trawler. At least other skippers would be aware of our possible plight. It became clear she was going to miss us now, but not by much. The rust streaks on her black hull and buckled plates on her starboard bow, the result of many years fighting Arctic storms, were a stark indication of the nature of her work.

As the huge ship drew level, only a boat's length away, a muffled figure appeared from her wheelhouse and looking down from her towering bridge, gave us all a friendly, unconcerned wave. There was someone in control of the *Northern Prince* after all. I breathed a sigh of relief.

Had the ship not altered course it would have been extremely difficult to avoid a collision, which would have split our vessel in two.

I could have altered course sooner to ease the situation but dragging a trawl, our general direction would have remained the same for a considerable time regardless. Also, according to the 'rule of the road', vessels running free should give way to vessels engaged in fishing. I was briefly left to contemplate the responsibility I had for other men's lives, before the airwaves filled with the crackle of skippers cursing and commenting on the close quarter drama we'd encountered.

Incidents of this nature were a source of entertainment for the tough men on the trawlers; an interlude to help break the monotony of the shipboard life in which they existed. These men spent twenty-one days at sea talking of nothing but sex and women, then on the short period spent on shore, spoke only of the bags of fish they'd caught on the previous voyage. They were indeed a race apart.

In a similar situation a few years earlier when I was with Bob Walker on his previous boat, *Success II*, a head had popped up from the wing of the bridge and a voice had bawled, "now lads." Half a dozen more heads came up from below the starboard bulwarks and a hail of beer cans had flown through the air in our direction. Some tins bounced off our side, others landed on the deck and one hit the wheelhouse.

Shouts of, "'ave a drink on us yer Yorkie bastards."

"See yer agen in three weeks."

And, "we 'ad yer worried there," could be heard above the noise of both vessels' engines.

The last caller was definitely right. They'd had us worried for a while.

Barney didn't seem enthusiastic with his new job and was reluctant to leave his bunk during the hours of darkness. He'd previously worked on large vessels where crews worked up to eighteen hours a day with a maximum of six consecutive hours below. Here on the *Pioneer* he was getting an hour and a half at the most between hauls and it was telling. He constantly mumbled under his breath and was becoming belligerent. Barney clearly wasn't going to be with us long.

Late in the afternoon of the second day, we hauled the trawl for a measly two kit and I decided to head for home to land our catch. We'd accumulated thirty-five kit of fish for our trip, which was pleasing and there was still a few days of the week left to catch more. It was a great feeling to steer the boat into the harbour with a catch on board. As we tied up at the pier, where several vessels were already landing, a small crowd of lobster fishers seeking bait, plus a few other onlookers gathered above the vessel to assess our first performance. Dad was among them.

" 'Ow'd it go?" he enquired as I climbed the ladder from the boat to the fish market. This question was followed by, "did yer save me any bait?" Dad was getting his request in early. Bait was always a problem for the potting men. He was in luck. The lads had saved a few boxes of mixed, unsaleable and undersized fish, which Dad had the pick of.

"We've thirty-five kit for our two days. It's not bad stuff, so we should do OK," I said, nonchalantly, but inside extremely pleased with myself.

"Well it's a start I suppose, but you've a long way t' go yet," he replied, instantly deflating my ego.

Next to request bait was Bill Sheader, universally known as 'Jitta'. Bill, tall, thin, with sharp, weather-beaten features and a large, hooked nose dominating his face, was a wonderful character. He was also Coxswain of Scarborough Lifeboat and had an immense reputation as a seaman. I'd served on the lifeboat many times with Bill and felt very comfortable under his leadership. I was pleased to help him in his quest for bait. I'd been in Bill's company in the 'Leeds Arms' on the previous weekend when someone said, "I hear Benny and his wife are going on a Rhine cruise, and it's costing a fortune."

Bill said, "if 'e'd gone durin' war like t' rest of us, 'e could 'ave gone fo' nowt."

Benny was one of the few fishermen who hadn't gone to war but had continued the no less dangerous, reserved occupation of fishing. Some men were not so honest. Donny carried a white cane for the duration of the hostilities but found he'd no requirement for the stick after VE day.

We commenced landing the catch. Raymond was below in the fishroom while Rusty, at the winch, hauled the boxes from the hold, two at a time. The landing pole, at an angle to the foremast, was plumbed over the hold and swung the boxes ashore easily. I weighed each box accurately to six stone of fish, allowing for the weight of box and ice; taking off or putting on a fish or two until the scales balanced. Barney, still complaining, helped Dad carry each weigh into the fishmarket. Our agent on the market would auction the fish on our behalf the following day.

While the lads replenished the boat with empty boxes, I took a moment to take stock of my first catch; almost sixty full boxes. The fish, in rows of twelve deep down the sloping market, shone brightly, reflecting the overhead market lights. I shovelled extra ice on each box then covered the catch with a plastic sheet. This would keep out the warm air and predatory gulls, which could empty a box of small fish in no time at all.

"It's not a bad shot lad," someone at my side said. I turned to see Tommy Luntley perusing our catch. I'd not heard his approach. Tommy 'Lunt' was a fish merchant who operated a small shop in the vaults of the town's market building and also supplied many customers in the area with fish from his handcart.

Clad in black trousers, a navy blue gansey, which accentuated his little potbelly and topped with a brown trilby hat, Tommy was small in stature but big in personality and enjoyed life to the full. This may have been because he'd nearly lost his life as a young man.

During the war, Tommy was stationed along with many of his fellow townsmen, in Harwich, serving in the Royal Naval Patrol Service. He tripped on railway lines in the dockyard, breaking an ankle and was hospitalised, forcing him to miss his ship. The minesweeper *Red Gauntlet,* on which he was due to sail, proceeded without him and was sunk by enemy action. She was lost with all hands on 5th August 1943.

Tommy was married to Florrie, who was a member of the Salvation Army prior to their wedding and a greater attraction of opposites never existed. Tommy was wild, hard-working, hard-drinking and forever in trouble, especially from Florrie when he arrived home the worse for wear. They raised a large family, mostly boys and there was never a dull moment in their home.

"You'll do all right if yer keep that up lad. I'll buy a bit o' yer fish meself tomorra," and with those encouraging words, he was gone as swiftly as he'd appeared.

Work finished, we walked from the pier together, though Dad remained behind to ice and store his bait. It was almost eight o'clock and normally I'd suggest going for a quick pint in the nearest pub to unwind but I was weary and didn't want to encourage Raymond, who once in the pub, would stay till closing time. "Three o'clock in t' morning lads, if we can get t' same again, we'll be in for a good week." Barney rolled his eyes but said nothing. He didn't need to speak; his eyes spoke the words for him.

Though knowing little about fishing, Dotty could tell I was pleased with my first trip and caught my mood. But for her support I'd never have felt able to leave the job I'd held on the *Jann Denise*. It was difficult for her at home, alone most of the time with two small bairns to take care of. Her parents, though very supportive, lived in Hull and she was far too independent to ask my mother for much help. Paula and Danny were fast asleep when we looked in on them. They'd still be asleep long after I'd gone out again. I wouldn't see them awake until the weekend.

There was no sign of Barney next morning and no amount of knocking on his door would rouse him. Someone in the house, his wife or youngsters must have heard Rusty banging. Plenty of others in the street were wakened, opening their windows to complain at the noise. I wasn't surprised when Rusty returned alone. I don't think our erstwhile deckie had any intention of turning up again. Deep sea fishing is extremely arduous and the ships work in much worse weather, but our type of fishing required men with a different type of resilience to turn out several times each week, in the early hours, and to work round the clock with only catnaps. There were good hands fishing from Scarborough, who'd made the transition to inshore work from deep sea, but Barney wasn't one of them. I wasn't too dismayed. Raymond was on time and sober; we'd manage with three.

If our first trip was easy going, this second one certainly made up for it. We'd steamed to grounds east of Scarborough, some thirty miles distant, where we'd caught some good hauls of cod with Bob in my previous boat. Every hour or two the net became snagged on the bottom and had to be hauled up. Each time we pulled the gear up, there were two or three boxes of fish; enough to encourage us to persevere, but though we persisted, we couldn't get a clear tow home. It was becoming frustrating and there was frequent net damage. We were losing too much time and eventually, after coming fast and tangling the net and bobbins in a big heap, which took over an hour to clear, we moved away to find easier grounds.

Our troubles were not over however. We did manage a few clear hauls, giving us a chance to eat and get a little rest, but in the early hours when attempting to haul the trawl, we discovered the winch wouldn't work. Inspecting the engine-room, I could see the shaft leading to the winch was turning, yet the flywheel in the foc'sle wasn't revolving. The problem lay somewhere under the fishroom floor. Rusty and I took up the fishroom boards, which we found to be black and exceedingly slimy on the undersides. It was apparent that the entire bilge in the fishroom was in a disgusting, stinking state and was in need of a major scrub out, but we couldn't do the job at present.

The immediate problem, which was now obvious, was a sheered flange on the shaft. At the joining point, where two sections of shaft were bolted together, a keyway on the coupling had sheered. This was a job for an engineer ashore. The dilemma was that the trawl was still on the seabed and I was exceedingly reluctant to release my gear. The equipment was new and even with a buoy attached to mark its position, there was a possibility my net could be towed away in the dark by large, foreign beam trawlers with whom I couldn't communicate.

I suggested to Rusty that we could try lashing the two halves of the shaft together with twine and rope. He was sceptical, but we would try. I disengaged the clutch to stop the half coupling rotating, then began to hitch the two parts together. First we used light line, fastening the butt ends with rolling hitches that would jam and not slip on the shaft. Next we used heavier rope and finally the boat's stern rope, still using rolling hitches. The end product was an unsightly ball of knots, but would it pass the acid test?

Gingerly, with the engine running at dead slow speed, I engaged the winch. The end drums of the machine began to rotate. I was elated. So far, so good. With the boat stopped in the water, lying across wind and tide, Rusty shipped the for'ard clutch home. The barrel of the winch also began to revolve, hauling up the wire warp. Very gently we seesawed the gear towards the surface, first on one end then the other, not daring to engage both clutches at once for fear of overloading the shaft and parting our makeshift connection.

The for'ard trawl door broke the surface and was hauled very slowly up the side of the vessel. I was greatly relieved to see it chained home. When the after door was secured, I knew we'd won. The doors were the heaviest part of the equipment. Rusty now engaged both clutches and gently eased the net up until it was alongside. We'd recovered the trawl and as a bonus, it contained a good haul of fish. On checking the rope on the shaft, I discovered more than half of our handiwork had parted under the load. I'd got my gear back by a whisker, but it was the end of the trip for fishing. We headed home with forty boxes of fish on board but more importantly, with my fishing equipment intact.

There was no sign of Barney when we arrived back home but he'd been to the agent's office to collect his share of pay from our first catch, which he was entitled to. As a share fisherman, he was due one eighth of the proceeds of the catch after the voyage expenses had been deducted.

The engineers had no trouble making a permanent repair on the damaged shaft, though they laughed at my use of twine and rope to fix a mechanical problem. I didn't care; the method had worked. I was to use a lashing of twine on more than one occasion in the future to good effect.

We took the opportunity of thoroughly cleaning the fishroom bilges during the downtime, creating a huge slick of stinking water in the harbour as the resulting effluent was pumped out. Rusty and I did the scrubbing and hosing, Raymond, on deck, manned the pump. We emerged from the hold looking like miners and smelling vile, having disturbed and disposed of years of accumulated seepage from the thousands of boxes of fish that must have passed through the hold. The fishroom bilge would never be neglected again. This was unhygienic but could also cause blocked bilge pumps, which could prove fatal in an emergency.

I crossed the busy road from the harbour into Eastborough on my way home feeling quite anti social, but I'd only be in this road for a few yards before turning off to the right, up the quieter, Pump Hill. This little cobblestoned hill was the site of the town's communal fresh water supply in medieval times. Eastborough was the main street, which led from the flat foreshore to the town centre and railway station. Years ago, in the heyday of steam, tons of fish were drawn by horse and cart up this steep road to the goods yard to meet the evening transport trains. The poor horses were often flogged hard as the drovers raced each other to meet their deadlines. These trains would take this freshly landed fish overnight to inland wholesale markets, where it would be distributed to retailers in time for the next morning's shoppers.

Here at the foot of the hill, leaning on his barrow waiting for assistance, was Fred Herritt. Fred, a large, rotund, red-faced, bespectacled, balding man, attired in a khaki overall, was a fish merchant. His hands were gnarled and deformed from years of pushing his barrow and filleting cold, slippery fish, while exposed to outdoor elements. Fred's fish-round covered a considerable part of the town, following a different route each day.

His immaculate, green handcart, with large, red cartwheels and white interior, was laden with fish fillets of varying species, cooled in crushed ice. A wooden tray atop sheltered his products from the weather and held a pan weighing-scale with brass weights in a box at its side.

I drew near old Fred and stopped for a chat, offering assistance, but the odour I was emitting was clearly dreadful and my offer was declined. I'd worked for Fred while still at school, delivering fish to various guest houses, hotels and cafés. My mind briefly flicked back and I gave a little shudder as I recalled the major tongue-lashing I'd once received from Freddy Coopland, while making a delivery to the popular 'Cooplands' restaurant. I'd leaned my carrier bike laden with fish, against the dustbins at the rear of the building. The only access to the premises was between the firm's delivery vans and the bins, I had no choice; there was nowhere else to park the machine. That wasn't how Mr Coopland saw things. I was almost tearful following his dressing down for my malpractice. The high-powered businessman wasn't going to listen to anything a small schoolboy had to say in his defence. I did remind Freddy Coopland of this incident many years later. He couldn't recall the occasion but the meeting left an indelible print in my mind.

While talking to the elderly fishmonger, I spotted Tommy Taylor hurrying down Pump Hill to rendezvous with the merchant. Tommy, a very timid man, dressed in an old, shabby suit, helped Fred to push his cart up the steepest part of the main street on a daily basis, for a small remuneration. Tommy had been a soldier in France during World War I and had returned home a broken man. People said he was shell-shocked but, sadly, the enormity of this bald statement didn't register much on my friends and me at the time and we didn't give this man due deference for his suffering. Now Tommy did odd jobs, offering to guide visitors round the town, helping boats to land fish and earning whatever he could, though he was unable to work at anything permanent.

Both Fred and Tommy were old enough to remember the heady days of the horse and cart and early steam trains and trawlers.

As replacement for Barney, Rusty suggested shipping up a Hull fisherman that he knew to replace Barney. Sid was another deck hand from the deep sea fleet who was keen to work inshore. He arrived on his motorbike at four o'clock on Sunday morning, having ridden from his home city, fifty miles away. He certainly seemed keen to join our crew. This was a journey he was to make hundreds of times.

Sid was willing and energetic, a refreshing change from his predecessor. He was also a superb cook. Throughout the next week and for a long time to follow, he treated us to home-made soups, wonderful steak and kidney pies and succulent roasts. He even found time to make steamed puddings with chocolate sauce, though he was first and foremost a deck hand. Sid never seemed to sleep and even found time to scrub the galley and its contents from top to bottom, a standard he kept and took pride in.

I was so enthusiastic about his cooking, that on several occasions when arriving home and sitting down to dinner, I'd observe, "Sid made us this on Sunday," or "Sid makes his gravy a little thicker." My tactlessness clearly rankled with Dotty, who with two small children was finding her days fully occupied, without planning special meals.

A small, innocent comment one evening, relating to some wonderful fish stew we'd enjoyed during the day brought the shrill reply, "you should have bloody well married Sid then shouldn't you?" I never mentioned our meals again, though we continued to be fed like fighting cocks.

* * * * * *

There was sadness and some disbelief around the harbour when news circulated that Herbert had died. He'd been quite a character and definitely one that everyone knew. Herbert had been a fisherman all his life apart from the war years, when he'd served all over the world as an engineer on several large vessels. He was a father of five children, three older girls and my friends, Herby and Brian. Self-opinionated, there was only one view on any subject in the universe and it was that of Herbert. He would contradict not only any member of his family who had opposing views, but anyone within earshot. His darkish, swarthy skin gave an appearance of not washing, which was probably untrue, though it was said his wife Gwen hid her money under the soap.

Gwen only discovered Herbert had passed away when she swore at him and gave him a push for lying on the sofa and not getting up to answer a knock at the door. The sofa was his favourite place when he wasn't at sea.

When younger, Herby and Brian were strictly controlled and dominated by their father, but as they grew older they began to rebel against his authority. One day an argument at home became so heated that Herby, who was a big, strapping lad, threw his father out of the house. He then held him at bay with a shotgun, which he used for shooting rabbits and pigeons, threatening to shoot him if he came near.

After several minutes of stand off, Brian arrived home to hear his father raving outside the door. "Don't shoot 'im Herb," Brian said, "an' let me in t' 'ouse." Brian entered the house and with a little persuasion took the gun from his brother. At this point Herbert made a move to re-enter the door. Brian turned the gun back on his dad and said, "keep out you old sod. Our Herb might not 'ave shot yer but I will." It took a visit from the police to calm the situation down and restore order.

At their mother's request, on the eve of the funeral, the two sons along with brother-in-law Ken, sat up in an all night vigil with their father, who was lying on the table in his open coffin. At about three in the morning, for no reason and without warning, Ken suddenly gave out a loud "whhooooaaa." Herby hit the ceiling and Brian shot out of the door.

On the morning of the funeral, with the coffin still open on the table and all his family gathered in the room, Herby turned to his mother, pointed at the box and said, "d' yer know Mother, this is t' first time we've ever 'ad a conversation in this room without that old bugger interrupting."

They all looked at the box, waiting for the deceased to say, "no it isn't."

* * * * * *

Throughout the summer we continued to fish well, to the delight of the *Pioneer's* owners, who were now pleased to improve on our performance by replacing 'Billy Smart' with a new, efficient machine and to modify the deck bollards, which had badly scarred the deck, despite our attempts to cushion the frequent blows with wooden padding.

During this lay up period I took up an invitation for a weekend trip to London with a group of sportsmen who I met each week in the bar at the town's sports centre, where I played squash and they played five-a-side football. From various professional businesses in the town, these people were a totally different crowd from my usual circle of friends but were fun to be with and I enjoyed their company. The group had arranged to play a couple of friendly matches while in the Capital against business associates. This was to be the start of an annual expedition, which would continue for many years.

Staying in a little hotel off the Bayswater Road, we were gathering in the bar early on Friday evening, ready for a night on the town, when I suddenly turned from the counter to find myself facing a rather short, rotund lady with straggly, straight hair and glasses which appeared to have been made from bottle bottoms.

"Mr Normandale?" she enquired, in a high-pitched, squeaky, Cockney voice.

"That's me," I replied, looking at the strange apparition before me and wondering how she knew my name. I looked round to my companions for some support but everyone in our group of twelve was now at a distance from me, watching the developing scene. From the grins of my so called 'mates', I realised I'd been 'set up'.

"Downt you remember me Mr Normandale. When you was in London last year, you slept with me, an' I've got a baby now."

The grins now turned to laughter as I visibly squirmed.

"Look Missus, ah've been in some drunken states in me time, but ah've never been that pissed, so bugger off."

The round lady didn't leave, but asked me to sit in a chair in the centre of the lounge and not wanting to be a killjoy, I complied. She then began reading a very badly constructed poem from the card in her hand. The short recital over, the woman began to undress. My companions now had tears streaming down their faces. Down to her underwear, it was obvious there were rolls of flesh to follow and I said, "yer don't 'ave t' continue fo' my benefit," hoping she'd stop, but the lady seemed quite keen to disrobe. With a twang, the powerful bra gave way and her huge boobs flopped to her waist. The audience, fortunately only our group, gave up a collective gasp, though not as loud as mine at the close proximity of this mass of uncontrolled flesh. The lady next suggested that I too should undress but I flatly refused, though responding to the booing from the spectators, I removed my shirt.

Fortunately for me, after removing her bulging tights, the stripper opted to retain her gigantic bloomers, though these only enhanced her huge belly. My final humiliation was when, from behind me, she hung her huge, sagging tits over my shoulders, to loud cheers from the gang.

For the remainder of the weekend I was on edge. Even though we had two great nights out and some good football, I couldn't help looking over my shoulder, waiting for the next surprise.

* * * * * *

Summer passed into autumn and with the change of season came football. On Saturday afternoons I played for the local amateur side, 'Penguins', in the District League, which gave me an interest other than fishing. I was keen to continue this hobby, though there never seemed much free time now I was a skipper. There were extra jobs to be done when the crew had gone home. Due to a combination of circumstances one week, when we'd missed a couple of days at sea due to bad weather, we didn't land our catch until Saturday morning. By the time we'd washed the boat down, taken fresh water, replenished the boxes and been to the office to settle the week's wages, it was almost midday. I arrived home at about twelve-fifteen to find Dotty had struggled through a horrendous few days with the kids and was very relieved to see me. She wasn't at all pleased shortly afterwards, when I said our match that afternoon was kicking off at two-thirty, and I was expected to meet at one-thirty at the town centre meeting point.

She wouldn't listen to anything I said and stormed from the house saying she was going out for some time on her own and that I could look after the kids for the afternoon and see how I coped. I would have to give football a miss. Paula and Danny seemed fine, though a little lively. I rang my Mum who only lived a few minutes away, asking if she'd mind looking after the kids while I went to play football. Mum was pleased to help and immediately put on her coat and left her house, heading towards ours.

Unfortunately for me, I'd rung too soon and Mum met Dotty heading in the opposite direction. When she saw Mum, she put two and two together and got the right answer. Dotty turned around, reaching the house before Mum. I was caught red-handed putting my football boots into a bag and received a severe tongue lashing, though she did relent and allow me to go off to the match, while Mum held the fort.

CHAPTER 2

CAREER MOVE

My brother-in-law Roland asked if I'd take his brother to sea on a fishing trip, as Martin was considering a career in the Merchant Navy and wondered how he'd cope with seasickness. I was happy to oblige and later that week, after being stuck in the harbour for two days, weather-bound, we sailed with Martin on board. My crew, as usual retired to the cabin to catch a couple of hours shut-eye en route to the grounds.

The wind was still blowing strongly from the south-west but the weather forecast predicted the gale would moderate later in the day. With the wind blowing off the land there was no heavy swell in the bay, just small wavelets, but the gusts were creating white water as they picked up the surface of the sea, throwing up clouds of spindrift. The indications were a little ominous. Maybe I should have waited a while longer till the gale had subsided, but I was impatient. I knew that further off shore the seas would be bigger as the power of the wind built up the waves, so I opted to steam to an area three miles off Flamborough Head, where we'd still be partly sheltered by the land. It was a place of strong tides but there were prospects of good fishing for cod. Martin seemed quite happy standing on the galley step, sheltering from the elements. He was watching the spray blowing over the boat as we steered south-east, broadside to the wind, parallel to the coast.

We were less than a mile from the land for the first part of the voyage and though there was lots of splashing, the *Pioneer* was quite stable, hardly rolling at all. This changed as we steamed beyond the shelter of the Brigg. This long promontory defended the town of Filey and its sweeping, sandy bay from the worst of the North Sea's excesses. At the south end, the rocky ledge tailed off quickly, becoming an underwater reef, marked by a bell buoy to warn off the unwary.

Suddenly, having lost the protection of this headland, we were now three miles downwind from the shore and still sailing across the swell. The *Pioneer* began to roll and Martin, still perched on the galley step and unprepared for the sudden movement, grabbed for the side of the wheelhouse as the boat lurched. Unfortunately for him, he was a little slow reacting and his feet slipped on the wet step. Seconds later he found himself sitting on the deck on the starboard side. A stream of icy water immediately shot through the scuppers, drenching his trousers and filling his short seaboots. His complacent smile turned to a look of terror and consternation as the cold water reached his skin. Ensuring the boat was on a straight course, I ran to the deck to assist him, keeping my footing to avoid a similar fate.

Martin was still gasping from his cold immersion as I helped him up and we quickly retreated to the galley, where he was obliged to strip and change into spare clothes and borrowed rubber boots. This was an inauspicious start to a career at sea for the potential mariner. We still had an hour to steam before we reached the grounds and Martin, now confined to the warm galley with its rattling cooking utensils, began to change colour, first white then to a pale green. It was clear he was going to be sick so I yelled, "if yer gonna be sick, jus' fire it out o' t' door. Don't worry about any mess. There's plenty o' water washin' about out there. It'll soon flush away."

Maybe this was auto-suggestion or just timing, but seconds later there was a loud retching sound and intermittent groans coming from the galley. I glanced back frequently, checking he was safe and making sure he was following instructions. I didn't want to lose him overboard attempting to be sick over the side.

The swell grew bigger as we reached the fishing grounds. We were three miles north of Flamborough Head now and the lads were finishing their tea when I eased back the throttle. A few minutes later we'd donned our sea gear, lifted the trawl doors out and though the *Pioneer* was wallowing, we quickly had the trawl over the side. I returned to the wheelhouse, passing our glum-looking, silent passenger in the doorway. Despite the poor weather, efficient teamwork by the crew soon saw the gear on the seabed. Our craft was steadier now she was harnessed, though she was still rolling broadside to the swell.

At this distance from shore the *Pioneer* was still given a measure of protection from the towering, white Flamborough Cliffs to the south-west, though it didn't appear so to Martin, who was attempting to remain in the galley while breathing air from outside. His neck seemed to be stretching to achieve this aim. Little did he know we were soon to lose the little shelter we were getting from the land. Our course was due south, with some allowance for the strong wind and within an hour we had lost our lee. Now it was eleven miles down wind to the nearest land and *Pioneer* began to buck and strain like a tethered animal as the effects of drag from the trawl, wind, waves and tide acted upon her. Again I wondered if I'd made the correct decision in sailing. It was too late now.

The whites of Martin's eyes seemed huge as they darted up at the wheelhouse between gulps of air. This was an uncomfortable course, but necessary if we were to avoid numerous wrecks and not tow across the tide, which would inevitably result in snagging the trawl on the rocky seabed.

I'd kept this heading for about six miles, holding twenty fathoms of depth but now had to turn the boat round on a reciprocal course. The water was shoaling and the nature of the seabed changing to sand, so there'd be fewer fish here. It was essential to turn into the wind. Forty-five degrees to starboard would put her head to wind and the elements would help with the remainder of the turn. If I turned to port the *Pioneer* would travel miles down wind out of control and I'd never get back to my chosen line.

I heaved at the wheel, pulling on every spoke to haul her up into the wind and was pleased when our course noticeably changed. Now head to wind she was much more comfortable, slicing through the waves with her sharp bow. I would allow her head to fall off the wind to starboard gradually and we'd be round. Suddenly a bang and a jolt from the stern indicated the net had snagged on the bottom. This was a major problem. We were across the tide with a gale of wind on the opposite side to the trawl.

Realising the problem, Sid and Rusty were quickly at the winch, hauling the gear back, but the trawl was stuck hard and the wind was blowing the boat over the top of the warps. I disengaged the engine to avoid fouling the propeller with the wires, but with no engine power, the tide began to act on the boat too. There was another loud bang and the after wire parted. The boat spun round with the remaining wire now leading forward.

I was sure we were going to lose our trawl, but at least the propeller was now clear. Re-engaging the engine I headed the *Pioneer* in the direction of the gear, easing the strain on the remaining warp. The for'ard door appeared and was chained in place but the net was still stuck fast on the seabed. It was essential to dodge the boat slowly into the tide. Gingerly, Rusty played the winch, easing up the cable leading to the net. There was a tremendous strain on the singing wire and I was sure it would part, but then, a slight jerk and the load eased. We were free of the fastener. It was pleasing to note the cable wasn't entirely slack, as this would have indicated we'd lost our trawl.

It was a relief to see the net appear on the surface, even though it was badly torn and in a tangled mess. Once recovered, a net can always be repaired, no matter how extensive the damage. Even now I couldn't assist on deck. On the seabed, the other trawl door was now acting as an anchor. The crew struggled and bit by bit, the pile of netting, floats and bobbins on the deck grew, as the gear was heaved on board. Each part of the trawl was lashed inboard to prevent the entire heap flying back overboard with the drag from the rogue door. Only when this board was lifted clear of the seabed could I knock the engine out of gear and help to recover the final piece of equipment. We'd been almost two hours manoeuvring, heaving and securing the gear and I'd completely forgotten about our passenger, until I stepped into the galley on my way to the deck.

I found him in total despair, lying on the floor, his head on the galley step, groaning intermittently. Even now I had little time to spend with him as I donned my oilskin. I could only assure him we wouldn't be long, then we'd be going home again. What a difference those few words made. A look of hope appeared on his face and he sat up, allowing me to pass from the galley onto the pitching deck.

Half an hour later we were steaming north, towards Flamborough Head, then north-west to home. It was a great relief to see the gear piled in a heap on the deck. The mound would need untangling and mending but was safe. The lads, having done all they could, were enjoying a steaming pot of tea and thick corned beef sandwiches, but our passenger couldn't be tempted. He clung to the galley door with a new zest for life. We sailed close in, under the sheer cliffs at Flamborough and immediately found shelter from the gale. We then had a pleasant cruise across Filey Bay on our way back.

We entered the harbour and were soon alongside the pier wall. Even before the ropes were secured, Martin was climbing the ladder to the quay. He stood very unsteadily on the pier, looking down at the *Pioneer*. I looked up from the open window in his direction. "Thanks for taking me," he croaked weakly, "it's helped me to make up my mind."

Shortly afterwards, I heard he'd joined the Royal Air Force.

CHAPTER 3

A VISIT TO GRIMSBY

Fishing was good a few weeks later, once more trawling south of Flamborough Head, where we'd caught a hundred and twenty boxes, mostly of cod. Other boats had also fished well and were on their way to land in Scarborough, which meant there'd be a substantial amount of fish on the market at home. I decided to land our catch in Grimsby. There was little difference in distance between the two ports from our present position, though they were in opposite directions. The buying capacity of the fish merchants in Grimsby was vastly greater.

This was the first time the *Pioneer* had been back to her former port since I'd become her skipper, ten months earlier. It was exciting sailing up the river in the dark. The lights of flashing buoys, the navigation lights of ships arriving and leaving the various Humber ports, plus the shore lights of Grimsby and adjacent Cleethorpes painted a very confusing picture, which required total concentration. At least the visibility was good. I could only imagine what it must be like in fog. In the dark we seemed to be racing towards the huge fishing port, yet in reality were stemming the ebbing tide. It was taking longer than I'd anticipated to reach the Lincolnshire port. With three miles to go I radioed ahead to the lock operators, informing them we were inward bound.

The reply came back, "*Pioneer*, this is Fish Dock Island, the gates are still open, keep coming, there are a couple of seine-netters about to leave. When they've gone we'll change the lights for you."

I thanked the officer and considered his reply. At least we would make the tide and the forthcoming market. There were two lock entrances into the dock, the lock-keeper's office was between them, hence when both sets of gates were open, the men were literally on an island. As for the lights, these were red and green traffic lights at the dock entrance. With so much shipping using the port, it was essential to control the flow.

The seiners' lights were easily discernible as they left the entrance and though it was dark, I could visualise these boats. There were hundreds of boats like these fishing from Grimsby. Traditionally painted a very pale blue, almost grey, these craft were no bigger than the *Pioneer*, but would be away from home for twenty days or more with only three men on board. They'd range all over the North Sea and in times of severe weather would drop anchor, lying head to wind, sometimes for days on end if the storm persisted. We never went far offshore and returned home when the weather turned bad.

These seine net fishermen fished for cod and plaice and only worked in daylight. Their method of fishing was ineffective in darkness. The days were short in winter but in summer these men worked twenty-hour days. I didn't envy them.

We passed the two vessels port to port and I gradually eased the engine. The lights on Fish Dock Island changed to green and we approached at slow speed, entering the lock pits as the outer gates closed behind us. We'd just made the tide and wouldn't be able to leave now for a minimum of eight hours. The huge port was only accessible two hours either side of high water; less on neap tides. The Dock Master yelled a number and wharf where we were to land but I didn't catch the message. I was too busy avoiding the concrete sides of the narrow entrance. Rusty had heard the relevant information and passed it on as we sailed across the busy dock, where fishing vessels could be seen in all directions. Gangs of 'lumpers' were discharging the catches from a line of seiners on our starboard side, while to port a row of black, rust-streaked trawlers lay idle, stem on to the pier. Their stay in port would be brief. The vessels I could see were only some of the craft at present in the massive dock. These in turn were a small percentage of the Grimsby fleet. The majority were at sea.

With the first streaks of dawn in the sky, we passed from the main section of the port into another, smaller part, again managed by traffic lights. This too was a hive of activity. In the far corner more trawlers were lined up, each waiting to be filled with ice from the huge factory with its overhead gantries. A berthing officer dismounted from his bike and waved, directing us to an empty slot among other vessels. Even before we were securely tied up, a young man on the quayside was trying to attract my attention. Our boat was level with the quay so I jumped ashore. Kurt introduced himself as the agent's 'runner', a shore assistant who helpfully briefed me on the landing procedure and asked if there was anything we required. "What about a couple o' mucky women an' some beer?" Rusty chipped in.

Kurt laughed and quickly organised a set of scales and the section of the market allocated for our fish. As soon as our landing pole was hoisted we began to discharge our catch. Kurt disappeared, returning with a case of 'Long Life' beer, "to assist you with your labours." He said, "there's no mucky women about yet, it's a bit early, most of 'em will have just gone to bed."

When the catch was ashore we tipped our boxes of fish into bigger, aluminium kits, weighing them into ten stone units. With our catch on the market, we could now relax. The lock gates were shut so we wouldn't be able to sail until four o'clock in the afternoon at the earliest. Leaving our two shipmates to wash our empty boxes with a nearby hose, Rusty and I decided to walk along the section of fish market where we were berthed. It was amazing to see the endless mass of fish of all types, and this was only part of the market. We came to a catch of cod; hundreds of kits, all giant fish, much bigger than the ones we'd landed. A man in a long, white merchant's overall, noticing our interest, told us this was the catch from the *Sonia Jane* and *Island*, two former seine-net boats. They were using a new innovative method of fishing, towing a single net between the two boats, 'pair trawling'. "They've only been at sea for eight days," he said.

This was an awesome performance. These boats were hardly bigger than ours. The *Island* was an old boat with only a 114 horsepower Gardner engine. This was a revolution in fishing.

A 'wall' of white coats was heading slowly towards us. It was the auction approaching. "You'd better move," said the single white coat, who was standing sentry on some fish he wanted to bid for. "They'll sell you, if you stand there."

We retreated to the edge of the market to watch the proceedings. I'd never seen a sight like this in my life. The merchants were like locusts descending on the display of fish. More than a hundred men, shod in wooden clogs with studded soles, moved slowly over the fish, walking on the edges of the aluminium boxes. A salesman in the midst of the multitude was chanting an undecipherable language. His assistant, with book and pencil, hovered at his side, scribbling furiously as the fish was swiftly knocked down to demanding buyers.

"Scarborough merchants wouldn't get a flake o' fish 'ere," Rusty observed. "It'd all be gone while they were suppin' tea an' talkin' about football."

He was right. There was fifty times as much fish here than at home and all would be sold in little over an hour. The auction at home sometimes went on from early morning till after midday when there was any quantity on the market. The ice, keeping the fish cool had long since melted and the quality of the catches deteriorated quickly. The buyers and salesmen back home could learn much from a visit here.

We called into a nearby teashop for breakfast and were pleased to see old 'Paddy', skipper of the *Scanboy*, an occasional visitor to Scarborough. We sat with him for a while, exchanging news and fishing gossip. He made us laugh with a yarn about one of the seiner skippers who'd recently returned to port unexpectedly.

The man was one of the port's top earners and a hard fisherman but his weakness was for jelly babies. He never sailed to sea without several boxes of the variously coloured sweets. Outward bound to the fishing grounds one morning, the new deck hand/cook went up to the wheelhouse to take the wheel while the skipper went below for his breakfast. The cook was amazed to find jelly babies standing in line like soldiers, on every window ledge of the wheelhouse. He thought it was a great joke when he bit the heads off all the little people. He nonchalantly waited to see the skipper's reaction. The skipper was apoplectic on his return to the wheelhouse and without another thought, immediately turned the boat round and returned to the dock. On arriving he promptly sacked the cook.

We bid Paddy good day and good fishing, returning to our boat to find Sid and Raymond had not only washed our boxes, but had stowed them on board too. Frank Chapman, one of the boat's owners was standing at the quayside waiting my return. He was delighted with our catch and that we'd landed at Grimsby, through his agency. He said we'd got an excellent price for our fish and merchants had commented on the quality. As most of it had been caught in the last two days, this didn't surprise me. Some of the fish we'd seen on the market had been out of the water three weeks. Frank walked off, pleased to hear we were planning to sail again on the next tide. This wasn't the normal practice in Grimsby. I didn't tell him we were going off to the pub for a few beers at midday and wouldn't be sailing until just before the gates closed early in the evening.

Ever-willing Kurt arrived with twenty pounds, an advance on our pay. The balance would be forwarded to Scarborough. He suggested we try the 'Coach and Horses' if we wanted to see a bit of life. We spent a couple of hours overhauling and mending our trawl and it was gone noon when the four of us, washed, shaved and dressed as best we could with our limited supply of clothing, wandered off to town.

The 'Coach and Horses' was the most dilapidated hostelry I'd ever seen. The remaining paint on the red and white facade was faded and flaking. Almost half of the small paned windows were broken, some of the gaps filled with cardboard, others had a more permanent fixing; parts of fish boxes, nailed into place.

We entered the dingy doorway with trepidation. There was plenty of noise from within, even at this early hour. Sawdust was liberally sprinkled on the worn, bare floorboards. We were welcomed like old friends by a smiling, buxom woman, who I presumed to be the landlady. Her exposed cleavage, wrists and fingers, were adorned with gold jewellery. Probably in her forties, her face, painted with crimson lipstick, mascara and powder was cheerful, but prematurely lined. Tired eyes, less sparkling than her personality, spoke of late nights and gin. Her permed hair was blonde, apart from the inch nearest her scalp, which was a mousy brown.

In a surprisingly cultivated voice the lady said, "hello boys, come in, don't be shy. I'm Elsie and I won't bite you. Well not just yet anyway," she laughed, "what can I get for you?"

Elsie moved out of the narrow hallway, to the bar at her side, exposing the dim, smoke-filled room behind. There were eight or ten men, in two groups, visible in the gloom. All seemed to be enjoying the atmosphere of the hostelry. Their tables were strewn with beer bottles, but a large number of spirit glasses were also in evidence. The ashtrays, tobacco tins in a former life, were overflowing. A chrome jukebox, incongruously the only object in the room which related to the twentieth century, separated the two parties.

Raymond, wiping his mouth at the thought of the beer to come, ordered four pints of bitter. "Go on through my dears, I'll bring them in," smiled Elsie. "Which boat are you off?" The landlady was clearly used to fishermen and had immediately realised that we were from a boat.

"We're off t' *Pioneer*, from Scarborough," replied Raymond, choosing to wait at the counter for the beer to be drawn. His eyes were firmly focused on the first pint, already being pulled by the lady's powerful arm.

"I wouldn't want a punch from 'er," I whispered to Rusty as we moved through to the back room. Elsie was clearly good at her job and kept up a cheery chat with Raymond, as she began pulling the other drinks. Raymond had already taken a large slurp from the first glass, which was now half empty.

"We get quite a few lads in here from along the coast, but not usually at this time of year. They come during the summer from Bridlington and Scarborough for the dog-fishing season." She chatted on in her friendly manner. "Those boys in the back room are Dutchmen and Danes. They both landed fish on the market yesterday. They were in here last night until well after midnight and were banging on the door again before I opened at eleven this morning."

Legal closing time was ten-thirty the previous evening. Elsie must have locked the door and continued serving. No wonder she looked a little weary.

Raymond brought our drinks through to one of the two remaining tables on an ancient, battered tray. A Dane, a huge man with a barrel chest, spanned by a pair of red braces which would've driven the *Pioneer's* winch, shuffled amiably along the threadbare seating to accommodate our waiter. The hulk's weathered face wore a booze-induced grin. He had tussled fair hair and wide, friendly, blue eyes, typically Scandinavian.

I noticed Raymond's glass was already refreshed, but I wasn't too worried. He'd earned the break. There'd be plenty of time for him to sleep it off. There'd be no work for him till we got back to the fishing grounds. One of the Dutch crew opposite loaded the jukebox with coins, selecting music from the sixties and everyone joined in singing. In less than an hour the back room of the Coach & Horses was like a United Nations Pop Convention. Raymond, having consumed a few more pints, was deep in conversation with the Great Dane, using the international language which drunks have no trouble with. Elsie, doing a roaring trade, continued to supply the company with their liquid requirements. Above the din I heard Raymond ask the big man his name. Pointing to his own chest he said, "me Raymond, who you?" pointing to the man's giant chest.

The Dane, grasping the gist of the question replied, "me Bengt."

Raymond thought this was hilarious and yelled across the table to Rusty, "oy, Rust, this bloke sez 'e's bent."

Looking at the size of the man and his state of inebriation, Rusty called back, "you can call 'im bent if yer want, I'm not gonna." Raymond's new found friend was a little perplexed, and suspected he was the butt of a joke. The Dane frowned and his demeanour changed. Sitting close by, I'd been enjoying the interchange between the two and was able to placate the big man. Tapping the side of my head with a forefinger then pointing to Raymond I said, "he crazy, loco." Bengt nodded, turned away and began talking to his shipmates.

The session continued and I felt the need to go to the toilet. Following a sign, I found myself outdoors in a back yard. The gent's urinal was behind a simple brick screen, sheltered by a dangerously sagging, freestanding, lean-to roof. I was joined moments later by Rusty, somewhat inebriated who, having followed the call of nature, thought he'd do something about the dilapidated roof. He promptly broke a nearby broom and wedged the brush shaft between the top of the brick wall and the sagging roof. As a temporary measure it was a good fit. The roof was supported and much of the sag removed. Pleased with his emergency handiwork, Rusty returned to the bar. I followed him.

The group of Danes were now amusing themselves with a pet mouse, which was scampering around their tabletop. It was fun watching its antics and I nudged Raymond, pointing to the little creature. I was horrified when, in his drunken state, Raymond reached over and brought his clenched fist down on the harmless rodent. I couldn't believe what he'd done. Maybe he thought it was a resident. I cringed, wanting to curl into a ball and disappear. The Danes stood up, all shouting at once and though I couldn't understand them, it was clear they were about to pull Raymond's head off.

The Dutchmen looked on with interest. Elsie was on the scene in a flash. She had clearly seen the incident and was decisive in her action. "Right you! Out! Now!" Grabbing Raymond by the collar she dragged him to his feet. In the same movement she spun him round and propelled him towards the door. "An' you lot can join 'im," she called over her shoulder in our direction. All signs of the well-modulated voice had disappeared.

"Come on you two, quick, we're off," I hissed at Rusty and Sid. They'd missed the original incident and looked confused. "We'll get filled in if we stop 'ere." They took in the situation at a glance, left their drinks and followed me to the door, where we found Raymond lying on the ground, where he'd been thrown. Elsie stood threateningly over him.

"I've just saved you from a bloody good 'iding, you drunken sod, now fuck off an' don't come back." She didn't mince her words.

The landlady looked in our direction and said, "he's trouble that one. Keep 'im away from 'ere. I'd take 'im back to your ship if I were you," and with that she was gone; back to offer her captive customers a drink on the house to pacify them, hoping to persuade them from leaving for another of the many hostelries in the area.

We returned to the boat, helping our drunken shipmate, who was burbling threats to the giant Dane. "Lemme go. I'll ave 'im, that big bassard." I looked at my watch. I couldn't believe it was only three o'clock. We descended to the cabin and were pleased to hit our bunks.

At six o'clock, with the tide now ebbing strongly, we left the dock; the gates again closing behind us. There were red, green and white navigation lights to be seen in all directions as we raced down river amid vessels large and small. These ships were sailing to or from the many ports on the Humber and its tributaries.

Strangely, amidst all the surrounding lights, I couldn't see the loom of red and green from our own port and starboard lanterns, usually showing on each side of the darkened deck. Rusty came on deck to deliver a mug of coffee and I asked him to check our sidelights. "Maybe t' bulbs 'ave gone," I suggested.

He climbed onto the wheelhouse top in the dark with spare bulbs in hand. Minutes later he returned grinning. "It's not t' bulbs that 'ave gone, it's t' bloody lights. Some thievin' bugger's nicked our port an' starboard lights."

It was true. Either while we'd been in the pub or while we were turned in below, someone had boarded the *Pioneer* and stolen the ship's red and green brass and copper navigation lights. At this point we'd been sailing for at least half an hour among a mass of shipping and we'd not been showing sidelights. It was too late to get back into the dock. Even if we did, we wouldn't be able to get replacement lights before morning, by which time the gates would again be closed. There was no choice but to press on with extra vigilance.

The next hour was exceedingly worrying and I gently manoeuvred the *Pioneer* out of the main channel, so we were passing all navigation buoys on the wrong side. I knew there was sufficient water and we were safer. Our luck held and three uneventful hours later, we were back on the fishing grounds. We managed a few more reasonable hauls during daylight hours and arrived back home on Friday afternoon with another good catch of fish to add to our earlier grossing.

Next morning as usual, I was down on the pier attending to the various requirements in preparation for the following week, and after settling our accounts at the office, I encountered Bob Sabin, looking bleary-eyed and hungover. Bob, a tall, gangly man with a pock-marked face and straight, swept-back hair, lived alone. He was an easy going, generous man and if he had any money, it would go through his hands like water.

"You look rough Bob. Did you 'ave an 'ard night las' night?" I enquired.

"Ah did that," he replied, "our bloody Alan drank me under t' table."

With some difficulty he went on to explain that the previous day had been his nephew Alan's 21st birthday and as a treat, Bob had taken Alan on a pub crawl. His nephew wasn't used to drinking and Bob thought it would be amusing to get Alan drunk.

The pair hit town dressed in style. Bob resplendent in a new suit, Alan in his Uncle's cast off, which fitted well and was still in good condition. Many pubs and even more drinks later and with closing time still way off, not only was Bob as drunk as a lord, he'd also run out of money. Alan was showing little effect from the huge quantity of beer he'd consumed.

" 'Ave yer any money wi' yer Alan?" his uncle slurred.

"I've got about three quid," came the reluctant reply.

"We'll 'ave t' spend that then," Bob said, "we're not goin' 'ome before closin' time."

Begrudgingly, Alan handed over his total wealth to his Uncle Bob. This saw the pair through to closing, by which time Bob was paralytic. It was Alan who helped his Uncle home and into bed, not the reverse as had been planned. As we stood together on the pier yarning, insult was added to injury for Bob when Alan, full of the joys of spring and showing no sign of the large quantity of alcohol he'd consumed, approached. His first words were, "can I 'ave that three quid back ah lent yer las' night?"

Several weeks later, Paddy, in the *Scanboy* was in Scarborough Harbour and was tied alongside our boat. Rusty called to him, "now then Paddy, 'ow's things goin' in Grimsby? 'Ave yer bin in t' Coach an' 'Orses lately?"

Paddy replied, "I was in the old dive only last weekend. The place is getting worse. They've got a brush shaft holding up the toilet roof now."

CHAPTER 4

STEERING TROUBLE

At sea during the next week, while turning hard to port to reverse our course, the wheel suddenly went slack. The *Pioneer* wasn't answering her helm and wouldn't steer. We were towing our trawl and were now out of control. There were other vessels in the vicinity, so leaving Rusty in the wheelhouse to warn off any shipping that may come close, I went below to search out the problem. Climbing into the tiny, dark, steerage compartment at the back of the cabin with only a box of matches for light, I discovered we'd parted a steering chain. The chains, attached to a yoke, linked the wheel to the rudder. It wouldn't be too difficult to fix the problem, but I thought it prudent to haul the gear first. I made a mental note to buy a torch.

Calling the other crew from below, we commenced heaving up the trawl. It was essential to haul the net with the wind on the starboard side, allowing the boat to blow away from the submerged equipment, which wasn't a problem. As long as I left the vessel going ahead slowly, she would travel in a great circle due to the pull of the gear on the starboard side. I'd stop her when the time was right.

Everything went to plan and with the net alongside, I allowed the *Pioneer* to circle until the wind was on the starboard quarter. Things were going so well, I briefly forgot about the broken chain and gave the engine a little check astern to take the weigh off the boat. There was a loud bang from below and the engine stopped dead. With the boat in stern gear, the flapping, wooden rudder, unfettered, had swung forward and the propeller had embedded itself into the loose steering blade. My language turned the air blue. The cursing would have made the devil blush. I'd scored a major own goal, from which there was no hope of a resolution without outside assistance.

At least we were across the wind and the net was alongside. I pulled the throttle to neutral and restarted the engine. The machine fired up first time, seemed to run well enough out of gear and didn't appear damaged. We hauled the trawl on board then I made a humiliating call to the boats fishing in the area, requesting a tow back to port. Had the rudder been swinging free, the broken link could have been repaired. At worst we could have made a jury rig, allowing us to steer the boat home with some makeshift device, but now, with our rudder locked hard to port and the propeller stuck in it, we were helpless.

Dave 'Bev' Bevan, skipper of the *Our Margaret* was going to Scarborough to land fish and volunteered to alter course to collect us and tow us home. We were only twelve miles distant but what a difficult passage this proved to be. Our craft continually wanted to turn hard to port, making the journey almost impossible. Bev solved the problem by suggesting he tow us from our port bow, compensating for the rudder angle. This proved successful, though unorthodox and he did get us home, but it was a long time before I was allowed to forget the incident.

Next morning, with the *Pioneer* high and dry at the top of the harbour, a few heavy blows with a sledgehammer released the offending article. It was fortunate the rudder was of wooden construction. Had the material been steel, we'd have required a new propeller too. We replaced the broken steering chain, the cause of our problems, then made for the 'Dolphin Hotel' for a lunchtime beer. It would be late afternoon before there was sufficient water to refloat our boat. Spring was in the air and the town was busy as we walked along the seafront. The local Council had arranged a Dutch Festival in the town to promote early season tourism. There were visiting flower girls from Haarlem, wonderfully painted ornate barrel-organs, various bands and other colourful, cultural events livening the streets.

We joined the company of a group of coblemen, including Bill Sheader and his pal Ernie. Bill, having recently returned from a visit to his wife's relatives in North Shields, was telling a tall tale. He said his brother-in-law, Wally, who sailed as master of a tug on the River Tyne, had been instructed to take his vessel out beyond the port entrance, to allow it to be used for a burial at sea.

The undertaker, plus family and friends of the deceased were gathered on the deck of the craft and following the committal, the casket was launched down the stern ramp of the tug to the watery grave chosen by the departed. Unfortunately the undertaker had forgotten to ballast the coffin, so instead of the box slipping gently from the surface with dignity, it floated high in the water, bobbing in the swell. The passengers were bereft but were assured by Wally that eventually the object would lose its buoyancy and sink.

The tug kept station alongside the drifting box for an extended period of time and though now settled in the water, the coffin still refused to sink. Wally, aware of the muttering and stares in his direction and looking again at his wheelhouse clock, eventually thought he'd give the casket a little nudge with the stem of his vessel, hoping to expel a little air and encourage its disappearance. A miscalculation in the speed of his ship became obvious when the tug hit the coffin with a crunch. There was a splintering of wood as the box broke into several pieces, despatching the contents to their final resting place, leaving only driftwood splinters on the surface.

Our group were helpless with laughter at this sacrilegious story and even Bill, who always enjoyed his own jokes, had tears running down his face.

Our merriment was cut short when a commotion at the bar caught our attention. The landlord Ces, was on his knees, cradling his elderly dog, which appeared to have taken a fit and died. The owner of the long-haired Alsatian was distraught, not knowing what to do, or whether it was possible to revive the poor creature.

With simply dreadful timing, a group of Dutch musicians with large, booming brass instruments burst through the door, playing a rousing tune. They instantly fell silent on seeing the tragedy played out on the floor before them. In the stony silence that followed, Ernie called out, "can yer play, 'Old Shep'?"

Pioneer berthed at the Vincent Pier, Scarborough. Circa 1972.
Photo by F G Normandale

Aerial photograph of Scarborough Harbour.
Courtesy of Max Payne MBE

Some of the many seine-net vessels that fished from Grimsby.
Courtesy of Grimsby Telegraph

Courage leaving Scarborough Harbour. Circa 1975.
Photo by F W Normandale

Chapter 5

The Courage

I left the *Pioneer* on good terms with her owners, having recommended another local fisherman, Jim Whitlow, to take the vessel. I'd been her skipper for almost two years, during which time I'd achieved some modest success and had paid off the outstanding account owed for my fishing gear, which was still in good condition. Now I was looking to acquire a boat of my own. Having checked several boats advertised in the 'Fishing News' without finding anything suitable, I became aware the *Courage* was for sale. She was one of the most successful vessels in the fleet, though she was now getting on in years. Her present owners were building a big, steel vessel, the *Admiral Van Tromp*, which would soon be ready. My crew meanwhile, had all found other berths. Rusty was now fishing in a coble. Raymond was shipped up in another trawler and Sid was fishing for mackerel in a huge, stern trawler in the Channel, off Cornwall.

I approached Will Pashby, who in partnership with son-in-law Frank, was joint owner of the *Courage*. They were willing to sell me their boat, but not for several weeks, until their new craft was ready. I discussed my plans at length with Dotty, explaining that if we were to buy the *Courage*, we'd have to borrow a large part of the required sum from a bank. We would have to risk our house as security and we had two small children to consider. My wife, as usual was unperturbed. "Do what you think is best for us all," was her only comment.

The price, eleven thousand pounds was agreed and a survey of the vessel arranged for valuation purposes. I made an appointment with my fishselling agent's bank manager, thinking I'd have no problems acquiring a loan. My positive, ambitious attitude was flattened when I was introduced to this thin, bespectacled, dour, unhappy man who, with a negative attitude, listed all the possible, probable and unlikely things that could go wrong with my plans, my life and my family. He finally agreed to lend me a sum that would leave me a thousand pounds short of my requirements, having taken into account our savings. My Mum and Dad promptly offered to lend me five hundred pounds each, making up the shortfall. I was unsure they could afford this money, but I was grateful for the loan and would repay them.

For the next few weeks I sailed as deck hand on the *Evelyn* with skipper Jackie Mann. While fishing about twenty miles offshore one fine day, a budgerigar dropped onto the deck, totally exhausted. This very lucky budgie took no catching and we kept the blue and white bird in a cardboard box until we returned to port. Jack took the friendly little chap home as a pet for his daughters. They named it 'Sailor'.

I took over the blue-painted *Courage* in late summer. She was fifty-four feet in length with a 152 horsepower, 'Gardner' engine. Though now over twenty years old, she was well-maintained and her lovely lines and easy layout made her the perfect boat for me. Her successful record was one I could only hope to emulate. I was very fortunate to ship up Bill and Bluey as crew, as both were good hands. Bill Messruther, in his early thirties, was small of stature with bright, piercing, brown eyes and short thin hair. He was bursting with energy. His whole manner exuded positive vibes and what Bill lacked in height, he more than made up for in enthusiasm. Tommy Sheader, known to everyone as Bluey, like previous generations of his family, had a shock of blonde hair, a round, mischievous face and a witty sense of humour. He was seventeen years old.

The three of us found an instant rapport and worked together well. The *Courage* was already fitted with trawling gear so there was little to do to equip her. We sailed on our first trip early in September. I'd chosen to fish a few miles to the north, offshore from Robin Hood's Bay. This distinctive inlet was known to generations of fishermen only as 'Bay Wyke'. Our first haul left me feeling I had a very large mountain to climb. The codend of the net had a jagged hole in the lower part, probably chafed through by a large stone. Any fish we may have caught had escaped through the hole. The damage wouldn't take too long to repair but we'd lost three and a half hours of fishing time and we'd have to trawl for a similar period again before we were likely to see any fish. Half the day would be gone. My two shipmates addressed the repair to the trawl while I steered the boat to the north-east, where I hoped our luck would improve.

No sooner was the net mended than a huge black mark, several fathoms high, appeared on the depth sounder. This target, hard down on the seabed, could only be herring. The dense mass was far too big to be a wreck, though there were plenty of those in the area. These fish spawned in countless millions along this part of the Yorkshire Coast during August and September and had been fished for centuries by many nations. The government had recently imposed a ban on catching herring in the North Sea, despite fishermen's protests that this drastic action would kill off the entire trade in fresh herrings and kippers in the country. The merchants would be forced to close their businesses.

A large fleet of Dutch and Scottish vessels had left the area earlier in the month but a fishery protection vessel was still patrolling the region, ensuring the enforcement of this decision. Though our mesh size was too big to catch these small fish, there was a likelihood that cod would be feeding on this massive shoal. I yelled, "come an' look at this," to the lads on deck, while taking an accurate position of the quarry from the Navigator console flashing in front of me. Two curious faces appeared at the wheelhouse window.

"It's 'erring," Bill confirmed, "there'll be summat feedin' on 'em." He echoed my thoughts. With the 'fix' logged in the notepad at my side, I steamed the *Courage* downtide to the south-east for five minutes then stopped her across the wind. We quickly scrambled the net back over and began trawling to the north-west towards 'the mark'.

I frequently adjusted the course to ensure hitting the shoal. Three sets of eyes stared, unblinkingly at the sounder, willing it to record the dense mass encountered twenty minutes earlier. A few scratches began to appear on the thin graphite line that indicated the seabed. These quickly grew to a height of ten fathoms and continued to mark.

"Come on you beauty, keep goin'," I appealed to the machine, hoping the mark wouldn't peter out. It didn't. We took ten minutes to trawl through this huge mass of fish, during which I continued to note the minute adjustment in our position, to help me record the extent of the shoal for relocation purposes. Even when the sounder had stopped recording fish, I still held the course. It would be another three or four minutes before the trawl was through the 'mark' and even then, cod would swim ahead of the net for some time before tiring. Twenty minutes after the last scratches had indicated the herring were astern of us, I hauled the wheel hard to port and began to turn the *Courage* around to target the shoal again.

It usually takes a while to turn, but it seemed to take forever to get her round on this occasion, and we were now going quickly downtide. No sooner was the compass lined up steady on south-east than the sounder again indicated the huge shoal. "We'll get through it this time an' 'ave a look t' see if there's owt in it," I said to my shipmates, still avidly watching the sounder through the open window. They were as keen as me to discover if we'd struck gold.

Twenty minutes later, oilskin-clad, Bill and Bluey shipped up the winch clutches and we began to haul up. It wasn't long before the trawl was alongside. We hurried to get the mouth of the net on board, all the time looking to windward in anticipation, waiting for any fish to float. The codend came up with a rush, showing a good haul of cod. Quickly we scrambled at the loose netting, and then dragged the bag alongside. Our catch must have been around a hundred stone of fish; ten kit. The codend was rounded like a giant ball as Bill, on the winch, hauled the bag over the side onto the deck. The fish pound overflowed as the catch of wriggling cod spilled from the net. "Come on me lads lets get it down ag..." the words died in my mouth as I detected Bill staring at me. He too had been at sea with Tom Pashby and was familiar with all the sayings and mannerisms of our erstwhile skipper. I raised my eyes to heaven, said, "sorry," and began preparing to shoot the trawl.

Looking up, I spied the navy gunboat heading towards us at a rate of knots. There was no point in throwing the net over yet. The 'bogeyman' would only insist we hauled it back for inspection, so we began picking up the fish into boxes on the fishroom hatch, while our visitor launched the small 'Gemini' rubber boat to board us. By the time the four sailors came alongside, we had picked the fish up into eighteen boxes, each weighing approximately six stone. It was a splendid haul of mixed fish but predominantly cod of varying sizes and I was itching to get our gear shot again. The boarding officer, young and flaunting his authority, was quite officious. "Don't you know there's a ban on fishing for herring in this area?" he challenged.

"We're not fishin' for 'errin'," I countered. "Look we've got all these boxes o' cod. Look at our codends; they're at least eighty millimetres. Yer can't catch 'errin' in 'em." The sailor wasn't convinced at all. He was sure we were concealing an illegal catch and insisted on inspecting our fishroom.

"There's bugger all down there," I tried to explain, "we've only 'ad one 'aul an' t' codend was out." The man remained unmoved, so we were obliged to move the boxes, which we'd recently filled, stacking them on the deck so the inspector could visit the storage space below. Even when he'd checked the empty hold and it was blatantly obvious there was no fish below, he moved a few empty boxes around to search for hidden cargo. I was disgusted at his attitude and he clearly embarrassed his fellow visitors, who delighted in making rude gestures behind his back. At least this cheered me up and I concurred with their sentiments while keeping a straight face.

Pointing to a whiting on the top of a box, the stroppy official said to Bill, "what's that?"

"A mackerel," came the reply.

Next he measured our nets but could find no fault. "We're going to be in this area for some time," was his parting shot, as he crossed our vessel back to his rubber command. "You'll be seeing more of us."

"I can't wait," I replied through clenched teeth and grimaced smile. We were throwing our net over even before these unwanted visitors had boarded their craft. We shot the trawl again, though we were now some distance from our quarry. Bill and Bluey quickly got stuck into gutting and washing the catch.

"What bloody chance 'ave we got when the buggers don't know a whiting from a mackerel?" Bill asked, though didn't expect an answer.

We continued to hammer the herring mark. With the fish put below and iced in boxes there was only time for a quick cup of tea and a sandwich before we hauled again, with similar results. There was no rest for anyone while we pursued this quarry. It was dark when we hauled for the third time but the catch was still good, though the shoal of herring had now left the bottom and was lost to us. The lads were now gutting in the glow of the overhead lights, strung on a wire between the wheelhouse and foremast. These bulbs, screened by enamel shades resembling Chinese hats, rolled gently with the movement of our vessel.

I continued to navigate the *Courage* though the 'Decca' was noticeably less reliable in the dark. The normally steady dials were wavering quite erratically. Concentrating on the radar, which would give me an approximate idea of our position, I noticed a large target approximately two miles away, which was gradually drawing closer. This was strange because the visibility was clear and this mysterious craft was showing no navigation lights. I tuned the VHF radio to channel sixteen to listen, in case this stranger attempted to contact us, while continuing to monitor the ship's progress as the blip drew closer. "I think we 'ave a visitor," I called to the pair on deck; their yellow, blood-streaked oilskins glistening in the cluster lights.

"It'll be that bloody navy boat again. T' crafty sod'll be sneakin' up on us," Bill yelled back above the scream of the hundreds of gulls, which were also enjoying our success.

Eventually the unknown radar target was lost in the clutter in the centre of the screen, meaning the darkened vessel must be very close on our port side. I put both strops on the wheel, making my way onto the deck to stand at the boat's side, near to where the crew were working. I said, "'e must be close now lads, I've lost 'im in t' clutter o' radar. Can yer see owt t' port?" Both men stabbed their gutting knives into the wooden boxes they'd been working from and joined me, peering into the dark. Suddenly the black night was pierced by the beam of a powerful searchlight, totally dazzling us.

Quickly regaining his wits, Bill, in the middle of our trio, grabbed my right and Bluey's left arm. "After three boys, one, two, three." He began a series of high kicks. Bluey and I grasped the situation immediately and joined in, kicking each leg alternately like the 'Television Toppers'. Our impromptu performance was quickly curtailed when the searchlight abruptly went out again, leaving us blind in the relative gloom.

Green and white navigation lights broke the blackness and began to move swiftly away from our side. "We 'avn't finished yet!" Bluey bawled through cupped hands, as the forward facing lights gave way to a single white, stern glow. Not a sound had been heard on the radio.

This was not the case just after daylight on the following morning, when radio silence was broken by the same patrol vessel, again heading in our direction. My two shipmates were below, having finally caught up with the supply of fish and were enjoying a much needed kip. They'd been below less than an hour. I was wedged comfortably on the wooden bench that spanned my little wheelhouse, one eye closed, the other glancing between radar, sounder, compass and 'Decca'. This was a technique I'd found helpful during prolonged stints in the wheelhouse. After a while I'd change eyes.

"*Courage, Courage*, this is the Fisheries Patrol Vessel approaching on your starboard bow. Do you receive, over?"

I picked up the handset from VHF, annoyed at the disturbance. "Yer, I'm gerrin' yer," I replied, with an economy of words.

"Can you haul your gear immediately. I intend to send my boat over to inspect your nets," came back the bossy instruction.

This was even more annoying. The lads had barely been turned in an hour and there was another hour to trawl yet before I was due to call them for hauling, then they'd sit for half an hour with a pot o' tea and a cigarette.

"We aren't due to 'aul for an hour an' 'alf yet," I replied in an equally abrupt tone.

"I really must insist you haul your trawl now skipper," said the voice of authority.

There was little point in arguing. These people can make things very difficult if they choose to, so without further communication, I went for'ard to call the sleepers below. Dropping down the cabin ladder, I switched on the light, calling out, "aye aye lads, t' bloody navy's 'ere again, 'e wants us to 'aul."

"Fuck 'im," came a call from the nearest bunk.

" 'E won't tek no for an answer," I said. "We're gonna 'ave t' pull it up."

Both men climbed reluctantly from their bunks as I filled three mugs with hot water from the ever-boiling kettle. "It's same bugger that was 'ere yesterday. Pity 'e 'as nowt better t' do. Tek yer time, 'e can bloody wait till we're ready." I left the lads sitting at the cabin table, still half asleep, and returned to the deck. The small boat was already on its way with the boarding party.

Not waiting till we hauled the trawl, the rubber boat came up our port side and our 'friend' from the previous day jumped aboard, accompanied by two assistants. He called to his helmsman, a very young sailor, probably newly recruited, to stand off and keep station close to our side.

Opening the wheelhouse door, our uninvited visitor was disappointed to realise he couldn't get into my domain, as the bench stretching the width of the little bridge prevented access. This seat, in position when I'd acquired the vessel, was highly polished. Years of bottom sliding too and fro by previous incumbents as the boat rolled, had smoothed the wood to a shine.

"Can you haul your trawl now skipper?" This was an order, couched in the words of a request, from someone used to being obeyed.

"What, on me own?" I prevaricated. "I can't manage on me own. You'll 'ave t' go below an' 'urry t' lads up a bit."

Little did he know what he was letting himself in for, as the officious little prat gingerly made his way down the cabin ladder. I heard both Bill and Bluey's raised voices emitting from the open skylight. Loud cursing and implausible suggestions rent the air, much to the amusement of the two sailors standing idly by. The officer shot from the cabin red-faced and fuming.

"We'll haul as soon as they're ready skipper."

Ten long minutes later my two shipmates, deliberately at snail's pace, arrived on the deck and prepared to haul. The two matelots, unseen by their superior, gave my deckies the thumbs up sign and one whispered, "wish we dared tell him where to go like that."

Fifteen minutes more saw the trawl alongside and the bag of fish dropped into the receiving pound. Of course there were no herrings. I'd have been amazed if there had been. There was a moderate haul of decent fish, which would now have to be gutted and stowed when the trawl was back down, before the lads could return to their beds. If they'd managed a two-hour spell below, it would have been my turn for a watch in my bunk, but it wasn't to be.

"Are yer bloody satisfied now?" snarled one of my lads to the inspector. He wasn't and insisted on another look in the fishroom.

"We can't leave t' 'atches off, t' ice'll melt," Bill told him as he went down into the hold.

The clunk of the heavy wooden hatch boards, dropping into place above his head must have had a claustrophobic effect, as the inspector had been below less than a minute when he was banging to be let out. The man was unable to raise the hatch himself as Bill was standing on it.

The tyrant probably didn't even see the sixty to seventy boxes of prime fish we had stowed below, as pale-faced, he emerged back into daylight.

"Now piss off an' let us get on with our job," said the other half of the double act on deck.

The frustrated officer, angry at this insubordination, looked towards me through the window for support. His plea was in vain. "They've only 'ad an hour's sleep in t' last twenty-four. What d' yer expect. I bet you've 'ad more sleep than that." I was totally unsympathetic.

The indignant chief, waved to the youngster in the small boat to come alongside to take his party back to their ship. Swiftly the small craft headed in our direction. This wasn't to be as easy as it seemed for the unsuspecting coxswain. Each time the poor chap attempted to come alongside, I put the *Courage* slowly into stern gear and he missed his target. On his third attempt, as he tried to allow for unseen elements, I put her in ahead gear. The poor fellow was having no luck at all in getting alongside. Bill and Bluey were now enjoying the ravings of the officer, who was almost apoplectic.

"Stay there, we'll come t' you," I shouted to the unfortunate helmsman. On his fourth attempt I did nothing with our engine. The rubber boat, now with an excess of speed to compensate for the mysterious currents, hit our side with substantial force, causing the poor young fellow to fall headlong into the bottom of his little craft. I averted my gaze and felt a wave of guilt and sympathy for the lad. It wasn't his fault he had such an ass for a superior. Two minutes later they were gone.

We soon had the gear down again and continued our routine. The pair got a watch below, and then Bill took the next trick at the wheel, so I too managed some shut-eye. We were still fishing moderately well but had seen no sign of herring marks, despite continuous blanket trawling of the area, looking to find another shoal. It was late afternoon and we'd recently shot our trawl for the finishing haul of this trip when I heard Bill say, "I don't bloody believe it. The buggers are back again." He wasn't wrong. Mr Plod was astern of our vessel and steaming towards us at high speed. The small boat was hanging in the davit, ready for fast deployment. Personnel could be seen preparing to launch the craft.

My two companions had just finished gutting our latest catch. The fish pound contained the remnants of the haul including a quantity of small fish, sea urchins, starfish, weed, shells, a few small crabs and a large quantity of fish guts. "I'll fix the buggers this time," Bill said. I was to discover that he was very good at fixing things, though never aggressively.

Bill put the deck hose-pipe, which he was using to wash the catch, into the pound with the accumulated dross. This dreadful mixture began to swill too and fro with the gentle motion of the boat. Turning to his willing accomplice, speaking theatrically through the side of his mouth for no evident reason, he whispered, "stand by t' scupper door Bluey and when I give yer t' nod, open it." The scupper door, a sliding hatch in the side of the boat at deck level, enables excess water, offal and debris from the deck to be jettisoned overboard.

A few moments later, unannounced, the inflatable with its unsuspecting crew pulled along our port side as the *Courage* rolled to port. "Now!" hissed Bill through clenched teeth, as he raised the port side pound board. The mass of slops flowed to port. Simultaneously, Bluey opened the scupper door allowing the continued movement of the torrent.

The results exceeded their wildest dreams. Looking over to port for the first time in answer to yells from over the side, Bill saw the inflatable and its deflated crew. The little craft was almost full to the brim with the dreadful soup. "Oh 'eck!" Bill said, "we never saw yer there, we didn't expect t' see you again. Y've bin 'ere three times in t' las' two days already. Sorry."

The prospective boarders were seen off, choosing to retreat with as much dignity as they could muster.

That evening we landed an excellent first trip; a good omen of things to come.

CHAPTER 6

MORE FUN

We continued to fish well throughout the autumn and into winter when the weather permitted, concentrating mostly on whiting, which we seemed particularly good at catching. Unlike cod and haddock, which showed as small, individual targets on the sounder, whiting would mark similar to herring, though not usually as dense or extensive. The two species also shoaled on our coast at different times of the year. I'd make three or four passes through the shoal once located, then haul up, rather than trawl for a full watch. Though we didn't gut the whiting, these fish were labour intensive, as we relied on quantity to make a good trip. They were a relatively low value species.

One particularly exhausting trip, while fishing many miles to the south-east of Flamborough Head, I crossed the deck to the cabin hatch, shouting, below, " 'aul oh! 'Auling time, come on me lucky lads, let's 'ave yer out." We'd been dragging the trawl for less than three hours, but I was keen to pull it up and was confident of a good haul. We already had many full boxes in the hold.

Bill tumbled from his bunk, sat on the seat locker and proceeded to roll a cigarette. There was no movement from the opposite bunk. "Come on Bluey, its 'auling time," Bill called to the inert teenager across the cabin. The call went unheeded. His young shipmate slept on, dead to the world.

Bill finished his smoke then proceeded to make three mugs of tea from the simmering kettle. He brought a mug to the wheelhouse then returned below to his own drink. "Come on Bluey, show a leg, it's 'auling time." Nothing stirred. He sipped his tea, growing more exasperated. This was happening more and more. Bluey was only a young man and though he worked hard on board, he also played hard, along with the other fisher lads, when ashore. He was burning the candle at both ends and needed more rest. "Come on y' idle little sod ger out o' yer pit," Billy bawled. Nothing happened.

His eyes lit on the wooden shutters at each end of Bluey's bunk and inspiration struck him. "I'll fix you me lad. I know 'ow t' get yer out." Bill picked up an old newspaper from the table, separated the sheets then covered the inert teenager, leaving only his head in view. Picking up his cigarette lighter, he set light to the bottom of the paper then shut the shutters, holding the doors closed. There was a delay of several seconds then thumping, kicking and shouting from behind the closed doors, quite unlike anything he'd ever heard. Bill released the shutters and Bluey shot from the bunk through a cloud of smoke, like a genie from a bottle. His eyes were streaming, he was coughing, spluttering and swearing. "That'll teach yer t' get out when yer called me lad." Following this lesson, if Bluey was reluctant to leave his bunk, it only took the rustle of a newspaper in his ear to raise an immediate response.

We took another good haul on board and then another. We now had over a thousand stone of whiting below, but we were a long way from home. It seemed logical to take our catch to Grimsby, as it was usually merchants from this port that bought the majority of whitings on the Scarborough market. I radioed our agent and he contacted a leading buyer to agree a price. Arriving early the next morning, we were waiting outside the lock pits as the huge gates opened to the flowing tide. On request we were directed to a space near the merchant's premises, where the berthing master, who'd cycled round, was standing to take our ropes.

We weren't long landing the catch and we didn't weigh the boxes. All were estimated at seven stone then tipped into the port's larger containers to be transported direct to the factory chillers by a fork-lift vehicle. The whole process took less than two hours.

I was feeling quite pleased with myself at this private arrangement and was happily washing our empty boxes ready to pass back on board, when John R, approached. I'd met John several times in the past at various fishing meetings, as he operated his own vessel agency. John was a rotund, red-faced, balding man, with only a thin strip of hair at the sides and back of his head, He was wearing a heavy overcoat, cap and scarf, muffled against the cold. He bid me good morning and said we'd made the right decision in bringing our catch direct to the port, saving time and transport. This would reflect in the price we received for our fish.

I agreed and said we may be back if the fishing continued. While we were talking, I gained the impression that John seemed a little thoughtful and not his usual self. "What's wrong John? Is there something on your mind?" I asked.

"Yes there is," he said. "I've just come from the hairdressers."

I found difficulty in hiding a grin.

He continued in the same serious vein saying, "I was the first customer through the door this morning and as it was jolly cold in the salon at that time, I asked the girl if she would mind if I kept my coat on. The impertinent young thing said, "you can keep your hat on if you like mister."

I found it impossible to keep a straight face at this comment and was spluttering and choking, though the poor man couldn't see the joke. He went off muttering inaudibly.

The berthing master, who'd been pleased to accept some fish to take home, continued to watch and to make general conversation as we landed our fish and replenished our boxes. He looked amazed when we cast off the ropes and prepared to sail again as soon as the last box was stowed. "That doesn't happen often round here," he observed. Most Grimsby boats were at sea for prolonged periods then spent time in dock.

The gates were still open and river traffic light as we made our way towards Spurn Point lighthouse, clearly visible six miles downstream. Breakfast was completed as we cleared the river, then Bluey navigated the *Courage* back to the fishing grounds.

Thirty-six hours later we were back in Grimsby again with a similar catch, again selling to the same merchant, who seemed delighted with fresh deliveries to his door. The dock-man on his bike was really surprised to see us back so quickly, but looked totally perplexed, removing his cap and scratching his head when once again we let go of the ropes to catch the tide; the gates closing behind us.

When we sailed in through the lock pit on the following evening for our third landing in four days, the same poor chap came along once more to attend to us. "Are you catchin' 'em in the fuckin' dock?" were his only words.

When we cast off on this occasion, it was to sail for home. We were totally shattered, but we'd had a good week, catching two thousand, seven hundred stone of whiting, though only a few boxes of other species. The predatory whiting, in concentration, are clearly avoided by other fish.

We arrived back off Scarborough having each had four hours sleep en route, to find we had a brief wait outside the entrance. The dredger *Skarthi* was taking her last few grabs of silt before leaving the harbour to dump her cargo of spoil in the bay. She was named after a legendary Viking warrior, supposed to have given our town its name. Her grey hull and buff-coloured superstructure were splattered with mud and streaked with rust. The old ship had clearly seen better days, though continued to give good service to our port. Her Master, Captain Sid Smith, who nursed the old girl along, was a remarkable, gentle, unassuming man. He gave his usual smile and friendly wave from the bridge, doffing his battered, old sea cap as he steamed past.

Sid was the font of all knowledge where local maritime history was concerned. There was nothing he didn't know about Scarborough Harbour. As a boy he could remember the German High Seas Fleet bombarding the town in December 1914. Sid had joined the Merchant Service on leaving school and eventually became a Master Mariner, sailing the world's oceans. During World War II he was Captain of a cargo ship supplying munitions to the troops and had discharged loads at five separate invasion landings, including Normandy and Sicily. Sid had crossed the Atlantic Ocean on a number of occasions in merchant convoys, which were attacked by German U-boats. As well as being a very able and competent seaman, Sid must also have been a lucky skipper. He never lost a ship and never lost a man. Now in his later years, he was very content as a dredger skipper and Deputy Harbour Master. Sadly, he and his wife had no children.

Allowing the dredger egress, we tied up and made our way from the pier. Coblemen preparing to sail requested bait, but on this occasion we had nothing to offer them. An early merchant asked if we'd caught anything and if we were landing our fish. He was quite surprised when we said we'd nothing to land, as we'd been missing from the port for five days.

We'd had an excellent week and I'd already decided to go chasing whiting again the following week. Things don't always go to plan, or as my old skipper Tom often said, "we plan an' the Lord decides." We sailed early on Sunday morning and steamed south-east to the whiting grounds and were soon back amongst them. We had a couple of good hauls, but unluckily caught an uncharted wreck during the third watch and couldn't get clear without chopping our trawl away. We were in twenty-six fathoms of water and had one door chained up in the gallow. The other was suspended somewhere in mid-water, clear of the obstruction. There were no other boats in the vicinity to assist us, so my only other option was to attempt to contact Terry Diltry.

Terry owned an ex trawler, *Madame Sands*, working from Bridlington and was a renowned diver. He spent his days salvaging non-ferrous metals, such as condenser tubes, copper pipe and propellers from many of the wrecks in the area, for which he had salvage rights, using a considerable amount of explosives. Terry had also recovered nets for the Bridlington fishermen and was a local celebrity for his diving achievements. On one occasion he'd placed an explosive charge on a wreck, three quarters of a mile from Flamborough Head. The ship had been carrying a cargo of war time bombs when it had been sunk and some of these were now strewn across the seabed as the wreck had decayed. Fortunately for Terry and the area in general, when his charge fired, these high explosives didn't detonate in sympathy.

Terry was relating an account of this episode to one of his friends in the pub on his return, later in the day. His pal replied, "bloody 'ell Terry, if that lot 'ad gone off, we would 'ave 'ad to re-name Flamborough Head, Flamborough Bay!"

On another occasion Terry had loaded his truck full of scrap, delivering the cargo to his usual scrap metal merchant in Hull. Part of the consignment included a brass torpedo tube from an unknown wreck. On arriving back home, his telephone was ringing so Terry quickly ran into the house to answer it. The caller was the scrap merchant who said, "this bloody torpedo tube has still got one up the spout. You've got twenty minutes to get here and take it away before I ring the police." The offending article was returned to the sea quickly and quietly.

I contacted Terry and his team by radio at six o'clock on Monday morning as he was sailing from port, on his way to his chosen dive site. He was happy to lend his assistance and arrived alongside the *Courage* two and a half hours later. We'd agreed terms of half the value of the equipment for recovery of the gear, on a 'no cure, no pay' basis. This was a reasonable deal if it saved the inconvenience of returning home with little catch, then having to assemble the dozens of component parts that went to making up our gear. That was a nightmare scenario and would take at least two days to complete; the week would be lost. If we got our trawl back we could re-rig it and be back fishing in a few hours. There were two spare nets on board in case of major damage.

Terry waited a while for the tide to slacken, then kitted up into his wet suit. He donned bottles, mask and fins then jumped overboard, swimming down our taut trawl warp, dragging a wire hawser with him. The colour of the water was dark grey and the visibility, even with his high-powered torch, was almost zero. I had immediate regrets at asking him to do the job. Here was a man, diving on his own, onto an unknown, deep wreck, surrounded by netting, in the middle of winter. Gear can be replaced at a price, not so a man's life.

Terry seemed to be down for ages but then surfaced and we hauled him shivering, onto the deck. "'Eave on that wire now and yer trawl should come clear," he croaked.

Bill engaged the winch and began to heave. At first the net seemed to be coming up, but then snagged again. Terry jumped back into the water and swam down the wire again, surfacing a few minutes later saying, "now 'eave on it." A second time the gear came a little, then caught. As he went down to the depths for the final time, he shouted, "the bugger will come up this time," and on his return, it did.

We had recovered all our equipment and with a good catch of fish still in the codend as a bonus. There was little damage to the netting and we soon had the trawl back on the bottom, fishing again. I arranged to meet Terry at the weekend with his payment and to buy him a few beers. He and his two assistants sailed off contented to their chosen site, where his buddies would dive on the next slack water. It wasn't until sometime later when I learned to dive myself, that I appreciated the amazing feat Terry Diltry had accomplished for us. He broke all the rules, but survived.

We stopped working this lucrative area shortly afterwards, when a Bridlington skipper gave me the many other wreck positions in the area, over the radio. No wonder we'd had these grounds to ourselves. How we'd missed some of these fasteners during the previous trip was a mystery when I plotted them on my chart.

CHAPTER 7

THE PASSENGER

On a lovely spring Saturday morning, I was standing on the fish market with Bill and Bluey, having minutes earlier settled our account in the agent's office. The local fisheries officer approached us, accompanied by a dark skinned, foreign-looking gentleman. He introduced the man as a Mexican fishing student, visiting Britain to study our catching methods and marketing system. The inspector asked if we'd be prepared to take him to sea with us the following week, saying all visiting students must spend a few days at sea, to gain catching experience at the 'sharp end' as part of their course.

I informed the officer, to whom we regularly volunteered catch information and who I thought to be a pleasant, amiable man that we'd be sailing at 0400hrs on Sunday morning. I don't think our prospective passenger was aware that four o'clock happened twice in a day. He seemed quite stunned when he'd grasped the message. However, he agreed to be present, ready to sail at the appointed hour.

I enjoyed my time ashore with Dotty and our two lovely bairns, who were now of an age where we could have fun together. As usual on the Saturday lunchtime, we had a pie and pea lunch in the local diving club, situated next door to the 'Leeds Arms'. This was now a regular venue, as I'd recently become a member and was keen to learn to dive. Having spent most of my time at sea and knowing the positions of hundreds of wrecks, I thought it would be terrific to be able to dive on some of them.

The members of the club were very competent divers and great fun. I felt quite at ease in their company, though on this particular occasion there appeared to be a rather heavy drinking session in progress and for once, I wasn't going to be a part of it. I chose to go home with my family instead. Arthur, one of the leading members seemed to be in particularly good form. At least he wouldn't have far to go home. He lived in the flat upstairs.

As always, the weekend went very quickly. I was already on the pier when Jose arrived at the harbour the next morning and a more unlikely looking fisherman I've never seen. He was very dark, fat and had a peculiar, distinct, spicy aroma. He insisted on shaking my hand. His palm was soft and clammy. It was like shaking hands with a warm, wet lettuce. Our passenger stood out like a sore thumb on the fish pier that morning. All the other crews arriving at tide time in their usual working clothes, saw a pair of white eyes staring from inside the hood of a brand new yellow oilskin. This figure also wore new thigh-length, white seaboots and a heavy-duty pair of rubber gloves. The question, "who's that?" echoed from one end of the pier to the other. Bill and Bluey rolled their eyes and tried to distance themselves from the stranger.

We sailed and steamed about ten miles from shore, then shot the trawl. The weather couldn't have been better; just a gentle breeze and a lazy swell. We did the usual four-hour tow and began to haul. With the doors up, a short touch in stern gear and the boat was lying comfortably across the gentle swell. As always, I looked to windward expectantly as the sweeps were drawn in, waiting for the net to surface. The thrill of anticipation was ever present. Every haul was like a present at Christmas. There was always a surprise awaiting, though not always what you hoped for or expected.

I looked skywards to see squadrons of gannets gathering, many more than we usually saw. It was the nesting season and tens of thousands of the creatures bred successfully on the sheer cliffs at Flamborough. They would be hunting food for their ravenous chicks. These birds too were looking for the net to appear but their aerial view was better than mine at sea level. Could they see something below the surface that I couldn't? First one, then a few, then scores of the magnificent birds rolled over and were falling out of the sky, black tipped wings swept back, primrose yellow heads and pointed beaks projected forward. Each perfectly aerodynamic form hit the water like a dart, leaving barely a ripple as it broke through the smooth surface of the sea. It was impossible not to enjoy the wonder of this spectacle and even our passenger was pointing to the diving stukas excitedly.

For a few seconds there wasn't a gannet to be seen, then, one by one they began to re-surface, the lucky ones bolting down small fish that they'd plucked from our net. Later these would be regurgitated to feed their young. On the surface, they flapped their v-shaped wings ungainly, struggling to get airborne, in stark contrast with their graceful entry.

The net was pulled to the surface and was soon alongside. The codend floated, containing a reasonable haul of splashing marine life. Dozens of heads from small fish were sticking out from the taut meshes and the beautiful birds, now diving shallow and surfacing, were dragging these tiddlers from the trawl. We hauled the footrope on board and began to drag the stocking containing the catch, towards the boat. Gannets, still diving, were now getting tangled in the slack netting which formed the mouth of the trawl and which was hanging in the water for'ard and aft. As soon as the catch was released onto the deck we set about freeing these four or five struggling, trapped birds. This wasn't easy as their vicious beaks were thrust in the direction of anyone approaching. Being cruel to be kind, the birds in turn were grabbed by the neck to prevent attack, then untangled from the netting and launched unceremoniously back into the sea. They swam about for a while, undignified with feathers ruffled, before flapping their way skywards again.

Fishing was quite good and we hauled the trawl three times during the day, as usual snatching a brief meal and a nap when we could. Bill took the second watch, Bluey the third stint in the wheelhouse. Jose had been on deck watching our fishing operations each haul during the day, but after dark he was nowhere to be seen. When we pulled up the trawl at ten o'clock that night, our student never got out of his bunk.

When it was time to haul again at three o'clock in the morning, there was again no sign of our passenger. Bill decided that if this person had come to see British fishermen at work, he should be on deck with them, not down below in a bunk, so he walked to the mouth of the cabin hatchway and at the top of his voice shouted, "arriba, arriba." This meant nothing to Bluey or me but had an immediate effect on the 'sleeping beauty' below. He emerged from the cabin like a shot from a gun. Two big, white eyes were followed by shirt-tails and baggy underpants as Jose tumbled onto the deck. At least he'd taken the oilskins and seaboots off to go to bed.

Our Mexican friend stared round with uncomprehending eyes. He'd heard this urgent summons from the deck yet work was going on as usual. "We've just 'ad a good 'aul," Bill said, "we thought you'd like to see it." Jose turned out for every haul for the remaining time we were at sea and certainly learned something of the way we earned our corn. We heard he slept for twenty-four hours solid when he got ashore.

It was the following weekend, in the Sub Aqua Club when I learned of my lucky escape from the party the previous week. Arthur told the story. He said his head was pounding, his hands felt sore and he was very cold. He slowly opened his eyes and blinked. All he could see was brick. "Where the hell am I?" He blinked again and looked up. His hands were clinging to guttering at the edge of a roof. He looked down. It was a long way to the ground and he hoped he was having a nightmare, but he wasn't. Arthur looked down again and realised that all he was wearing were his underpants. "This can't be happening," he thought. "I'm hanging from the roof of a three story building with no clothes on." His last recollection was of boozing with his mates and some fishermen in the club bar.

Arthur realised the roof he was dangling from was that of the diving club. Looking to his right, he could see the sash window, which he must have climbed out through. It had dropped down again. There was no chance of reopening the sliding sash panes from the outside. Looking left, he saw a drainpipe and edged his way towards it gingerly. Reaching the fall pipe, he unhooked his throbbing hands, clasped the pipe, then gradually, hand over hand, was able to slide slowly to the ground.

Arthur stood trembling, unable to believe his lucky escape, then realised he was in an enclosed yard, full of beer crates. "I must be in the backyard of the pub next door," he thought. Looking through the glass door, he could see people sitting talking and drinking. "Oh hell, they're open, it must be evening." He was aware this door was his only way out from the enclosure and he was very cold. Arthur took a deep breath, opened the door and strode into the pub. All eyes turned in his direction as he walked in from the yard, surprising the clientele. His eyes were looking only at the floor as he made his way through the lounge into the bar, then out through the front door. He shot down the steps of the pub and into the street, quickly realising he was bare footed, then hobbled over the cobblestones to the diving club steps and safety. He was through the door and up the stairs to his flat in an instant. It was quite some time before Arthur felt able to drink in the 'Leeds Arms' again.

Bill joined the diving club for a while and enjoyed the local underwater landscape and occasional wreck dive, though he seldom visited pubs and spent most of his free time at home. Always mischievous, early one morning, while his wife was still in bed, Bill placed his diving bottle under the bedclothes. Cracking open the valve, the intense pressure contained within, blew the bedclothes completely off.

On Saturday, at six o'clock in the evening, alone as usual, I took the *Courage* to the icehouse for our week's supply of ice. There was no sign of the pierman but Dennis the iceman assisted me to berth the boat. Returning to his ice plant in a first floor, refrigerated chamber above the fish market, he began shovelling ice down the chute to the deck of the *Courage*. Below, in the fish hold, I trimmed the freezing particles with a brush, pushing the mass of small flakes to the back and corners of the ice locker as they dropped through the bunker-lid, preventing the deck scuttle from blocking before the pound was full.

The ice stopped flowing and I heard a shout from above. "Where are yer going? Bloody Bear Island?" It was Dennis, shouting his usual comment from the small window overlooking the chute when he thought we'd got our allocation.

"Just another slack 'alf ton?" I made my regular plea.

The iceman grunted his affirmation and returned to the conveyor, sending down the balance of our requirements. The three tons of thin, flaked ice would last us through the week, unless fishing was heavy or the weather particularly hot.

The *Courage* was the last boat to take ice over the weekend. Most boats took their needs during Saturday morning, but I preferred to pay Dennis a fee to turn out after hours, when the machines had made further supplies so I was sure of our full quantity without queuing. I planned to leave the boat berthed alongside the fish market. No one would want to land fish on a Saturday night and we'd be sailing in the early hours before the coblemen turned out, wanting the quayside berth to load their bait.

On completion of his work Dennis bade me good night and good fishing then left me to batten down the *Courage's* fishroom hatches and shut down her engine. Ten minutes later I was climbing up the pier ladder intending to make my way home. As I stepped onto the quay I spied the pierman heading in my direction at speed. He was an aggressive, unpleasant man with few friends and was new to the job. Most of the pier staff were helpful, friendly and obliging.

"You can't leave yer boat there, it's a landing berth, get it shifted," he yelled nastily, as he drew close.

"We're sailing at three," I reasoned, "no one'll want t' land or get bait before then. I always leave her there on Sat'dy nights."

"I don't bloody care, get it moved. You're not leaving it there today."

Bowing to his authority and not wanting confrontation, I said, "ok I'll move 'er t' outside of them three boats astern. You'll 'ave to 'elp me with 'er 'ead rope."

The horrible man snarled, "that's not my job, go an' get yer crew out."

I saw red. "Well fuck yer then, she can stay there," I yelled back at him, pointing to my boat alongside the quay. His attitude wasn't necessary. He was being difficult and thoroughly unpleasant for no reason whatsoever. I wasn't prepared to struggle on my own without reasonable cause just to appease this bully.

He was equally aggressive, shouting back, "trouble wi' you son, is you've got a fuckin' big 'ed."

Probably for the first time in my life, the response came as required, when I needed one, not as an after thought. "I might have a big 'ed but it would rattle in your mouth."

The horrible person realised I wasn't going to back down and I knew he wouldn't want to fight. He turned abruptly and sloped off without another word. I'd won the verbal battle. Mr Nasty didn't last long in the job. Complaints of his manner and attitude ensured his dismissal soon after this confrontation.

Late during the following week, while lying across a light breeze, mending our trawl, we observed a large vessel approaching from the north. It was soon obvious the ship was a large Hull trawler, homeward bound. She was only steaming slowly so we presumed she was idling, saving fuel and timing her arrival at St Andrews Dock for high water. We were not unduly worried at this close approach, as these vessels posed little threat when homeward bound. All on board would be sober. As the huge craft drew closer, her name, *Arctic Cavalier* was clearly distinguishable on both sides of the beautifully flared bows. This was a famous trawler with a reputation as one of the top ships from the port. As she steamed very slowly past, her skipper, high up on the bridge yelled, "can you come alongside?"

I was intrigued and curious, wondering why he hadn't used his radio to contact us. The *Cavalier* had slowed to a stop by the time we'd pulled our dangling net ends on board and soon we were lying alongside the magnificent ship. Her skipper was now on deck and offering us a bundle of floats and line which had been tangled in his trawl somewhere off the North Cape of Norway. I thought this very generous of him, but then the real reason for his dallying and strange lack of communication was revealed. He asked if we'd take a parcel of cigarettes in for him. He would come to Scarborough at the weekend to collect them. Though not happy about being involved in smuggling, even for a few hundred cigarettes, I felt obliged and consented, though swore I wouldn't get suckered into this trap again should the circumstance arise.

* * * * * *

The year was moving on quickly with but a few weeks remaining. I was now confident I knew my vessel well. All boats have their own little idiosyncrasies and the *Courage* was no exception, but between us we could usually keep the boat running for the duration of a trip with temporary repairs when necessary. Bill was adept at fixing things, and people. We carried spare fuel pipes and filters for the engine, as well as various sizes of belting for the numerous pumps and dynamos powered from the machine. Most of the wheelhouse equipment was duplicated or not vital to the continuation of the voyage, but one day we were faced with a problem we couldn't fix, and for which we had no spare.

The boat wouldn't steer at all. She wasn't answering the wheel, though there seemed normal pressure on the helm. It couldn't be a broken steering chain this time, as I'd recently had hydraulic steering equipment fitted. We hauled the gear and I remembered not to go astern this time as the drag of the trawl pulled her across the strong south-west wind. I'd learned from my previous mistake. With the trawl on board, we began trouble shooting, checking belts and pipes, looking to solve our problem. It was a poser till Bluey, hanging over the stern shouted, "no wonder she won't bloody steer, t' rudder's fell off." He was correct. The three of us gazed into the water at the place where we could usually see the rudder top, below the surface. There was no sign of the maroon painted blade and our vessel wouldn't steer without it.

What were we to do? I'd heard of skippers guiding their boats home by towing fish baskets on either side, causing drag, depending on the required direction. I didn't think this method would work in the present circumstances, as the wind was too fresh, so I wasn't surprised when it didn't work on this occasion. I'd also heard of deep sea skippers bringing their craft home hundreds of miles using a trawl board as a rudder, jury-rigged, steering the ship with blocks and tackles on the stern of the vessel. We couldn't attach the after trawl board to the rudderstock, but maybe by towing the board astern we could get steerage. It was worth a try. If all else failed we'd have to call for assistance.

Bill and Bluey shackled the board to the steel warp then lowered it into the water, paying out ten fathoms of cable. I engaged the engine and lifted the throttle. The *Courage,* her head pointing south-east, began to turn to starboard with the drag from the door. Our required course was south-west, directly into the wind so this was going to be difficult. Her head continued to swing, south then to south-west. The wind was soon on the port bow and her heading quickly swung to west, north-west and she continued circling.

Totally frustrated, I put the throttle down hard. The swing to starboard stopped immediately as the door was lifted half out of the water by the boat's momentum. She began to creep back to port, into the wind. I was jubilant. By increasing and decreasing the revolutions of the engine, averaging half speed, I was able to hold her head in the direction of Scarborough Castle headland, a mere seven miles distant. This was great. We wouldn't need a tow after all. I was euphoric, but hadn't thought far enough ahead. We covered the distance with no trouble at all but as I eased back the throttle, close to the pier end, the *Courage's* head came to starboard. Her head was soon lined up for the harbour entrance. I had no alternative but to increase the revs again if I was to gain entry. On reflection this was a stupid move. I should have stopped outside the harbour and ask for help, but I'd got this far and wanted to get into port without assistance. Once in the entrance to the harbour I had to ease the engine down again; I couldn't go at half speed any longer.

Her head immediately turned to starboard and my boat bumped into the lighthouse pier. Fortunately there was no damage but on recovering the door, I had to accept a short tow across the harbour from the visiting Bridlington vessel *Crusader.* Forever after, when we met, her skipper Tom Cowling would remind me he was owed salvage rights on my boat though he'd always settle for a half of beer.

The shipwright would take a few days constructing and fitting a new rudder so each morning was spent overhauling our trawl, and then repairing a damaged net in our gear store on the pier.

Mid-morning on the second day, rather than go to the teashop, Bill suggested we went to a little transport café he knew of in the town, beyond the station. We'd go in his Morris 1000, the latest in a succession of these vehicles Bill had owned.

I got in the back seat leaving Bluey as front seat passenger. "Can I 'ave another go at driving Bill?" he asked, when sitting in place.

"Aye OK," Bill nodded his assent.

I tapped Bluey on the shoulder and said, "you 'aven't got a licence."

"I don't need one the way we do it," he replied.

Bill relinquished the wheel, which Bluey grabbed with his left hand. He released the hand-break then said to Bill, "clutch," at which, Bill, hands on knees, put his foot on the clutch, while Bluey, somehow, engaged first gear with his right hand. "Clutch out, we're in first, accelerate an' indicate left as we leave t' pier." This was real teamwork and the pair had clearly practised this performance before. If Bluey forgot any instruction or didn't pay attention to the small amount of traffic, Bill would berate him seriously. I was both horrified and impressed. I don't know how often the pair had done duel driving and it was both highly irregular and obviously unlawful, but when Bluey eventually did get a provisional licence, it wasn't long before this became a full version.

CHAPTER 8

AN EARLY CHRISTMAS PRESENT

We were soon back at sea, though were looking forward to tying the *Courage* up in a few weeks and spending some time ashore with our families. Christmas was almost upon us. The weather became unsettled with a biting, cold, easterly wind, which stayed in that direction for days on end, creating a niggling, uncomfortable swell. The old fishermen called these lingering easterlies, 'sheep's 'ead winds'. That was the only meat affordable when they couldn't get to sea for weeks.

We were heartily sick of rolling about; there wasn't much fish to catch and it was hauling time again. We heaved the trawl up and the orange coloured net was straight up and down, bar tight alongside, obviously containing something very heavy. This couldn't be fish as they're semi-buoyant. It would probably be a rock; perhaps some lost fishing gear or maybe an old anchor. Bill and Bluey heaved on the quarter ropes, dropping the bobbins onto the deck. This eliminated the anchor theory. An anchor would always be hooked over the ground gear.

The combination of swell and weight in the net was causing the bobbins to swing back overboard each time she rolled to port, so while the two men held their respective ropes in position, I lashed the wayward ground gear to the inboard side of the boat with the stern rope, preventing it from jumping back into the sea. Together we passed another rope around the entire net and drew it tight. With Bill hauling on the winch, Bluey and I, with two short rope strops, were able to slowly seesaw the long sleeve of the net up the boat's side. Eventually the thick, green codend appeared in view. There was certainly something large and unusual in the bag. It was uniformly cylindrical in shape and about two feet in diameter, probably a piece of wreckage.

The lifting hook was eventually deployed and as Bill hauled the catch slowly from the water, our vessel leaning to starboard in sympathy, we attempted to identify the object. I could see the bottom end of it, sticking out where its weight had chafed through the net. The thing was round and bullet shaped. "Stop 'eaving," I yelled to the winch man, "it's a bloody bomb!" There was no way we were pulling a bomb on board. I knew from past experience, it's easy to get these things on board. The problem was getting them off again.

We stopped to take stock of the situation. Here we were, three of us, the week before Christmas, rolling about with an unexploded bomb dangling over the side. We couldn't take it into the harbour. If the thing went off, the result would be catastrophic. It would do untold damage to seafront properties and the harbour master would be most unhappy. We could simply cut the unwanted catch adrift. The loss of the codends was a small price to pay, but there was a high probability the ordnance would be caught again by another vessel in due course.

After some discussion we decided to drop the bomb on a nearby wreck where it wouldn't be a danger to anyone. The plan was that Bill and Bluey would hook the boathook into the quick release clip on the codend. I'd stop the boat over the wreck, identifying the sunken ship on the sounder. On the shout of "now!" the lads would pull the release clip, allowing the object to drop free. I would immediately set the engine to full speed ahead, so if the bloody thing went off on hitting the seabed, at least we wouldn't be directly above it.

The wreck was soon located and I stopped the boat. "Stand by lads. Now!" They heaved together, the clip opened and the bomb fell. I shoved the throttle to full and we instantly picked up speed. Unfortunately the device had only slipped half out of the net, then jammed and was banging on the boat's side as she rolled heavily at full speed ahead. The high explosive remained stuck for about half a minute, though it seemed much longer, before finally falling free. We looked astern, waiting for the massive, CRUMP and gigantic fountain of water but nothing happened. It didn't explode on impact with the bottom, which now we were safe, was a bit of an anticlimax, but the bomb didn't hit the wreck either.

Much relieved, though mentally drained from the drama, we headed for home, arriving in the early evening. Quickly landing our meagre catch, we secured the *Courage* then hurried to the nearest pub to celebrate our survival and an early start to Christmas.

A few months later, the *Success II*, fishing in the same area caught the contraption again. Her skipper Jim Lawrence and his crew were incautious enough to haul the bomb on board, then inform the Coastguard by radio. The Royal Navy bomb disposal unit was sent for and the skipper anchored a mile off shore to await their arrival. The naval officers, on seeing the huge cylinder were horrified. "This isn't a bomb, it's a very sophisticated mine, with numerous booby traps." The disposal team were amazed the device hadn't previously exploded with rough handling. A light sensitive cell, which would cause the weapon to explode, was blocked by a barnacle.

After much deliberation and delicate exertion, the mine was manoeuvred back overboard and *Success II* was allowed to return to port. At two o'clock the following morning, the deadly weapon was detonated by remote control. The sonic boom from the massive explosion rattled the town's windows, causing widespread consternation, even from ten fathoms down. We'd had a lucky escape.

Christmas Eve lunchtime was always the start of the 'Bottom End' celebrations, so along with a large group of pals, mostly fishermen with money in their pockets, I was out on the town. On tour from pub to pub, we were having great fun. Promptly at 1430hrs the landlord called 'time', and having consumed a large amount of booze, we were reluctant to end the party to go home. Collectively we decided to visit Rich and Sandra, who had recently moved back to the 'Bottom End'. Sandra had spent her early years in the area and we were sure they'd be pleased to see us.

En route we passed the little butcher's shop in the square, close to the 'Leeds Arms', where a mouth-watering display of pork pies featured in the window. Cyril, an engineer and one of our group, dashed in, quickly purchasing a large, standing pie, which he thought would be appreciated by our soon-to-be hosts.

"Shall I carry that f' yer Cyril?" I volunteered, as he caught up with the group.

He handed over the brown bag without a second thought. I dropped back from his sight, opened the bag and took a large bite of the delicious golden crust. Someone at my side took the parcel from me and also took a mouthful. Gradually, as we made our way along the street, the pie was handed from person to person, each one taking a bite. The remains, back in the bag were handed to Cyril as he stood on the doorstep of the new residence. As Sandra opened the front door, greeting us all with sincere pleasure, Cyril removed his purchase from the bag and said, "we've brought you this ppp... A look of horror came over his face as he realised he was holding a dome shaped blob of pink meat. Not a scrap of crust was left on the pie. Thinking on his feet he continued, "we've brought you this brain."

The hospitality offered by the couple was very generous and later than planned I left the party, setting off for home. It was already dark. A clear thought came to my befuddled mind. I hadn't yet bought a Christmas card for Dotty. There was no excuse for this heinous crime so I decided to go to the local Boyes chain store, normally a ten-minute walk away. This regional store is a real treasure trove. The company motto should be, "if Boyes don't have it, you don't need it."

It was getting very late when I arrived at the store and the hard-working staff were already preparing to leave to attend to their own last minute needs. Luckily for me, a friendly counter girl, noticing me wandering aimlessly along the aisles, took pity on me and asked what I was looking for.

"A Christmas card fo' my Missus," I said hopefully.

"I'm afraid they've all gone," came back a sympathetic reply.

My face fell. I hadn't time to travel further into town, even if I'd been capable of making the journey. The shops would be closed before I got there.

This wonderful lady said, "wait a moment, I'll look in the stockroom, see if there's anything left." Minutes later, though having little sense of time, it may have been longer, this paragon returned with a small card which was marked 6d. This was pre-decimal currency and we'd been using new coins for a few years.

"I was 'oping fo' one in a box," I said, not wanting to inconvenience my ally.

"There are several boxes in the store, but they all seem to be empty." she said.

Inspiration struck me. "Could I 'ave t' biggest empty box you've got. I'll put t' little card in that."

Smiling, either in sympathy for my wife or imagining my fate when the box was opened, she brought me a large, white, empty card box. I signed the card with the assistant's pen, put lots of kisses on it, paid the two and a half new pence, gave my saviour a kiss in gratitude and set off for home contented.

Somewhere on my way home, everything went blank, because my next recollection was of Dotty grabbing me roughly by the collar and taking me the final fifty yards home. She'd received a phone call from neighbours round the corner saying, "can you come and collect your Fred? He's swinging on our gate."

Dotty was exceedingly angry, and quite rightly. I'd said I'd not be too late coming home, but even with the loose description of 'too' giving me a little leeway, I was still miles adrift. She wasn't very keen on the card either, which, miraculously was still in my possession. Furthermore, I was supposed to construct a doll's house for little Paula, from a flat pack. Dotty had already put some of the kit together and I was in no state to offer assistance with its completion. I suggested maybe Paula could do it herself in the morning. She was a very clever girl.

The glare I received in return should have frozen me to the spot, though didn't. My bad timekeeping wasn't the full extent of the bother I was in either. We were due to go out that evening, together. Dotty had been to the hairdressers and was not about to be swayed otherwise. We now had a wonderful, young schoolgirl, Patsy, who was a regular babysitter. Despite her mere fourteen years and small stature she was very competent, reliable and loved the kids. Patsy was due to arrive at eight o'clock and it was now well past six.

"Go and get in the bath NOW!" I was ordered.

Obeying without question, I made my way unsteadily upstairs and sat in the ready filled, hot bath, which Dotty had prepared. I was glad to close my eyes. The next instant I received the biggest shock I'd ever had in my life. This was delivered in the form of a bucket of cold water, poured over my head. It was freezing and I gasped for air. If I'd had a weak heart this dowsing would have killed me off. I sat in the now tepid water, eyes vacant, teeth chattering, unable to speak.

"There's some black coffee at your side, drink it," was my next instruction. Again I obeyed. The strong, syrupy mix burned my mouth. Fifteen minutes later, in bare feet and clad only in a towel, I was frogmarched round our little backyard in the cold, fresh air.

At eight o'clock we went out together. I vowed not to drink again, but as our first port of call was the 'Leeds Arms', this proved to be impossible. A little later, we decided to wander further into the main town, an unusual occurrence for us, but it was Christmas Eve. We found ourselves in a pub called the 'Aberdeen'. I was delighted to see Ernie Williamson, also a little wobbly, with a group of his pals also on a tour of the town. I was standing talking to Ernie at the bar when the adjacent phone rang.

Before the landlord could reach the handset, Ernie grabbed the phone and said, " 'ello."

He listened attentively, replying, "naw silly sod, it's Scarborough," then carefully replaced the receiver.

The hovering landlord, annoyed, asked, "who was that? I've been waiting for an important call all evening."

"It weren't important," Ernie said grinning, "some daft bugger askin' if it were Aberdeen."

For Christmas I bought little Danny a junior tool-set as a present. Within an hour of opening the parcel, while playing on the path outside the house, he'd damaged the next door neighbour's glass door with his little hammer. Dotty was quite cross with him for this act of vandalism but I suggested he was only playing, as little boys will. Ten minutes later, when he'd smashed a further window inside our house, the toolbox was confiscated. This Christmas, Danny had also received his first set of wheels in the form of a small plastic trike. In no time at all he was carrying the little three-wheeler to the top of our very steep hill, then riding back down, lifting his feet from the ground to gain speed. He put fear into everyone's hearts as he shot down the street, people believing his bike was out of control as he belted down the path. Danny continued to wear his shoes out every few weeks, as his feet were his only means of stopping.

New Year's Eve was upon us and as had now become a tradition, we had a terrific party at home. These riotous celebrations began as quiet family affairs at first, and were held at home because we couldn't get a regular babysitter. Now they'd become quite wild events; the house seemed to rock and the walls move to the music of 'Status Quo' at full volume. The two bairns were asleep in their beds before anyone arrived and despite the subsequent racket, didn't stir, even though at one point we had between seventy and eighty people in the house. It was gone four in the morning when the last guests were pushed out through the door, then Dotty and I put the house back together again before going to bed.

We were up again at eight o'clock next morning, quite bleary-eyed as Paula and Danny, having had a full night's sleep, were demanding attention. Soon after lunchtime, with Patsy in control, we were in the 'Leeds Arms'. It was always very busy in the pub on New Year's Day. The landlord, Les, was a strange man; fifty some, balding, bespectacled with a round face and greying beard. He could be quite charming to the ladies and always lived in the hope of pulling a bird. Leslie could also be quite difficult and obnoxious when upset. His major attribute was that he kept excellent beer, sold good wine and always had a well-stocked ice bucket on the bar.

Among the crowd, propped on a stool at the end of the bar was Ken, a chef who worked in one of the larger hotels in town. Ken had been on duty the previous evening and was now determined to celebrate his New Year. He'd been first through the door at noon, having already consumed a quantity of drink. He'd then drunk several pints of beer and was showing no sign of slowing down. Sometime between one and two, the skirl of pipes outside signalled the arrival of Barry. Seconds later the piper, formerly a soldier in a Scottish regiment and dressed in full regimental regalia, entered the premises playing 'Scotland the Brave' to loud applause. The lone piper then continued with several other wonderful, traditional renditions and received full attention from the packed house. Much to the landlord's dismay, Barry slowly marched behind the bar, Les's exclusive, inner sanctum and helped himself to a quadruple whisky from the optic.

The landlord was clearly infuriated, both with the invasion of his space and the loss of drink. He immediately became the centre of attention for his attitude to the musician and was the butt of jokes and comments, which he had difficulty coping with. Twenty minutes later the solitary piper played himself out again with the 'The Skye Boat Song'. It wasn't clear how many pubs Barry visited on New Year's Day, but if he managed nine or ten of the many establishments in the area, he would have consumed in excess of a bottle of whisky.

There was lots of laughter and joke telling in our company. Men and women were enjoying the opportunity to relax in the atmosphere of what was essentially a village pub. The 'Bottom End' of Scarborough was in every way a village and the 'Leeds Arms' was for many people, the focal point and community centre.

A crash from the end of the bar drew everyone's gaze and it became clear that Ken the chef had fallen off his bar stool. He was lying flat on his back on the floor and wasn't moving. "No one touch him. Leave him alone. Keep clear," called the landlord as he grasped the situation and rushed from behind the counter to the inert customer on the floor. A space cleared around the unconscious Ken as the host appeared through the crowd. Everyone was keen to watch Les, not renowned for his sympathy or nursing skills, administer to the casualty.

Arriving on the scene, he picked up a soda syphon from the bar. Pointing the nozzle at the poor man, still stretched full length on the floor, Les squirted the jet of fizzy water full in the face of the hapless victim, emptying the entire contents of the bottle on the prone figure. The corpse miraculously opened his eyes, sat up and shook his head. Ken looked round the room confused, wondering what the fuss was about, then climbed back onto his bar stool and picked up his drink.

"I've always wanted to do that," said Les to the nearest of the many incredulous people, gaping open-mouthed at his ministrations.

Shortly after midday on the second of January, our last day ashore before returning to sea, and nursing a hangover from the accumulated days of excess, I again found my way to the pub, looking for like-minded people. I joined the company of Bill Sheader and pals, which guaranteed entertainment. Bill and his large circle of friends were the landlord's best customers.

"Why aren't you at sea?" Bill asked, knowing well we wouldn't be sailing until the following day.

"Yer don't get medals fo' goin' t' sea," I glibly replied, then realised I was talking to our lifeboat coxswain, who had several awards. "Except in your case," I quickly added.

As usual Bill was holding court and everyone was listening to him intently. "Last year ah came in this pub every dinnertime and every night except one," he announced to his group and the clientele in general. His distinctive voice filled the room.

Inevitably I was the one to ask, "what 'appened that day Bill?"

"Ah never got 'ome from t' dinnertime," he guffawed loudly at his own joke.

Minutes later the telephone on the end of the bar rang loudly. Les answered in his usual pretentious phone voice, "Heelloo, this is the Leeeds Arms, can I heelp you?" Disillusioned on this occasion, he called out to Bill, "it's Julie fo' you."

Three strides in the little pub brought Bill from a window-seat to the bar and phone. In earshot of everyone, he bawled into the handset, " 'ow did yer know where t' find me?"

It was a wonderful atmosphere in the pub that day and Bill, in top form, was holding the crowd in his finest style. It was well-known that Bill never went shopping. He seldom travelled beyond the market, then only to visit different pubs. If Bill needed anything from the town's shops, he sent long-suffering Julie. He told us of the occasion when he was in need of a new suit. His own grey, square-cut suit, which he'd had for years, was looking shabby. Bill wrote a brief note, sealed the envelope, then instructed Julie to take the message to the popular tailors in the main street.

The manager of the shop opened the envelope, read the contents then laughed loudly saying, "do you know what this says Mrs Sheader?"

"No I don't" she replied frostily, "but if my Bill has written it, it'll be right."

"But Mrs Sheader, it says, same as last time but with another inch round the arse."

This caused great merriment but then Ernie spoke up. "Aye but she got 'er own back on yer, didn't she? Rachel told me t' story."

Bill turned to his little pal looking perplexed then scratched his head under his cap.

Ernie told of the occasion, unknown to Bill, when Julie had been sent to buy a new pair of shoes for him. On arriving back home from the town centre with his usual style and size, Bill had insisted they were too small and that she should take the shoes back to get a larger size. Julie argued strongly that they were the right size, but Bill had been adamant. "Tek 'em back an' get me t' nex' size up."

Leaving the house with the shoes, Julie appeared to set off back to the shop but only went as far as her friend Rachel's house around the corner. There she stayed for an extended chat and a cup of tea before returning home again with the same shoes. Entering the house she handed her husband the footwear again saying, "try these on yer Bill."

He put the pair on, walked back and forth across the room before saying, "these are alright, ah told yer them others wer' too small."

This brought the house down and was the catalyst for much more banter. Even the landlord attempted to join in the repartee but someone said, "d' yer remember when Les asked Bobby Walker for a monkfish t' mek some fish stew wi'?" Eyes turned towards Les and he shuffled uncomfortably in the limelight. "Bob brought one in weighin' about three stone. Its 'ead was on 'is shoulders an' t' tail was nearly on t' ground. Its mouth was like t' 'arbour mouth," he exaggerated wildly.

Ernie chipped in, "aye, an' that lobster 'e asked fo' Nommy. Didn't you bring 'im a big un in, on a lead?"

Attention now fell on me and through tears from the previous story, I described how, on one busy summer evening, when I was a deck hand in the *Jann Denise*, skipper Bob had walked into the pub, announcing loudly to Les and all in earshot that I'd be in shortly with the lobster he'd requested. He informed the host we'd caught one in the trawl earlier that day. Meanwhile, I was outside the door tying the creature to a fathom of twine.

A minute later I walked through the entrance dragging a huge, dead, barnacle encrusted, old lobster on the bit of string. "Come on in matey, don't be shy," I called behind me to the lifeless crustacean. "Come an' meet your Uncle Leslie." I had no trouble getting to the counter. A path opened up immediately for me in the busy pub. It wasn't difficult to get a place at the bar when you'd been at sea for a few days without a wash, but on this occasion I think the lobster helped too.

The landlord, who loved to dish out humour at other people's expense, had now fallen silent. This was an ominous sign and unfortunate timing for two male strangers, who at this point innocently wandered in from the street.

"Can we have two pints of bitter please boss? One with a dash of lemonade."

"There's nothing wrong with my beer," snapped the landlord.

"I'm sure there's not," replied the unsuspecting customer.

"Then you'll either have it unadulterated or you're not having it at all."

"Just two pints of bitter then," said the poor man, unaware his host had recently been wound up by his regulars. His friend stood open-mouthed but silent. The pair quietly drank their beer, which was in its usual, excellent condition. These two men, frequently looking in our direction, were unable to understand why everyone else in the place seemed to be enjoying themselves.

A few minutes later, at two-thirty on the dot, five bells was sounded, navy style, by Les who shouted, "tiiime."

"Any chance of another?" the second of the visitors enquired quickly to the adjacent barman.

It fell quiet in our corner. This was shades of Oliver Twist.

"Would you like to drink a little longer in my pub?" asked the landlord softly but clearly audible to our group.

"Yes please," said the strangers in unison.

We cringed collectively.

"Well get yer fuckin' selves in earlier in future," bawled the publican as he snatched their empty glasses.

Les Jenson, landlord of the Leeds Arms.
Courtesy of Bob Walker

Bill 'Jitta' Sheader, Tom 'Denk' Mainprize and Tom Rowley.
These three men were all awarded gallantry medals by the
RNLI while acting as coxswain of Scarborough Lifeboat.
Courtesy of Scarborough Evening News

Skipper Will Pashby arriving home with the 'wonderful' news that the 'Heath Government' would give the fishing industry 'due consideration' in the negotiations to join the Common Market. Left to right: Pete Somers, Ken Fishburn, Will Pashby, Ernie Eves, Ray Thordason, Charlie Plummer, Terry Hunter, John Normandale, 'Jocksey' Scales.
Photo courtesy of Bill Pashby

CHAPTER 9

LOWS THEN HIGHS

The New Year at sea brought new problems. We didn't get to sea often in January as the weather was exceptionally poor. Occasionally, when we did sail during brief lulls, we were usually pleased to get back as the wind freshened yet again. One afternoon in early February, when beating another retreat in a northerly gale, I left it too late to attempt an entrance and missed the tide. There was insufficient water for a safe passage in the deep swell. All the other vessels were snug in the harbour while we waited half a mile offshore for the tide to ebb then flow again. The wind had risen to severe gale and we could only dodge head to wind and be patient. I played my newly acquired searchlight on the coming seas then adjusted the engine speed to keep steerage on the vessel and keep her comfortable. She was a fine sea boat and I never doubted her.

At eleven o'clock in the evening, after taking advice from the watch-keeper in the lighthouse, I deemed it was safe to enter the port. Apart from some severe rolling and heavy spray, we had no problems getting round the pier end. We tied our boat up, the lads putting double ropes out against the strength of the gale, then I stopped the engine and we left the pier. I was soon on my way home up the hill to "the lee side o' Bum Island." This was an expression Jackie Mann, skipper of the *Evelyn* often used, when referring to being in bed with his wife, Dinah.

Dotty was in bed when I arrived at the house, though not asleep and there wasn't much of a lee anywhere near Bum Island. She'd seen us outside the harbour and was horrified and frightened at the searchlight's erratic movements. Nothing I could say would sway her from thinking that we might have been lost. I repeated over and over that we were in no danger and it was only the searchlight playing tricks, but she would have none of it and vowed never to watch us again in similar circumstances.

"If you want to kill yourself, don't expect me to watch you." That was her final word on the matter.

Next morning at breakfast, little Danny, who knew we'd been caught out in poor weather, innocently asked, "were you frightened, Dad? Did you find a smooth bit?"

It was a hand to mouth existence in these early months. To compound our problems, when we did get to sea, fish prices were very poor. It wasn't just a local problem. The country was swamped with cheap fish from all over the northern hemisphere. There was even talk of importing frozen fish into Scarborough, along with the timber, fertilizer and potatoes which were regularly shipped in.

The end of February brought more gloom when skipper and respected leader Will Pashby was taken ill on his vessel, *Elisabeth* while fishing offshore from the Tyne. Will and his crew had caught a huge haul of dogfish, an unknown occurrence at that time of year. Usually, these were never seen in large numbers before early summer. Will and his crew were wrestling with the intense weight of the haul, attempting to get the catch on board when Will suddenly collapsed with a suspected heart attack.

One of his crew, Eddie Temple immediately radioed for assistance, then chopped away the bag of dogs, allowing the massive haul to sink to the bottom of the sea. A helicopter was soon on the scene and Will was taken into intensive care at Ashington hospital.

This wasn't Eddie's first experience of handling medical emergencies at sea. Years earlier while sailing as mate on a Grimsby trawler, he'd been required to perform a tracheotomy on his skipper, who was unable to breathe unaided. With radio assistance from ashore Eddie cut the man's throat and inserted a plastic tube into the exposed windpipe, saving his skipper's life.

After a few days in hospital and still very ill, knowing he'd never go to sea again, Will Pashby insisted on being taken home, where he died. His death was a great loss not only to his family but to the entire fishing community. Will's skill, tenacity, knowledge and leadership were an example to a generation. His funeral, in a packed St Mary's Church, was attended by fishermen from the Tyne to the Humber and was a very sad day indeed. Will was fifty-nine years old.

March too was a dreadful month. Against the trend, we landed a good trip in the first week, a catch I was delighted with, but the fish sold cheaply on the market and we earned little money from it. The next two weeks again brought constant bad weather and on the only day we got to sea, I caught a wreck a few miles from Bay Wyke and lost the trawl. I was finding it difficult to meet my bank and mortgage repayments and was facing an uncertain future. Considering selling the *Courage*, my pride and joy, I informed my crew we were facing troubled times but they were prepared to stay as long as we could keep going.

It was at this point, when things were really low, I was given a vital pep talk by Dotty. Mostly my wife kept her own counsel, but as I was well aware, when she had something to say she didn't mince her words. "That's our boat, you've worked hard to get her and you're not going to throw it all away now. Things will get better."

They would too, but they were going to get worse first. There was talk nationally of blockades to stop imported fish and also to attempt to secure a fifty-mile limit for British fishermen within the new Common Fisheries Policy, which was under negotiation. News came that Grimsby fishermen had blockaded both Grimsby and Immingham Docks to prevent further cargoes of imported fish getting into the country. Other fishermen throughout Britain were holding meetings with a view to taking similar measures.

'Denk' Mainprize, one of the leading skippers in the port, the man who'd picked up the mantle of the late Will Pashby, called a meeting at the 'Lord Nelson Hotel'. The room was packed with worried fishermen, who were struggling to keep going. A unanimous agreement was reached to blockade Scarborough Harbour in support of the other protesting fishermen and to request the Borough Corporation not to allow any frozen fish into the port.

Thirty boats blocked the harbour entrance from early on the last day of March and four watches of crews were appointed to guard and protect the vessels. By evening on the first day the weather freshened and it was necessary to reduce the number of craft, but the watch-keepers kept to their shifts.

The blockades were receiving national publicity. Television and newspapers were filled with fishing boats creating havoc at ports around the country. I attended a protest meeting in North Shields with 'Denk' and Colin Jenkinson, his son-in-law, skipper of the *Our Rachel*. The Shields men were considering blockading the Tyne but were given assurances by the Bergen & Olsen lines that their ships wouldn't transport frozen fish into the river while the dispute lasted. George Crawford, a very articulate Shields skipper spoke well, saying fishermen had never had a single voice and it was time to form a national association of fishermen.

Back home again, I'd drawn the 1800hrs to midnight watch each day and along with Colin and several others, was able to spend the evenings on watch in the comfort of the Yacht Club, situated in the lighthouse building, overlooking the harbour entrance. Colin's generosity made sure I wasn't short of a few beers while we stood our spell on the picket line and I wobbled home each evening.

Talks were held with top civil servants in London but legal injunctions were also served on skippers in some ports, but the blockades held. It was the evening of April 2nd when our boats returned to their berths, allowing entry to the *John Bluhm*, a regular trader to the port, carrying a cargo of timber. In exchange, the local shipping agents agreed not to handle frozen fish from outside the Common Market. Still no one sailed until finally, the main action committee in Aberdeen gave the word. The problem of frozen fish from outside the Common Market would be addressed and there would be some cash assistance for fishermen.

We sailed again the next morning and very slowly, things did begin to get better. The spring gluts of fish from third countries dried up and catches and prices improved, but for me, it had been a close run thing. This was as close as I'd get to selling up. Even then, I spent a weekend helping out my brother-in-law Ian on his farm during a small mechanical breakdown. I found this experience totally alien to anything I'd ever tackled before and this helped to underline my newfound determination to keep going.

In early summer, following some good weeks fishing and better prices, but dogged by machinery problems, I was faced with replacing the *Courage's* engine. Her old, Gardner 152 horsepower was worn out and there seemed little point in spending money to keep the old motor going. With the help of a small government grant and loan, I was able to buy a new 230 horsepower engine of the same make and size. Scarborough Marine Engineers would take three weeks to install the engine but the loss of fishing time to upgrade the machine would be well spent, and we could use this period to paint and generally maintain my lovely, old lady.

The *Courage* was tied up conveniently for the workforce alongside the Golden Ball slipway, where she would be left high and dry twice daily at low water. The engineers arrived first thing on Monday morning to make a start on their project, led by Jacky Redman, a large sledge-hammer slung over his shoulder. This looked ominous. Jack wasn't even a qualified engineer. He usually delivered diesel fuel to the motorboats and cobles in five-gallon, metal drums. Some of the cobles would use up to fifteen gallons of fuel a day. On quiet days Jack used a carrier bike, carrying two cans. Today he was going to rip up the decking of my 'pride and joy'.

Jack, thin and alert, was red-faced with black, curly, unkempt hair. Ever cheerful, he had a ready smile. Nothing seemed to bother him and he was always ready with a joke or quick reply. Jack was always scruffily dressed at work, to the extent that he seemed to take a perverse pleasure in his untidiness. He would often find what he considered a perfectly wearable article in the many boxes of engine rags, which the company distributed to the fleet. His favourite garment, the one he was never seen without and was wearing now, was a full length, heavy duty, mottled brown, tweed overcoat. No matter what the weather, for years Jack wore this trademark garment.

Jack's coat was the first talking point when anyone met him round the harbour. " Jack, will yer leave me yer coat in yer will?"

"Don't fall in t' 'arbour Jack, you'll cause an oil slick."

"Yer could get ten gallon o' diesel if you wring yer coat out."

"When are yer gettin' a new coat Jack? Can I 'ave yer old one?"

He'd heard all these stories and many others and enjoyed the humour his coat invited.

As he approached I called out, " 'ow much fo' yer coat Jack?"

"Yer can't afford it," came back the instant reply and pleasant grin.

By mid-morning, the squad had cleverly removed two thin strips of sacrificial decking, one each side of the fishroom hatch. They were about to lift off a complete section of deck, intact, to expose a gaping hole in the centre of my vessel, when they realised some essential tools were required and all the men tramped back to their workshop. This was perfect timing of course, as the shortage of gear coincided with their tea break. I soon realised there would be a dearth of vital gear midway through every morning and afternoon.

At the end of the first week, the engine-room bulkhead had been taken down, the clapped out, old machinery had been removed via the hole in the deck and we were awaiting the arrival of the new motor. Late on Friday afternoon, I met a lorry carrying the eight-cylinder engine and greeted the driver, who introduced himself as Gavin. A small, round, rosy-cheeked man, with thin, blond hair, Gavin parked up his vehicle close to the slipway, in readiness for the crane and with thermos flask and bag of sandwiches, sat for a private picnic on the slipway. Following his alfresco meal, the driver showed an interest in our boat and I give him a tour round her, though she was clearly not at her best in this state of transition. I explained to him how we usually did thirty-six hour voyages, with every second night at home.

"I wouldn't mind a trip sometime," Gavin said enthusiastically, "any chance of coming with you when I get my holidays?"

I said he'd be more than welcome to come with us any time, but explained it would be at least two more weeks before we were ready for sea, possibly longer. I gave him my home phone number then forgot about the conversation.

Our task of refitting the *Courage* continued steadily. Each morning, while the engineers were busy working below on the engine installation and pipe-work, we'd work on the outboard sides of the vessel, her deck or masts, until she was spick and span. We didn't hurry or rush the work and took frequent strolls to the little tea shack on the outer pier. The 'Tea Pot', a small, wooden construction, served takeaway drinks and snacks. Here we'd mingle with the dozens of visitors, watch the anglers, observe passing craft and enjoy the warm sunshine at leisure, or joke with Chris and Sandra in the tea stall.

One day, at slack water, with a flat calm sea, Bill observed an angler having difficulty recovering his fishing tackle, which was fouled on the seabed, some distance offshore from where we stood. He whispered quietly to Bluey and me, "watch this." Putting down his mug, Bill climbed over the railings and jumped, fully clothed into the clear water, much to everyone's astonishment, including ours. On surfacing he held his throat, shouting to all in earshot, "it's the tea that's done it. It's the tea." He then swam easily to where the angler's line was fouled, performed a duck dive to the bottom and cleared the snagged gear. He then simply climbed back up the stepped, outer wall to rejoin us and the stunned, grateful angler. The whole operation took only three or four minutes and was very amusing, enjoyed by everyone around, except the ladies in the 'Tea Pot', who were quite indignant at the slight on their product.

This break was a pleasant interlude in my usually busy life. I was able to watch the day-to-day activities around the harbour during the easy routine. Late one morning, as I wandered along the seafront, I noticed the traffic was at a standstill. The cars and buses were usually slow in summer but at present they were stopped and I could hear a car horn blaring, further along the road. The reason for the stoppage became clear when I arrived at the source of the problem. In the centre of the main thoroughfare, halfway along Sandside, Ethel was conducting the traffic, while waving her walking stick at drivers who attempted to run her gauntlet. A crowd had gathered on the pavement and were enjoying the entertainment. Ethel was a small, elderly lady, who suffered a permanently stiff leg. She lived alone in a little cottage in the narrowest part of Quay Street, running parallel to this main road. The poor woman, who always wore the same old coat and dark headscarf, was mentally disturbed and didn't usually communicate with anyone. Only occasionally did she have these outbursts and it was quite sad to see her carrying on like this. Minutes later, with an angry motorist yelling at her to get out of the bloody way, while keeping a safe distance from the swinging stick, a policeman came along and gently persuaded her to move off the road.

Her next line was predictable. I'd heard it many times before. "It's that man in t' café over there officer. 'E killed my 'usband." She gave the name of the poor restaurant owner, whose life was regularly plagued by the old woman with her wild accusations and frequent confrontations. The policeman promised he'd look into the matter, then escorted Ethel back in the direction of her house, stopping the traffic himself to enable them to cross the road.

I also took the opportunity to cross the road, my good humour returning as I bought an ice-cream from the bustling 'Harbour Bar' ice-cream parlour. Crossing back, I stopped to lean on the railings at Sandgate Corner, while enjoying the delicious snack. High water slack had recently passed and the now receding tide had left a band of wet cobblestones as the water slowly ebbed away.

It was great fun watching the cut and thrust of the boatmen operating the small passenger craft as they plied their trade from ramps on both sides of the slipway. The motorboats, offering forty-minute rides around the bay on the left side, and rowing boats, taking fishing parties for hourly trips to the right, were bobbing lightly at their berths. The many boatmen, eyes constantly scanning the three approaches to the slipway, would vie for the opportunity to ask potential passengers if they were sailing. It was fascinating listening to their constant interaction, which occasionally led to blows.

"There's a bloke an' a lad comin' on t' Foreshore," 'Blondie' Wood, owner of the *Venture*, called out.

Albert Fishburn, from the motorboat *Heather*, an old hand at the slipway, faced 'Blondie' and said, "they're mine, they were wi' me yesterd'y an' said they'd be comin' back t'day." Albert's spectacles must have been really powerful to recognise these people a hundred yards away, but he was seldom challenged, and ushered the perplexed pair down the slipway quickly, greeting them like old friends.

When not working at the slipway, Albert was always in a hurry. If anyone was looking for him they could scour the piers and harbour, only to be told, "you've jus' missed 'im, 'e was 'ere a few minutes ago." Someone suggested that if you wanted to find Albert, stand still and he'd find you.

It was Albert Fishburn who was recommended and sought out when occasionally, visiting anglers fishing from the piers, turned up at Sandgate Corner foul-hooked. The casualty was usually hooked through the hand, though my Uncle Robbie once got a hook through his nose. They would be distressed and unable to remove the barbed implement. Reluctant to go to hospital, they'd seek local assistance. Albert would cleverly hitch a piece of light line around the crown of the hook, then while holding the shaft straight with his other hand, would momentarily distract his patient. While the unsuspecting victim of misfortune looked the other way, Albert would give a quick yank on the twine, neatly plucking hook from flesh. The yell of pain was immediately followed by relief when the patient realised their ordeal was over. Grateful thanks and a pecuniary award usually followed.

When I was a youngster, Albert was the first person my friends and I knew who owned a television set. Some days there'd be ten or twelve kids, sitting cross-legged on the mat of Albert and Ethel's little flat on East Mount, watching, 'The Lone Ranger' or 'William Tell' during 'Children's Hour'. We were always fairly well-behaved and relatively quiet or we'd be asked to leave. Once outside, we'd re-enact the episode we'd avidly viewed.

Finishing my ice-cream and moving past the group of men, I chuckled as a potential fisherman approached Bill 'Bagsy' Johnson, enquiring what bait he had available.

"Do you have any lug?" the man asked.

"Aye, I've got these," Bill replied, holding both ears.

Bill's eyesight was now failing, and his ability to find the harbour mouth in his little rowing boat was due more to instinct than vision. His boatman's licence was probably issued as an act of goodwill. The previous day, Bill had lost a five-pound note, given to him by a customer in payment for a fishing trip. He'd put the note in the top pocket of his jacket, and it was now missing. "I bet t' bugger that gi' me it 'ad it on elastic," he commented to his mates, philosophically.

Ken 'Punch' Eade towered above the others on the slipway. With wavy, blond hair and craggy features, he operated his motor boat, *Two Sons*, which he was later to change to, *Three Sons*. Ken had been an apprentice officer in the Merchant Navy during the war. His ship was part of a convoy, which was severely attacked by a U boat wolf pack, suffering many losses.

When asked what it was like he replied, "ah don't know, t' skipper kept us young uns permanently pissed up wi' rum, so if we got torpedoed we wouldn't know owt about it."

There were dozens of these boatmen and all were able to make a living from their quick wits.

As I wandered on the West Pier, at the back of the fishmarket, I passed Teddy Ward, who gave a reluctant nod of acknowledgement. Ted, almost bald, pale-faced with sharp features, was one of the most argumentative people around the harbour. He would argue black was white and with such conviction, you would doubt your own mind after a while. "It's right what ahm sayin'. Ahm tellin' yer." Ted's memory was phenomenal. He could remember things that happened years before he was born. His son Malcolm had similar amazing powers of recollection. It was occasionally suggested, out of earshot, that they'd both worked on the building of Scarborough Castle, though the son was only an apprentice at the time. The construction was completed in 1268.

Ted would visit the 'Leeds Arms' daily, where he'd sit in the same seat in the back room and have the same number of pints of beer. When eventually, Ted passed away, people in the pub spoke to each other in hushed voices, saying Ted was dead, but would look to the seat in the corner, expecting, "no ahm not."

I continued along the back road, to where some youngsters were 'dabbing' pigeons. These thirsty, racing birds would be attracted to the harbour, where they'd attempt to find drinking water. Nothing had changed since I was this age. My pals and I would throw mixed corn onto the roof of the fish market, luring the birds into the gutter, where one of our number would be clinging to the downfall pipe, ready to grab a bird as it fed above. If the pigeons could be lured to the ground, we'd catch them in a box trap; an upturned fish box, baited with corn and propped with a stick. A sharp tug on the light line attached to the stick would allow the box to drop, trapping the birds.

There were many pigeon fanciers in the area. Some of the more serious owners were members of the local clubs that raced birds throughout the summer. Several of my mates had home-made lofts and would try to emulate these respected people, though their collection of pigeons originated from the harbour.

At sea, we often had pigeons alight on the boat for rest and sustenance. Bill would catch the birds and give them succour, then attach a note under the rubber racing-ring giving the date and saying, "fed and watered on board fishing vessel *Courage*, off Scarborough." If it was late in the day, Bill would keep the birds in a fish box overnight and release them the next morning. He'd occasionally receive letters of thanks from grateful owners, via the Harbour Master.

I sauntered to the pier end where a fresh summer, south-easterly breeze was now blowing on shore. This was a localised, natural phenomenon, occurring on really warm days on the coast. The land would warm quickly and the heat would rise, creating a convection effect. Cooler air would be sucked in from the sea in the form of a fresh breeze. The wind would fall away again later in the day as the temperature dropped.

Standing near the harbour mouth, I noticed two subdued, young girls, probably in their late teens, at the pier edge. One was holding what I took to be a tea caddy. Before I was able to grasp the situation, the pair exchanged glances and the nearest of the duo unscrewed the lid from the container, inverting the tin and tipping the contents out over the end of the pier.

The grey powder contained within, didn't fall into the sea. The half gale of wind picked up the dust, blowing the cloud into the stack of fish boxes behind them. The pair looked aghast and simultaneously burst into tears. I realised they were intending to scatter ashes into the sea but had been confounded by the wind. I waited a few minutes then approached the pair, now red eyed and holding hands, asking them if they were alright.

It appeared the girls were from Bradford, in the West Riding and had been sent by their family to carry out a last request of their grandfather. I was able to assure them that the pierman would be washing down the pier later in the day with his hose-pipe; that the dust would be washed into the sea when the wind died. This cheered the girls up no end, their eyes sparkled again and they thanked me for the information. The pair left the pier content that Grandad's wishes had been fulfilled, if indirectly.

CHAPTER 10

BACK AT SEA

With the new engine installed, we worked continuously to make up the time we'd lost, and to pay off the accumulated expenses, incurred while we'd been tied up. Landing very late one evening on an ebbing tide and unable to sail, I suggested we went home for a few hours. I took with me a lobster, which we'd caught in the trawl and which I'd boiled during the day. Arriving home, I wasn't surprised to find all in darkness, as our two little ones were very lively and tiring. Dotty usually went to bed early when I was at sea. I left the crustacean on the draining board, had a quick shower, set the alarm then went to bed. Early next morning while still dark, long before my family awoke, I was out of the house and making my way back to the harbour.

As I passed his house, I gave a friendly wave to old Dick Sheader who, as usual, was leaning on his window-sill. Dick was a retired cobleman who, for several years hadn't slept in his bed. He suffered from terrible bronchial problems and spent all his nights resting on this ledge. The old man was always awake when I passed and returned the salute.

On Friday evening, when I returned from my week at sea, Dotty told me how she'd boiled a pan of water, then bravely dropped the lobster into the steaming vat. The creature didn't turn blue, but the air did, when I laughed on hearing of the double cooking.

Weeks later, a phone call and a reminder of my offer of a voyage, resulted in the arrival in Scarborough of Gavin, the driver from the Gardners engine company, for his fishing experience. We gave him overnight accommodation at home and sailed at four o'clock in the morning, on a lovely fine day. By six o'clock we'd reached the chosen site and were streaming the trawl, though our passenger didn't appear very interested in watching the fishing operation or the handling of the gear. Gavin was much more interested in how much food we had on board and where it was stowed.

At hauling time four hours later, things were no different. Bill and Bluey were on deck to haul the net and after a cursory glance at the catch, our tripper returned to the cabin, again rummaging through the food lockers.

This pillaging and scoffing continued throughout the day and was most annoying. We'd brought this person, at no charge, for an experience not available to most people and his sole interest seemed to be the depletion of our food stocks, which were supposed to last us the week.

Bill, usually mild-mannered and easy going, was incensed at this rudeness so when he noticed Gavin had taken a slice from our chicken dinner, while it was still cooking in the oven, he vowed to 'fix the prat'. Picking up some small lengths of jellyfish streamers from the deck, he spread them on the engine exhaust behind the wheelhouse to dry. A few hours later, with no resolution to the locust-like antics in sight, Bill scraped the now-dried particles onto a piece of paper. Even when dry, jellyfish give a severe itching sensation.

While our fat passenger was paying a brief visit to the deck, Bill seized his opportunity. He hurried for'ard where he buttered six slices of bread, making three large jam sandwiches, carefully sprinkling the contents of the paper onto the middle piece. Emerging from the cabin Bill carried the snacks aft to where Gavin was leaning on the side of the wheelhouse, talking to me through the opened window. The first round from the 'fixed deck' was dealt to me with a wink, the second was handed to our passenger. "It's special jam, me missus meks it," Bill said, taking a large bite from the remaining one.

With a surprised, "oh! thank you," Gavin began to devour his snack. Long before the last of the bread had disappeared the driver developed an itching of the lips, though he continued munching. Shortly after the sandwich had vanished, he complained of a ticklish throat, then stomach cramps.

"It's all t' grub you've been eatin'," Bill said. "Yer might be better lyin' down." He pointed to the cabin hatch.

As Gavin shuffled down to the cabin holding his stomach, I said, "yer might 'ave poisoned 'im," but was amused at the way he'd been 'fixed'.

Our passenger climbed into the spare bunk and we hardly saw him again for the remainder of the trip. I frequently visited the cabin to ensure he was still breathing. An enquiry if he was hungry, brought only a grunt. Gavin didn't stay to watch us land the catch when we arrived back. Finally feeling better and ravenous, he went off to buy some fish and chips. We never saw him again.

* * * * * *

The new engine was performing well, our catches increased and with them, our earnings. We were doing really well and needed another hand, so my Dad tied up his coble for a while and came to sea with us.

It was during this period I made the potentially fatal mistake of going out to a nightclub on the eve of sailing. Though usually having two or three beers early on Saturday evenings, I always went to bed for at least a couple of hours before sailing, but this was a special occasion. The 'Penguins' football team were planning a trip to the 'Outrigger', a large cavernous nightclub on the edge of town. Dotty and I always enjoyed the company of the players, their wives and girlfriends. Their humour was zany and we had a wonderful team spirit.

As always we had great fun, dancing, playing practical jokes and drinking. The club closed at two o'clock in the morning and it was a quarter to three when I finally arrived home. Foolishly, I'd ordered my crew for sea at three o'clock, so had to change and immediately go down to the harbour. Half an hour later, with the first strands of daylight in the sky, we let our ropes go and as luck would have it, it was my turn to take the first watch. I intended to steam twelve miles due north, to where we'd taken a good haul prior to stopping fishing for the weekend. My crew were soon below and though I received a pot of tea, ten minutes later I was on my own.

The flood tide was running against us, but we also had a light northerly wind on the nose. For the first three or four miles I steered a straight course, the wheel strops were in place and only required a spoke or two either way but then I began to lose concentration. No matter how hard I tried, I couldn't keep awake and continued to dip. Each time I bobbed off, the *Courage* veered slowly off course one way or the other due to the adverse forces on her bows. One minute I'd be going north, then I'd look at the compass again with a start, to find I was heading west. I'd alter a few spokes to starboard but before I knew it, I was going east. On one occasion I went full circle before regaining my heading.

It took two and a half hours to get to the position I was making for, when normally, even against the elements, the passage shouldn't have taken more than an hour and three-quarters. The sun was high in the sky when I slowed the boat down to shoot the gear. There'd been no other shipping anywhere in the vicinity to worry about, so I thanked my lucky stars and forgot the incident, vowing never again to go partying before sailing. I'd overlooked the numerous coblemen hauling their pots inshore, to the west of my meandering course. When Dad met his fellow potters next time we were in port, having observed my erratic course, they asked him what we'd been doing early on Sunday morning. Dad quickly came to find me and gave me a well-deserved rocket.

Dad didn't stay long with us on the *Courage*. It was nothing to do with this incident. He was quite right to bawl me out. It was a salutary lesson and a one-off incident, which I learned from. We were just two different generations with differing opinions. We hadn't got on when I'd worked with him in the coble when I was younger, and we still couldn't work together now. We were good friends ashore and it was better for us both if we didn't sail together.

Our new crewmember, John, hadn't done much fishing before though he was a willing worker. He was about Bluey's age and size and had black hair and a dark complexion.

At the same time as Dad was with us on the *Courage,* Bob on the *Jann Denise* was experiencing similar circumstances, though both Bob and his dad, Sid Walker were probably less argumentative. Sid said he was unable to sleep on board the boat. Even when they'd been at sea for two or three days, he was adamant he never slept. Other members of the crew knew differently. They'd often heard him snoring while he 'rested his eyes' in his bunk.

Tom and Terry thought they'd brought the debate of Sid sleeping or not sleeping to a definite conclusion when, while he was 'resting' one day, they stitched him to his mattress with heavy-duty needle and thread. For good measure, they also placed the week's supply of groceries in the bunk with him. When hauling time was called, the two culprits waited by the winch for Sid, occasionally calling for him down the cabin ladders. After a prolonged wait, Sid finally arrived on deck, breathless. "Where 'ave yer been? What took yer so long?" Tom asked, smirking.

"I was cutting meself loose with me knife," said Sid. "I knew you were sewin' me in all t' time. I jus' thought I'd let yer 'ave yer little joke."

CHAPTER 11

DISASTER

Early one morning, Bluey called me from my bunk urgently. He'd heard Frank's distinct voice calling, 'Mayday'. There was a dense fog and a deep, but lazy easterly swell, though not a breath of wind. Bluey was on watch and wedged on the bench against the constant motion, keeping an eye on the radar for traffic. We were fishing about six miles from the North Cheek of Bay Wyke, a very distinctive landmark and radar target.

I arrived in the wheelhouse quickly and reached for the radio handset as Frank was repeating his message. "Mayday, Mayday, this is the *Admiral Van Tromp*. We are ashore near Whitby Lighthouse." This was strange as she'd sailed from Scarborough several hours earlier and should have been many miles out to sea by now. I'd heard Frank on the radio, shortly after the vessel had sailed, informing someone of the result of Scarborough's evening home football game. Frank was a keen supporter of his new team and had attended the match.

Frank was born in Holland but had moved to Scarborough to marry a local girl and was now a naturalized Englishman. We'd studied together for our skippers' tickets only two years earlier. I'd bought the *Courage* from Frank and his father-in-law when the *Van Tromp* was new. She was named after a famous Dutch Admiral who'd carried a brush at the top of his ship's mast. He said he'd sweep the seas clean of English vessels. Now sadly, this lovely new boat with five men on board was ashore under 'Whitby High Light', two miles from the port's entrance and in a very precarious situation. With this easterly swell running, big seas would be breaking on the rocks ashore. The cliffs where the vessel was stranded were immensely high and in places there was no direct way down to the water's edge. At high water the sea reached the foot of the cliffs.

I checked the tide table, discovering it was low water ashore. Maybe if they could get an anchor over now, the hook would hold and they'd be able to haul themselves off again as the tide flowed. I called to Frank, and on confirmation that he was receiving me, suggested this course of action. He replied that the swell was breaking over the stern and there was no possibility of deploying an anchor.

We were the nearest vessel to the casualty and though there was nothing we could do to assist the men on board, we hauled our gear and set off for the stricken craft at full speed. I radioed to the Coastguard, letting them know we were on our way to the scene. They had already alerted the Whitby lifeboat crew, who were now mobilising. The fog was still dense and we were running down hill on the swells. I shuddered as I thought what these seas must be like on shore.

It was still dark and foggy as we approached the coast. The tide was flowing quickly and would be pushing the *Van Tromp* shorewards. Her skipper was very concerned for the lives of his crew, as his vessel was now holed and there was water in the fishroom. He fired a distress flare to indicate his boat's position and we were able to see the red glow in the gloom, though couldn't see the land. The Whitby lifeboat crew were on their way, but were in an RNLI reserve boat, as their own vessel was undergoing repairs. This older craft had no radar and no recording paper in their sounder, so they were relying totally on coxswain, Bob Allen's local knowledge.

We were in radio contact with the rescue boat and were able to direct her to the *Courage* with our radar as they approached from the north. The *William and Mary Durham*, the former Berwick lifeboat, appeared out of the fog and came alongside, her crew holding fenders to protect both vessels from damage in the deep swell. I quickly pointed her coxswain in the right direction. Bob said he'd go inshore to reconnoitre, then drop a kedge anchor from his bow and work his way further inshore, stern first to the stricken trawler if possible. Though we were unable to see the land, I now had my radar on half-mile radius and was marking the coast and the breaking swell clearly to the south-west. By keeping just beyond these waves I was able to keep station and monitor the proceedings, though there was hardly any water under our vessel in the troughs.

The little craft left our side to vanish once more into the mist, heading shorewards. The airwaves were quiet for a few minutes then I heard Bob Allen call to the Coastguard, saying he'd been hit by a huge breaking wave, which had flattened his craft's after guardrails. He'd located the wreck and immediately brought the lifeboat's head into the swell, dropping the kedge anchor. He was going to let his vessel gradually work its way inshore towards the casualty, in a controlled manner.

I located a box of white parachute flares, which I'd bought for emergency use and asked Bill to fire one in the direction of the attempted rescue. With a whoosh, the rocket soared skywards, bursting into a white, incandescent glow that penetrated the fog and partial daylight. The sight we saw before us was awesome. Each breaking sea was throwing Scarborough's biggest and strongest vessel around like a toy. The lifeboat was bouncing around like a cork secured to a thread.

"That's great, keep 'em comin'," shouted Bob Allen over the radio. My crew took turns to fire the parachute flares to illuminate the scene for the lifeboatmen. Their brave little boat was now only a few yards from the casualty. As they closed on the doomed ship, lying on her starboard side, one of the lifeboatmen was able to fire a rocket line across the wreck. The thin cord snaked across the battered wheelhouse and was grabbed by someone reaching from a port side window. Though very strong, this light line snagged and parted in the surge. Two more lines were attempted in vain.

The lifeboat was constantly being battered and bounced on the rocks beneath her as the giant waves rose and fell. Suddenly, with no warning, the rescue craft's anchor appeared to break free from its hold, creating a potential disaster for the rescuers.

Bad weather at Scarborough Harbour entrance.
Photo by F.G. Normandale

Albert Fishburn on Sandgate slipway.
Courtesy of Gordon and Ken Fishburn

Admiral Van Tromp, ashore under Whitby High Light.
Photo by Ken Wigg

Our Heritage. Steaming head to wind on a fresh day.
Photo by F.G. Normandale

The lifeboat broached broadside to the huge breakers, surging shorewards and throwing the crew in all directions, though luckily, no one was washed overboard. It was only the quick thinking of her coxswain that saved the day. He slammed the throttles to full ahead and with the wheel hard over, forced his vessel's head into the next foaming swell. His crew were again thrown off their feet, one man was knocked unconscious, another dislocated a shoulder, but now at least they were safe from imminent peril, if badly shaken. Not so the hapless crew on the *Admiral Van Tromp*, whose lives were now in mortal danger.

The lifeboatmen recovered their thick, nylon cable to discover that though the anchor was still attached to the line, it was broken. The solid steel fluke had completely snapped off at the crown, leaving the remainder of the anchor virtually useless. How much load had been on this hook to cause it to fracture? The valiant crew came back alongside the *Courage* and we were able to provide them with soup and hot drinks. We also gave them our anchor. The injured men were taken to Whitby by the *Jann Denise*, which had now arrived on the scene. Bob also loaned his vessel's anchor. The lifeboat was now short of crew so Bill immediately offered his services, which were accepted. They could have got no one better. Bill was a good man to have at your side in a crisis. Before the lifeboat had arrived, Bill asked if he could don a lifejacket and swim in to the stricken craft, taking with him a thin rope, in an attempt to help the endangered men. He said he'd hold on to an inflatable fender for extra buoyancy.

I'd refused point blank to allow him to do this. The seas were throwing the stranded vessel around, so Bill would have had little chance of surviving the passage or gaining access on board the *Van Tromp* without injury or worse. He was fearless enough to want to try and it was the stuff of heroes, but he had a wife and two bairns at home. I wasn't going to be the one to tell his wife I'd lost him. Bill was pleased to get onto the lifeboat and the crew fitted him with a lifejacket. I heard him say, "tie a line on me and I'll swim in to 'er." I knew Bobby Allen wouldn't allow this mad scheme either.

It was daylight now and the fog had thinned slightly. We could see the ship ashore through the haze, though it was a very grey morning, reflecting everyone's mood. The small rubber RNLI inshore rescue boat had now arrived on the scene and was also patrolling close to the breaking seas. The coastguards were on the cliff top and were in radio contact with the lifeboat and other vessels in the area, but though they could now see the ship ashore, radio contact had been lost with the casualty. The engine-room must have flooded, killing her batteries. Frank's last report had been that he and his crew were confined to the wheelhouse. The situation was exceedingly ominous.

With both anchors out, the lifeboat again attempted to make her way shorewards. Due to the buffeting on the rocks, a cooling water pipe burst on one of her engines, causing the machine to overheat and stop, but the sturdy little craft was still able to battle the elements with the remaining motor. The rescuers were now within touching distance of the *Van Tromp* but were unable to see any sign of the crew in the wheelhouse.

A radio message came from the coastguard, saying there were men in the water, washing ashore. This was encouraging to all listening, but shortly after, they said there were only two of them and they were now safely ashore. It was awful speculating who was missing. Apart from Frank, there was Alan, a seasoned deck hand, 'Scots John', an ex shipmate from my early days in the *Whitby Rose*, George, a middle aged man, who normally sailed on cobles and was temporarily shipped up on the *Van Tromp* and Tony, a young lad of seventeen, who hadn't been going to sea long.

The lifeboat crew heard someone shouting for help to the south in shallow, more sheltered water and summoned the inshore rescue craft which, following directions, found Frank, semi-conscious, clinging to a large rock. They were able to haul him on board and quickly deliver him to the larger lifeboat. The two men now ashore reported there was no one left alive on the doomed vessel. The wheelhouse had flooded completely and they'd been forced to leave. There was no possibility of any more survivors, so Bobby Allen and his gallant men took Frank to Whitby.

There was nothing anyone could do to assist further and the feeling of helplessness was overwhelming as we returned home. Bill would get a lift back by road. During the passage home, we heard over the radio that John Addison and George Eves were the missing crewmen. It was a very sad homecoming back in Scarborough. The dreadful news had already reached the 'Bottom End' and was on everyone's lips when we arrived in port. There was an almost tangible gloom pervading the 'village'.

When she was rehoused it was evident the lifeboat had taken a massive punishment. She was holed in several places and half her rudder was missing. That she survived at all was a tribute to her designers, builders and the skill of her coxswain. Bob Allen was decorated by the RNLI, who awarded him their silver medal for his endeavours on this black day.

The coastguards recovered the first body from the wreck when the tide ebbed. The body of the second missing fisherman was found a few days later. The tragedy was the sole topic of conversation and speculation throughout the area for weeks. In this close community, a loss at sea was felt by everyone and was labelled 'the true price of fish'.

CHAPTER 12

A LAUNCHING AND INSPIRATION

Much to our surprise, Dotty and I were invited to a new boat launching in Scotland. Colin Jenkinson had commissioned the building of the *Our Heritage* from the prolific yard of James Noble in Fraserburgh, and she was almost ready to leave the womb. This yard had a reputation second to none for building sturdy, successful vessels, which were pleasing to the eye. We'd been to Fraserburgh previously when the *Jann Denise* had been launched and I'd been one of her crew.

Colin was the most determined, single-minded fisherman in the port and this was his third new boat. He'd previously built the *Our Margaret*, named after his daughter and the *Our Rachel*, his wife's name. In contrast, I was skipper of a twenty five year old craft and didn't compete with any of the top skippers. I wasn't in the same league, but we'd received this invitation and were delighted to accept.

The format was similar to the previous time we'd travelled to the 'Broch', as the town was known by its inhabitants, though this time there were many more guests. Rachel was a great party organiser and would spare no expense to make sure the occasion was memorable. Leaving Paula and Danny to be spoiled by grandparents, we joined around a hundred guests, to be transported from Scarborough, four hundred miles north to Fraserburgh by coach. Some parties were making the journey independently, by road or rail. The accommodation for everyone

114

had been organised by Bessie, James Noble's hardworking secretary. This lady had taken almost every spare bed in the town's hotels for the many guests.

This excursion to the north-east of Scotland was great fun with a lively crowd of revellers on our bus. There was lots of joke telling, innuendo and banter, which made the journey pass quickly. Though it was evening when we arrived, the first of several parties was about to begin. The little bar in the 'Alexandra Hotel' was packed to the doors and Jeannie, the barmaid was rushed off her feet as booze flowed like water. Rachel insisted that no one was to pay for drinks. Everyone present was a guest, and it was she and Colin's pleasure to play host to all. Colin didn't argue, he just went with the flow and enjoyed his good fortune.

A delicious four-course meal was served in the large function room, then for some it was an early night. For most, including Dotty and me, it was back to the bar. The hotel's interpretation of the licensing law meant everyone had consumed more than sufficient before Jeannie finally said, "haway now, I'm finished f' the nicht an' ahm away t' ma bed, and so are all of yous." No one argued. Maybe no one understood, but with the shutters on the bar closed, the message was clear.

Next morning, for those requiring food, there was a huge fry-up breakfast, preceded by porridge, though there were few takers. There was plenty of coffee consumed as those who'd overindulged the previous evening, including me, kick-started their systems ready for the day ahead.

During the forenoon the females of the entourage could be found at the hairdressers and shops, while the men gravitated to the harbour and James Noble's boatyard. I related to the group I was with, how I'd first come to Fraserburgh as a teenage schoolboy with the crew of the herring drifter *Hazael III*. They'd been fishing from Scarborough and had returned home for a long weekend, taking me with them. I'd visited this very yard then and little had changed since.

The corrugated iron building, like a giant hangar was situated at the eastern end of the massive harbour. We could see the bright green transom stern of the new vessel, long before we reached the open shed. Her huge, four-bladed, polished propeller, to be powered by a 375 horsepower Kelvin engine, shone brightly. Below her waterline the antifouling paint was deep maroon. A thin band of white separated the red from green.

The yard was a hive of industry. The entire workforce was busy preparing for the afternoon launch. It would be a big day for these men too. They and their wives would join the evening celebrations when their day's work was complete.

At high water the entire group, dressed in their finery, made their way to the hangar bearing the name, 'James Noble', in large white letters above the entrance. Inside, at the bows of the new craft, a rough stage decked in bunting awaited the launching party. The smell of new wood and fresh paint filled the air. Proudly, Colin, Rachel, her mother Maggie and father 'Denk' mounted the stairs for the official business. Close behind hovered the builder, Jimmy Noble and his wife Madge. The crowd attentively gathered around the platform to hear the naming of the beautiful vessel by Rachel, the appropriate name, *Our Heritage*, had been her choice.

When Rachel had asked God to bless her and all who sailed in her, she released the champagne bottle, which unluckily, didn't break. On hitting the new vessel's stem with a dull thud, the bottle fell from its harness to the floor, where fortunately, it still didn't break. The thick container was handed back to Rachel, who, on the second attempt, belted the bottle with such force across the iron band on the boat's stem, the glass shattered into a thousand pieces, wetting all in the vicinity.

The yard foreman nodded to the waiting men beneath the craft and together they began hammering at the chocks retaining the vessel in position on the ways. The wedges were quickly knocked out, allowing the new vessel to commence her first journey. The workers quickly moved away, having assisted in the birth. Festooned in coloured bunting, *Our Heritage* emerged slowly from the shed into the sunshine to loud applause from guests, locals and workers. Young family members were on her deck enjoying the adventure and being part of this memorable occasion; a moment in time they'd remember throughout their lives. Yard workers were on board also, to help secure the vessel once afloat and to make sure she had no leaks. There were often small seepages on new boats but they invariably took up as the planking swelled when immersed.

The vessel was at present an empty shell with no machinery, wheelhouse or masts. The Scottish flags, 'Saltire' and 'Lion Rampant' were flying proudly from temporary poles on her stem and stern. She was Scottish built and her builders, justifiably proud of their construction, demonstrated it. A lone piper played an evocative Scottish tune, which produced goose-pimples down my spine as the vessel gathered speed. The *Our Heritage* hurried down the ways, keen to be in her natural environment. She splashed into the murky harbour water, rolling heavily for a few seconds before steadying and bobbing lightly in the water.

It was an emotional moment for most observers as this beautiful craft took to the water for the first time. It was a privilege to be a guest on this wonderful occasion; how must it feel if the vessel is your own? I looked at Colin, who was shaking hands and being congratulated by all within reach. "Could this possibly happen to me?" For the first time in my life, I thought, "maybe?"

The shipwrights were already clearing the yard of debris ready for the start of a new construction. The keel sections of this craft and the frames for the skeleton were already in an adjacent shed ready to be laid. The dozens of yard workers would start on this new project the following morning. Today these fine craftsmen, as thanks for their skill, would enjoy a 'wee dram or twa' of finest malt to mark the launching.

The *Our Heritage,* now floating lightly in the water, was surrounded by broken timber. These were the supports that had held her upright on her first journey, until she hit the water. The light construction then split apart, floating free, away from the new craft. Two men in a small boat were gathering this timber, most of which would be used again for the next vessel. The bright green, lifeless hull, already wreathed in redundant tyres on her starboard side, was hauled alongside the stone pier.

Guests who hadn't been aboard the craft while she was in the yard now clambered onto the now secure boat, though as yet there was little for them to see. Though fully decked, *Our Heritage* was empty of equipment and it would be several months before she was finally ready for sea. In through the gaping hole in the centre of the vessel would go fuel tanks, main and auxiliary engines, a hydraulic system, two banks of batteries and all the hundreds of other component parts to bring her alive before she was ready for her maiden voyage.

With the new craft safely berthed close to the builder's yard and curiosity fulfilled, the entourage returned to the 'Alexandra Hotel', where a magnificent, formal dinner of many courses was followed by several speeches, each ending in a toast. Glasses were raised to Colin and Rachel, to the builder, to the fine new vessel, to the hotel for the excellent meal and efficient service, then anyone who cared to propose a toast on any subject, even loosely relating to the day's events, had the opportunity.

Finally Rachel, a wonderful raconteuse, had everyone laughing with an impromptu performance telling of the many and varied predicaments and scrapes she'd been involved in. Her timing and humour were impeccable. For her finale, as ever, Rachel stood on a chair to sing a rousing, 'Land of Hope and Glory', insisting everyone join in. This lovely lady was exceedingly patriotic and needed little persuasion to perform this song. On one occasion this had unexpected results. Rachel and Colin had been invited to the housewarming party of a successful, local businessman, where she was easily persuaded into giving her unique rendition. Standing on a chair, Rachel thrust her fist into the air for the chorus, unfortunately punching a hole in the polystyrene ceiling.

It was early evening before the afternoon programme finally drew to a close. In fact the two sessions seemed to merge together, except some of the guests appeared to have changed into fancy dress; notably, Colin dressed as a monk and Rachel a nun. A ceilidh band struck up playing rousing Scottish reels, which found everyone's approval. It was easy to tell the English from the Scots when the dancing began. The visitors were mostly sitting watching, while the locals were slick and aware of all the moves. The few Sassenachs, fuelled by drink, who attempted to join in 'Strip the Willow' were clumsy, their improvisations disrupting the entire formation.

Midway through the evening the lights were raised to enable tea and sandwiches to be served. Surprisingly, considering the amount of food consumed earlier in the day, these too were devoured before the dancing recommenced. During this tea interval I found myself sitting next to Jimmy Noble, the builder of the new craft and of dozens of other magnificent fishing vessels. Jimmy spoke with a very broad Scottish accent, difficult to understand and it was necessary to concentrate on his every word. Unfortunately, Jimmy also wore a very obvious hairpiece, which distracted my attention from his conversation.

Only casually at first, I enquired what the cost would be of a similar, maybe slightly fuller vessel. As Jimmy went through a rough specification and guide price I began to get more interested, forgetting his wig. He in turn, sensing maybe he was talking to a potential future client, went into greater detail of the grant and loan schemes available for new vessels. At the end of our short, but in-depth discussion, which no one else in the room took for anything other than polite conversation, I had a definite desire, somehow, to build a new ship of my own.

As the evening progressed, some of the guests began to tire. It had been a long day and the celebrations had been almost continuous. Several people were staying in smaller hotels near the harbour and the hosts had arranged taxis to transport them to their accommodation, while in the 'Alex', the party continued. The fiddler, accordion and drummer gave way to a young disc jockey playing the latest pop music. Soon the floor was filled with English visitors strutting their stuff. It was the Scots' turn to sit and watch.

Shortly after the departure of the early leavers, a deputation returned from the harbourside saying their hotel door was locked and no one was answering, despite constant ringing of the bell. Rachel, angry at the inconvenience to her guests, rang the offending hotel's telephone number. After five frustrating minutes of receiving no answer, her patience snapped. Having summoned Colin to get her a taxi, Rachel, jumped into the vehicle as it arrived, setting off for the inhospitable hotel. En route she lit a cigarette, in an unsuccessful attempt to calm her rising temper. Observers at the scene were amazed to see the cab screech to a halt, a smoking nun rush from the vehicle to the hotel entrance, then proceed to bang loudly on the door.

The nun, cigarette in hand was shouting, "open this bloody door. If yer don't open it soon I'll knock the soddin' thing down." Despite her efforts to gain entry, the mission was unsuccessful. It transpired that the manager lived off the premises and presuming his guests were all abed, had locked the door and gone home. Back at the 'Alexandra', these unfortunate few with no accommodation were found camp beds and spent an uncomfortable night in the upstairs corridor, while the party continued to rock below.

Next morning, with the celebrations over, the evidence of the party was still plain to see as the erstwhile revellers drank even more black coffee, refused solid food, then crept into their various vehicles for the long journey back to reality.

Once home my discussion with Jimmy Noble was going round and round in my head at every free moment. I asked Dotty her opinion on the possible opportunity and explained it would mean a second mortgage on our house and there were risks. As always she was unfazed by the fuss and said, "you know you want to do this, get on with it."

While in the wheelhouse during the following weeks, I spent much of my time with pen and paper, jotting down the requirements for my dream boat, though at this point it was still an illusion. I'd struggled to raise the funds to acquire the *Courage* and now had little spare cash, though I'd long since repaid the one thousand pounds loaned to me by my parents. In my favour, our house value had increased substantially since we'd bought it. The old boat, which we owned, now had a new engine, new winch, hydraulic steering and some excellent wheelhouse equipment. She would never be worth more. It was now or never. I arranged an appointment with Mr Mitchell, the regional representative of the White Fish Authority, the body that administered government funds. He kindly consented to visit me at home one evening when I'd be in from sea.

Mr Mitchell was a strange man, who saw no problems whatsoever with me acquiring a new vessel. He was quite encouraging and explained, step by step the route I would have to take. He was much more concerned about the explosion of the grey seal population in the North Sea and the damage they were causing to fish stocks and of the disease they spread to fish, via their droppings. Mr Mitchell visited our home several times subsequently. Dotty would take the phone message then say, "the grey seal man's coming to see you again."

The approximate price for a new boat from James Noble, depending on the machinery and electronics required, was one hundred and sixty thousand pounds. This was a king's ransom, but Mr Grey Seal seemed unperturbed. I'd require twenty-five per cent of the cost as my deposit. If I could find this sum, I could have my new vessel. Of the remainder, fifty per cent would come from the White Fish Authority as a fixed interest loan, repayable over ten years. The balance would be paid in the form of a grant from the same agency.

The *Courage* was valued at thirty thousand pounds now, though I'd be unable to sell her in the near future, even if I found a buyer. A new craft would take ten months from the laying of the keel and I'd have to continue fishing for as long as possible.

I made an appointment to see my bank manager to explain my ambition, plans and hopes. After waiting an age beyond the time of my appointment, uncomfortably hot in suit, stiff collar and tie, I was finally brought before the same dour man who'd explained to Dotty the possible, probable and implausible pitfalls that could confront us, were we to buy the *Courage*.

In the brief period I'd skippered her, we'd fished exceptionally well and I was confident I could make a new vessel pay. His bank was also our fishselling agent's bank so our accounts were available for him to examine. I was bereft when, after listening to my ambitions he curtly said, "I don't think I can help you at this moment in time."

I was devastated. I'd raised my hopes to the sky and now here I was plummeting earthwards again. No longer caring, even if he was a bank manager and annoyed at his choice of, "at this moment in time," I asked when he thought he might be able to help.

"Young man, your present boat *Courage* is registered under part four of the Merchant Shipping Act. I am unable to take a charge on the vessel, so you cannot use it as security." He said this without sympathy, then stood up. My interview was over. I'd been given the bum's rush.

My plans were shot through. I couldn't sell the *Courage* now. I needed to keep her fishing, so I was in a dilemma. I decided to confide in Colin and ask his opinion. As yet only Dotty was aware of my hopes. I met up with 'Dilt' at the weekend in the pub and taking him aside from the main group of drinkers, explained how I'd spoken to Jimmy Noble at the launching, that I'd got an estimated price for a new boat, but my plans had been confounded by the bank manager.

He said, "yer crafty young bugger, yer kept that close t' yer chest. I saw yer talkin' wi' Jimmy, but didn't think owt about it. Don't worry, that miserable prat in t' other bank turned me down as well. Mek an appointment t' see Noel White, at Barclays. 'E's great, yer won't 'ave a problem."

My heart soared at his words. I was under the impression that if one bank wouldn't loan me the cash, then none would. I was naive and hadn't realised that banks varied in their policies and managers had differing attitudes to their customers. I was walking on air again, my ambition back on track. I felt positive and again had hope for the future.

Lunchtime in the pub was another great session. The lifeboat coxswain was, as always, on his best form, telling another dubious, but hilarious story. He said earlier in the week, he was mending a crab pot on board his boat the *Constance*, while she was berthed alongside a small cargo vessel, discharging potatoes at the North Wharf. The pot required a new piece of wood to replace a damaged section on the bottom frame. He had no spare wood on his boat but had lots, varying in length, in his store across the road in Quay Street.

Arms apart, the palms of his hands at each end of the pot, Bill gauged the size of the piece of lath required. Then, fingers pointed, his hands fixed in position to the size needed, he set off for his store. Of course, he had to climb across the little Dutch coaster, so briefly had to move his hands, but was sure he'd got them back in the exact spot. Once ashore he crossed the road, arms still apart, nodding to friends and acquaintances. There was a slight problem when he had to take his keys from his pocket, but again he was sure he'd got the right size. Ten minutes later he was back in his boat with a piece of wood three inches too short. He took his cap off and scratched his head, perplexed.

Bill continued his tale, saying, Geoff, one of the stevedores discharging the ship had called down to him shouting, "oy Bill, d' yer want some taties?"

Not one to refuse a bag of spuds, Bill replied, "aye that'd be alright." In return he offered the man some crabs. The arrangement was, Geoff would leave the potatoes in Bill's boat under a canvas cover and on the following day the crabs would be left under the same sheet. Bill said he would return to his boat that evening to collect the promised potatoes. After dark he boarded his little craft on his way to the pub, but to his consternation found there was nothing under the canvas.

At the very moment Bill was speaking, Geoff walked into the pub. All eyes looked in his direction, then at Bill. Bill looked at the stevedore and loudly called, "oy Geoff, what 'appened to me taties? Yer said you'd leave 'em under t' cover in me boat."

The stevedore went very red and swore he'd left some potatoes on board and they must have been stolen. Geoff then asked Bill why there were no crabs left for him beneath the canvas the following day, when he'd investigated.

Bill said, "Ah left yer some crabs. They must 'ave been nicked by t' same bugger that took me spuds."

* * * * * *

Rachel had taken the trouble to make an appointment for me with Mr White at ten o'clock on the following Friday and had given me an introduction. It was with some trepidation I entered Barclays Bank, dressed once more in my best suit. I'd been waiting only a few minutes when a bespectacled, rosy-faced man with a pleasant manner and a twinkle in his eye came from his office to greet me. The contrast couldn't have been greater from my previous experience. This banker was human and sensing my nervousness, immediately put me at ease. Once seated, he asked me about my plans, my history and what cash and collateral I had available. Mr White didn't seem in the least bothered when I explained that his bank wouldn't be able to take a charge on the *Courage*. "Are you going to sink her?" he asked, smiling.

Dumbfounded at the suggestion of such a thought, I spluttered that I needed to work her till the new boat, if I ever got it, was ready. This was more of a conversation than an interview. I couldn't believe how comfortable I felt in this man's company. "Yer can tek a charge on our 'ouse," I suggested. "It's worth a lot more now than we paid for it," hoping to add weight to my case. He made a note on his pad to this effect.

Our discussion went on for some time and when the subject was completely exhausted he said, "go away and do some fishing. Come back next week at the same time and I'll give you my decision. Before then I'll do some homework on you," then added, "and you don't need to dress like something from 'Burtons the Tailors' to come and see me either."

I left his office hopeful, but sweated all through the next week, wondering what sort of homework Mr White would do. Who would he ask? What would he ask them? What would people tell him? Who did he know who knew me? Until that day I'd never met him.

Friday eventually came round again and I turned up at the appointed time, dressed casually in clean shirt and slacks. Mr White's manner seemed no less serious, which I took to be a good omen. He made sure I was comfortable before giving me his decision. "Now then young man, I've done my homework on you and I think we can do business."

His next few sentences were lost to me, I wasn't listening, just saying, "YES, YES, YES," to myself over and over again, wanting to punch the air with my fist.

Back down to earth, I tuned in as my benefactor was saying, "I believe you need another ten thousand pounds towards your deposit, apart from the thirty you'll get from the *Courage*, which you're not going to sink."

I nodded, preparing to reiterate my case from the previous week, that we had some savings and I was earning good money regularly. My new found 'Godfather' then presented me with a letter which I was to show to James Noble and Mr Mitchell, stating he was providing me with a bridging loan for thirty thousand pounds, until the sale of the *Courage*, and should I require it, he was prepared to lend me a further nine thousand pounds towards my deposit. I only needed to find a thousand pounds to commission the building of my dream boat. I couldn't believe my luck. I wanted to hug this man who, by putting his faith in me when others had turned me down was, apart from Dotty, to make the biggest single difference to my life and fishing career. I didn't even have an account at Barclays, yet.

He had a little more to say. "You'll not find out where I did my homework. I've always had a principle of backing the man and I've refused people in the past who've had plans and money. You won't be bothered how much interest I'll be charging you, but I'll be fair. Next time you make an appointment to see me, make it eleven forty-five and meet me in the 'Alma'. I do more business in the pub round the corner than I do in the bank. Oh and by the way, you'll be buying the beer."

He still had one more shock for me. "Oh and I won't be requiring a charge on your home. You've got two small children and I don't want to disrupt their lives, should your plans not work out." He explained that the free equity available would only be a small part of the vessel's cost and wasn't important.

I was on cloud nine. My head was buzzing as I dashed home to tell Dotty the wonderful news. I then rang Jimmy Noble and Mr Grey Seal in turn. The builder immediately posted me an official specification form, which I was to complete. This comprehensive document would detail every component part my new vessel would require. The specification would cover size and style of vessel, engine and gearbox type, propeller, winches, hydraulics systems, generators, size of water and fuel tanks, electrical and wheelhouse equipment and even cooker and hot water heater for the galley. If I forgot anything or deviated from this formula at all, I'd be charged extra for the alterations. This really focused my mind during the next week at sea. My head was spinning with details. Every watch

I'd go over my draft requirements to the smallest degree. I was very fortunate to be able to draw on Colin's knowledge and previous experience of building vessels and was able to view his vessel's specifications, though not costs, and was able to duplicate many of his ideas. This would have an added advantage as we could have a pool of mechanical spares which could be drawn on when needed, then replaced.

When my form was finally completed, I returned the script to the builder for his costing. Jimmy's original estimate was almost exact and his quotation was only a few hundred pounds below his rough price. I'd now submit this document to Mr Mitchell who would scrutinize it, then forward the approved version to his head office in Edinburgh, where a decision would be made at the next meeting of the White Fish Authority Board of Management. This would take some time, as their meetings were held quarterly and the next was not due for eight weeks. Mr Grey Seal was convinced there would be no problem; that my application was sound, but I was on tenterhooks waiting. Meanwhile I'd carry on fishing, but say nothing about my plans till I'd heard from Edinburgh.

We continued to get good catch results and were pleased with our performance, but I was unsettled and edgy until word came by post in the form of official approval and offer of grant and loan facilities. These were quickly turned round and Jimmy Noble and Madge arrived the following weekend with a contract for me to sign.

Both were sitting on the sofa, drinks in hand, when I arrived home from the harbour. We chatted for a while, asking about their journey down, where they'd be staying and if they planned to stay the weekend. The conversation was amicable, easy and flowing when our youngsters, Paula and Danny, entered the room and stood behind the seated visitors. Both were carrying fishing rods and were asking if I'd take them fishing in the harbour. A look of horror came over Dotty's face and I caught her thought immediately. Both kids, grinning, had fishhooks dangling precariously close to Jimmy Noble's acrylic hairpiece. In a flash Dotty was up from her chair and ushered the pair into the back room to play, explaining that Dad was busy and would take them fishing later.

With the polite conversation and the kids out of the way, Jimmy said he had some bad news. Fraserburgh Harbour Commissioners had decided to deepen the harbour where his boatyard was located. I couldn't see the problem but Jimmy explained that the contractors intended to cofferdam the entire section where his shed was situated. They planned to remove the spoil then dig down into the bedrock to make a berth for the deep drafted purse seiners, now plying a thriving trade from the port. This work could take up to a year and was to commence when the vessel currently under construction at his yard was completed. Our new baby would be next in line, but there'd be no water in the harbour to launch into for a year. "But dinna worry," Jimmy said, when he saw the disappointment on my face, "I've gotten permission tae build her on the paint slip."

This was a relief. I had visions of my new vessel, framed, planked and decked, standing idle for months awaiting water to float her. Looking ahead, I realised it would be a while yet before they'd be able to lay the keel, so it meant his workforce would be constructing my vessel through the winter on the exposed slipway. I didn't envy them. Scotland's weather can be bleak and in winter the days are short, but Jimmy was confident he could build the boat on this site, so I signed the contract. There was no going back now.

We sailed into the harbour one afternoon to see a crowd of people gathered on the pier end. Most were recognisable from the launching we'd attended a few months earlier, so it was obvious the *Our Heritage* was due home, on her maiden passage from Fraserburgh. It would have been a dreadful passage south for her. South-west winds of severe gale and even storm force had been battering the north-east of Scotland for the previous two days. We'd been fishing not far from home and had experienced gales, though we'd been fishing in the lee of the land.

Colin was certainly testing his new command from day one. He'd only have been able to hug the coast as far as Buchan Ness then would have been exposed to the elements as the land fell away almost south-west into the Firths of Tay and Forth. The *Our Heritage* would have taken a beating nearly fifty miles out to sea while crossing the Firths, if steering direct for Scarborough.

An hour later, as we finished landing our fish, a cheer rang out from the harbour entrance and shortly after, the beautiful, green vessel turned into her home port for the first time, her supporters enthusiastically flocking along the pier to where she would berth. Though now decked from mast to mast with flags and bunting, these had only recently been hoisted. Her decks were washed clean, she was covered in salt residue and she'd had a pasting. Boxes of drink were quickly passed on board the sturdy little craft by Rachel and her helpers, so the crew and all the visitors could drink to her safe arrival.

I spoke to Colin on his new vessel shortly after the arrival and his first words were, "I think we've bust 'er. She's certainly leakin'. Mek sure t' bloody bottle breaks when your lass christens your new un." He was convinced his first trip was an unlucky one due to the champagne bottle not breaking first time at her launching. I wasn't going to doubt him or flaunt superstition. He said the weather had been atrocious, the wind screaming and they'd been forced to seek some limited shelter closer in across the Firth of Forth. It must have been poor weather indeed, for Colin was fearless and trusted his boats implicitly. They'd had a rough ride home for sure.

I'd recently announced to my crew that I'd ordered a new vessel from Noble's yard and the keel was soon to be laid. I think they'd suspected something was in the wind with all the paperwork I'd been doing in the wheelhouse in the past months. It's almost impossible to keep anything confidential on a fishing boat, as there's virtually no privacy, apart from your own bunk. Bluey was enthusiastic about the new project but Bill less so. It was going to be a radical change from what we'd been used to, but it wasn't going to happen soon. It would be spring of the following year before she'd be ready. We hadn't chosen a name for her yet.

CHAPTER 13

A CLOSE ENCOUNTER

Summer arrived and with it the first of the herring. Large shoals were gathering between nine and twelve miles offshore and were attracting many predators. The total ban of the previous year had been amended to three prohibited areas in the region, where the silver darlings usually spawned. Though Britain still had a twelve-mile limit within the new Common Market, Dutch herring fishermen had negotiated tradition rights to fish between six and twelve miles from our coast, though they no longer used traditional gear. Huge Dutch trawlers were now scooping up the herring in vast quantities, even during the day. Previously these fish had been inaccessible, only rising from the bottom in the dark, when they swam mid-water and were vulnerable to drift nets.

These large ships with SCH marked on their sides, indicating they were registered in Scheveningen, were intimidating the inshore trawlers by fishing line abreast and stopping for nothing. The smaller local boats, fishing for cod and haddock, which were feeding on the herring, were unable to get near the marks for fear of being run down or having their gear towed away by the big ships.

We were trawling about a mile ahead of a large Dutch ship, SCH 23 when our gear became fast on the bottom. There was a strong tide running and we were struggling to retrieve our net, which was almost new. The gear was reluctant to come clear from its fastener no matter how hard we heaved. The relief valve on our winch was blowing off at maximum pressure and the big clogger was coming ever closer. I could now read her name, *Jacob Van de Swan*. The ship wasn't going to hit us on her present course, but was going to pass so close, her net would go under our boat and was sure to catch our fastened gear.

I attempted to contact the ship by radio but could get no response, despite trying all working channels and the international distress channel, sixteen. This was frustrating. I was sure they could hear me calling, but were standing on their course regardless. We were going to be subjected to a potential life or death situation through sheer bloody-mindedness. Other vessels, hearing my urgent calls responded to my message, saying they could hear me transmitting. There was little time to say more, other than "we're about t' be towed away by a fuckin' big Dutchman."

I was sounding a continuous blast on our foghorn, which was deafening, but to no avail. I shouted instructions to the lads on deck to hang on, as the huge vessel passed twenty yards down our starboard side. There were figures visible in her wheelhouse, but they refused to look in our direction, despite our noise and gestures. A minute later we experienced a sudden jerk and the wires at our side went from vertical to horizontal. Our net was no longer fast on the seabed, we were being towed sideways by this monstrous ship.

Fortunately the *Courage* was a very stable vessel and our wires were leading out from our starboard side and not under the boat. She didn't capsize, but we were dragged for several scary minutes while Bill and Bluey, hanging on, hurled abuse at the Dutch vessel's stern. I called on the radio again to all Scarborough vessels, telling them of our plight. Faces could now be seen at the ship's rear wheelhouse windows, observing our predicament, but not attempting to alleviate the situation. Eventually something parted underwater and we stopped moving. I announced this to the local skippers in the vicinity, who were filling the airwaves, expressing concern for our dilemma.

Lying across the wind, we were able to recover our ground gear, now in a heap. I was distraught to find only a small section of my new net remaining. The big Dutch bully had taken most of the trawl. I was incensed and steamed the *Courage* at full speed in the direction of the super trawler, now almost a mile distant.

When close alongside I blasted our foghorn again, while my crew waved and shouted to attract the attention of the watch-keepers, who again ignored us. Finally one of wheelhouse inhabitants deemed to come to the window, looking in our direction.

"'Eave up, you've got 'alf our net," Bill was shouting, gesticulating revolving winch drums with both hands.

The ignorant Dutchman shrugged, as if not comprehending the message, waiting for us to go away.

I was now almost apoplectic. "Get t' anchor ready, shackle it t' after wire. I'll show t' bastard summat 'e will understand." He'd destroyed our net and now I was going to wreck his. Our anchor, which had previously been borrowed and returned by the Whitby Lifeboat, was an admiralty pattern type with folding stock, which could comfortably be lifted by two men. John and Bluey carried it aft in full view of the watching Dutchmen. Bill assembled the stock while Bluey shackled the warp to the iron ring. It was dawning on the foreigners that we were about to fight back. My crewmen were in the process of hanging the 'hook' over our stern, allowing the winch to take the strain, when a man appeared on the platform outside the bridge.

Waving both arms above his head frantically, in perfect English, he shouted, "we 'eave up, we 'eave up." He'd finally got the message.

Five minutes later his massive white nylon net was on the surface. In contrasting orange, clearly visible hanging from the lower, leading edge of his gear, tiny in proportion, was the section of our missing net. A small sack of fish was hanging below the footrope. Three of the Dutch crew pulled our gear clear onto their main deck as the giant trawl was hauled up the stern ramp of the ship, to be wound onto a receiving net drum.

Several tons of herring were quickly and efficiently taken on board from the long sleeve of their colossal net, then we were able to get alongside the slow moving vessel. With no words spoken by the men above, our lost equipment was unceremoniously bundled overboard, falling on our starboard side, to be pulled into the middle of our little craft by my three crewmen. No fish was returned. The man, who I now presumed to be the skipper, again appeared on the bridge deck, high above us. With hands cupped to his mouth he shouted, "you should stay inside ze six-mile limit, zat is ze best way."

There was no point in arguing with him. Nothing I could say was going to make a difference but I found a little solace in shouting, "fuck off yer 'errin' yafflin' bastard," as I put the wheel over to port and disengaged the engine, allowing the bully to continue on his way. The white net was already streaming from the stern of his ship.

Feeling angry, helpless and totally frustrated at our inability to fish among these foreigners, who thought everything beyond the six-mile limit was exclusively theirs, I went on deck. The lads were already removing the remaining net from the bobbins in readiness for a spare one. "Where's t' bloody navy when yer want 'em?" I shouted to no one in particular, echoing the sentiments of every skipper on the coast.

"If they turned up now, they'd probably board us and leave them buggers alone," Bill said, equally annoyed at our loss and enforced extra labour. He was right as usual.

I reported the incident to the fisheries officer when we landed our fish, showing him the severed trawl. He appeared sympathetic but wasn't optimistic of any redress for our loss. No one in authority was interested in pursuing an international prosecution or claim on our behalf. We were insignificant as far as bureaucrats were concerned, but we'd keep going and we'd keep trying to get among the herring marks.

CHAPTER 14

A DIVING EXPERIENCE

Forgetting fishing problems for a while, during the weekend, as well as spending time with Dotty and the kids, I went out in a small, privately owned boat with two divers from the Sub Aqua Club. Strangely, they came to our house, saying they required my assistance to dive on a wreck, about two miles from the harbour. I thought this unusual, as I hadn't been diving very long and there were plenty of other, more experienced divers than me they could have asked, but these were very good divers and I wasn't going to say no to them.

The pair even helped me to carry my kit, as theirs was already on the boat. I was given a small, but heavy shoulder bag to carry. This expedition was beginning to appear suspicious. When I asked what wreck we were going on, I was told, "you'll see when we get there. We have a little job to do."

Intrigued, I went along happily to see what was going on. We were soon on board the little craft and cast off the mooring lines, which were permanently attached to the pier. Passing the lighthouse as we steamed from the leisure section of the harbour, I gave a friendly wave to the lighthouse keeper, Jack 'Jacka' Sheader who, not knowing who was in the little motorboat, gave a little, unsure salute, then recognizing me, shouted down, "what are you up t' young Nommy? Don't yer spend enough time at sea?"

"We're on a secret mission," I bawled back, adding mystery to a trip I knew nothing about. The feeling of friendliness and the witty interaction of the harbour users was one of the most pleasurable aspects of our community.

Jacka gave a big, amiable wave then called, "save us a fry." This was a request for some fish, if we were to get any. My crew often threw fish up to the watch-keepers on the lighthouse pier as we entered the harbour. Jacka had been a trawlerman in distant water vessels when younger and had fingers missing to prove it. He later sailed in steam trawlers from our home port before swallowing the anchor and becoming a lighthouse keeper.

Once out of the harbour, I was informed I could open the bag. The holdall contained five, cylindrical, cardboard tubes. I looked perplexed. "It's explosives; five, five-pound sticks of jelly," Paul said, grinning. "We didn't tell you earlier, in case you changed your mind."

I'm sure I would have. The pair went on to explain they'd been approached by a salvage company with information of a possible cargo of copper, on a wreck off Scarborough. The divers' assignment was to confirm or reject this data by examining the wreck. The sunken ship's open hold was coated with silt so the pair had decided to blast the midships section to clear this fine layer and identify any cargo.

En route to the dive site the lads told me of a prank, which had recently been played on Colin, the diving club Chairman. Gordon, one of the club members, had found an old bedpan with the name, 'Boots, Nottingham', in a dusty attic, when moving house. While on his next diving trip, he'd placed the piece of porcelain where it could easily be found. Subsequently, he'd taken Colin and others to dive on the same wreck and led him to the 'find'. Colin was ecstatic with his trophy and with great fanfare, produced the artefact from under a cover at the weekly club meeting. The object was acknowledged with great acclaim by most of the members, and not a little chuckling from those at the back of the room who were in on the joke.

The club Chairman was so taken with his specimen that he wrote to the head office of the major chemists, sending a photograph of the object and informing the PR department that he'd found this magnificent bedpan on a shipwreck from World War I. Colin waited anxiously for the reply but when it arrived the response wasn't what he was expecting. The letter informed him tersely that 'Boots' had not commenced production of this model until 1928.

There was a tense atmosphere in the club at the next meeting on the following Wednesday evening. Everyone was now in on the joke and the Chairman was not a happy person when he addressed the packed house of members. Normally an easygoing, pleasant man, Colin had a very serious demeanour. "I suppose you all think this practical joke is funny?" he said to a silent audience. "Well I've got to say," he paused several seconds for effect, "so do I. What a bloody great wheeze." There was an audible, united sigh of relief in the room. Colin was never one to be negative. His popularity soared to even greater heights.

The sunken ship took little finding. The transit points on shore to the west and south, denoting its position were clearly definable and we were soon grappled into the wreck and secured. As the tide began to ease, Paul and I kitted up then attached torch lanyards to our belts. Paul, holding his mask to his face, flipped backwards over the side and I followed. Surfacing alongside the boat, we were handed the bag of explosives, which now also contained a reel of thin electric cable. Together we swam down the grapple line leaving Pete on board as tender. Paul was leading, but I was very close behind as the visibility, even in powerful torchlight, was only five or six feet and not knowing the wreck, I didn't want to get lost.

The grapple was hooked into the wreck near the seabed, close to the ship's rudder. The prongs on this hook were light-gauge, mild steel, designed to straighten and pull out when required. Foreside of the huge rudder was the rusty, old, iron propeller, from an age before non-ferrous screws were developed. Two of its four, ancient blades were buried in the sand. Sitting under the boss of the rusting prop was a large, crusty, old lobster, its feelers frantically twitching at an approaching enemy. At any other time this delicacy would have been snapped up into a 'goodie bag' for the pot, but as we were on a serious project and not fun diving, the creature won a reprieve.

It was now slack water so there was no tidal effect acting upon us. We swam along the starboard side of the wreck then up to the deck level, which wasn't far from the seabed. The bows of the old ship appeared to be sinking into the sand. Our goal, the hatch coaming, was easily discernable, though the slightest flap of our fins caused the silt to billow in clouds, ruining the already poor visibility. The hold appeared full, but full of what? I could hear myself breathing rapidly and could feel my heart pounding as I took the explosives from the bag, passing them to my dive buddy.

Paul had assessed a likely position for the bomb and set about securing the sticks to a broken, unidentifiable girder crossing the cargo space. Gently paying out the cable embedded in the explosive, we retraced our path. The old lobster was forgotten as we slowly allowed ourselves to surface up the grapple line. It was essential not to rush this passage. The saturated air in our bodies must be given time to dissipate or we'd suffer decompression sickness; the dreaded bends.

All was quiet on the surface and Pete was now kitted up in his diving gear. He'd turned off the radio and disconnected the boat's battery while we were in the water, not chancing any external electrical source to prematurely detonate the charge. He took our air bottles and fins from us, allowing us to climb the aluminium ladder back into the boat more easily. Next Pete paid out the entire length of grapple line, which had been hauled tight above the sunken vessel, then tied even more cable to the bare end to extend our distance from the wreck.

High water slack had now given way to the ebb, though the tide wasn't yet strong. The little boat moved gently downstream until the grapple line again tightened. The electric cable had also been allowed to stream out freely and was hanging lightly over the boat's side. It was only now, when our little craft was well away from the wreck that Pete connected the two exposed wires of the cable to the twist grip detonator. Following a count down from ten, he twisted the handle and immediately there was a dull thump, and a severe shock wave instantly shot through our little vessel. Seconds later, a circle of white water, which quickly turned to brown, contaminated by silt, appeared on the surface. In the centre of this expanding ring, floating belly up and dead, was a large, bloated ling. This cod-like fish must have made the wreck its home and had been blasted to the surface by the explosion.

I gaffed the fish as it slowly drifted close to the boat on the gentle ebb, throwing the slippery creature into a fish box on the deck. Pete was now donning his diving bottles while Paul hauled on the grapple line, pulling the little craft back close above the wreck again. The brown cloud had now been carried downstream on the growing tide, so Pete wasted no time in dropping over the side, on his way to examine the results of the big bang. The tide was now ripping so he'd have to fight against its force to reach the site.

Fifteen minutes later he was back on the surface and after spitting out his air demand valve, began to laugh. Spluttering, as sea water splashed around his mouth he said, "there's an old lobster sitting under t' propeller, and it seems to be shakin' its 'ead and thinking, what the 'ell was that bang?"

Back on board and now more serious, Pete said the ship's hold was empty, that the whole cargo space must have been filled to the brim with silt. The ship was sailing 'light'. This was disappointing news, but no loss to the lads. They had been engaged to assess the potential, not salvage any cargo.

The grapple was hauled from the wreck by the boat's capstan and recovered back on board. The tines had straightened as designed and were soon bent back to shape by Paul, using a section of hollow bar. The instrument was now ready for use again and was stowed away, along with the coils of rope. As we steamed slowly back into the harbour, we again passed close to the lighthouse, and with considerable effort, I was able to throw the large ling onto the stone steps, leading up to the pier. Jacka swooped on the big fish like a seagull on a herring, shouting a big "thank you" in our direction as we continued back to our mooring.

In a very short while the boat was back on its berth, and we were off to the diving club to recharge our bottles, then wash the taste of salt away with some liquid refreshment next door in the 'Leeds Arms'. When I saw the friendly lighthouse keeper a few days later he said, "that ling was t' tastiest and tenderest fish I ever ate. Its flesh was so soft, it almost melted in me mouth."

I didn't tell him it had been softened by twenty-five pounds of gelignite.

CHAPTER 15

BONANZA

In the early hours of Sunday morning, we again went in search of herring. Steaming off ten miles to the likely area, I found a massive fleet of ships ahead of us. At least fifty foreign and local vessels were evident on the radar screen within a six-mile diameter, indicating the discovery of a big mark. The VHF was deafening on every frequency with Dutch, Scottish and the various Yorkshire dialects from Bridlington, Whitby and Scarborough. With the memories of our close encounter from the previous week still fresh in my mind, I decided to look for another shoal, away from the madding crowd.

After more than an hour of zigzagging in a south-easterly direction, attempting to cover the maximum search area, my eyes aching from constantly looking from sounder to compass and with the first light of dawn in the sky, I was beginning to despair of finding an exclusive patch. Reconciled to joining the melee of shipping now miles astern, I detected a slight thickening of the bottom line on the sounder. It could be something or nothing, but it might just be spawning herring, already hard on the seabed with the coming light. I took a precise fix then eased back the engine, which was the signal for the men below to turn out. There was no time for tea. I allowed the *Courage* to continue south-easterly for a few more minutes while the lads appeared then we shot the gear, heading back to where I'd noticed the possible signs.

There was nothing to be seen on the sounder when we trawled over the area again, not even the slightest waver on the bottom. I was confident I'd hit the right position, so looked again at the slight scratching on the original section of sounder paper. I still wasn't sure whether I was imagining the swelling and seeing something that wasn't there. If there was anything to be caught, at least we'd trawled over the area and would have an indication when we hauled the gear.

Three hours later and almost back among the mass of boats, we hauled the trawl. I'd almost forgotten the little blip shown on the sounder, so was gob-smacked when the net burst to the surface, containing a huge haul of cod.

"Bingo," I yelled to my shipmates as the mass of fish, buoyant, floated in the net, spreading to fill the whole trawl on top of the water.

"Bloody 'ell," said Bluey.

There must have been at least three hundred stone of big fish, many spewing partly digested herrings. We'd hit a bonanza.

Bill just rushed for the for'ard quarter rope. Following his example Bluey hauled on the after one while John and I began to pull the headline, hurrying to get the mouth of the net on board and closed off so fish couldn't escape. Soon the large catch was trapped down the long bellies and in the codend. There was too much fish to heave on board in one lift, we'd have to divide it up, taking three separate lifts of about a hundred stone each. It took more than half an hour to get the huge catch on board and all the time I kept looking round, hoping no boats were close enough to see us.

If even one skipper observed our operations, he'd be on the radio telling the fleet we were on a 'fish shop', and our secret would be out. Every vessel in the area would be homing in on the *Courage* and our private party would be no more. If we could get the fish on board unnoticed, we could steam back to the south, away from the busy traffic, where I was now convinced we'd stumbled across this windfall.

It was with relief that I saw the third bag swing inboard. As the fish spilled from the codend across the decks, levelling out to fill every available space, I returned to the wheelhouse. The wing ends of the trawl were hauled onto the deck and I set a course to where I'd seen the thickened bottom line. My shipmates were soon busy filling boxes on the port side of the wheelhouse, getting the decks clear so they could start gutting operations. There was a good sprinkling of quality haddock among the catch. These were kept in separate boxes and would be gutted after the cod. Haddock kept their colour better. The greenish skin of the cod would soon turn white if not quickly gutted and washed.

There was still nothing to be seen on the sounder where I thought we'd caught the big haul, but I was determined to trawl over the same ground again. I hadn't expected the little mark on the paper to yield this deck load of fish, so I wasn't worried when there was no obvious sign. If there were herrings spawning hard down on the seabed, we'd get a definite sign in the dark when they swam up again.

The catch was nearly all packed in boxes, only a few fish remained in the pound when I eased her down to shoot again. The *Courage* had a ten-degree list to port with the extra weight on that side. This increased to twenty degrees when we threw the fishing gear over the starboard side. We were soon towing back in the direction of the phantom cod. The lads on deck rounded up the remainder of the catch and commenced gutting. They had fifty-two boxes to get through.

I aimed the *Courage* in the required direction then put the strops on the wheel. For the next half hour I dashed back and forth from deck to wheelhouse, gutting a few fish then adjusting the course, making sure I hit the hot spot. Once past the zone I allowed the boat free passage for about fifteen minutes, then went back into the 'shed' to turn her round. Three times in the next three hours we passed over the same piece of ground. The men on deck were racing through their work and much of the catch was below, boxed and iced. There were ten boxes, mostly haddock, to process when I delivered the lads a pot of tea and a sandwich.

The trio munched on the alfresco snack with relish and were ready to carry on, but I didn't want to trawl any longer. I was worried that if we were hammering a mother lode, we could burst our net with the weight of fish. Equally, we could be wasting our time if my intuition was wrong. The remaining boxes were stacked on the fishroom hatch. These would be the first to be gutted next haul. We took our stations and began to heave the gear up again.

All eyes were looking to windward in anticipation as the wing ends came in view and together we spotted the bubbling, creamy water as another, even bigger bag of fish surged to the surface.

"Fuckin' 'ell, there's more than las' time," from Bluey.

"Don't bust! Please don't bust," I screamed at the bulging codend, straining to hold five hundred stone or more of similar sized fish.

"It's not ours till it's on board," advised Bill; shades of Tom Pashby appearing, which I ignored, as he again dashed for his quarter rope.

We struggled to get the bobbins on board this time. The weight of fish in the net was pulling them back over, forcing us to lash the ground gear inboard before we could pull on the headline. Several large cod had washed out of the net while we were wrestling with the bobbins and were now floating belly up a few yards from the side of the boat. The helpless fish were surrounded and being pecked at viciously by a cluster of fulmars. These birds, squawking and cackling loudly, assaulted the hapless, flapping fish aggressively.

Normally I'd be miffed at losing good quality fish but with a netful alongside, I had more than enough to worry about. There were no other vessels within three miles of us, so we were able to take our time, methodically lifting five bags of cod on board, filling the *Courage's* every available deck space with fish.

We couldn't shoot the trawl again, as most of the netting was buried under fish. Instead we lay across the light breeze and the four of us began picking up our bumper haul into boxes. We soon exhausted our supply of containers on deck and were forced to bring almost the entire stock of empties from below, after shifting the remaining ungutted fish from the fishroom hatch. There was much work ahead of us, but this was a nice problem to have. We were already guaranteed a very big pay packet at the weekend.

With all the catch boxed and the net clear, we decided to have one more haul before going in to land, so shot the trawl away again. This was an opportunity some fishermen never saw in a lifetime and I was determined to milk it. There was no chance whatsoever of the men on deck clearing this haul, but they'd shift what they could. If we caught any more I'd organise some assistance when we got in the harbour. Another four-hour trawl captured another four hundred stone of fish and though the boys had got through the remains of the first haul and more than half of the second bag, they could do nothing with this final catch as we'd run out of empty boxes to put fish in.

I set the course for home and we had another pot of tea and snack before the lads carried on gutting while I steered the sagging *Courage* for harbour. Every ten or fifteen minutes, Bill would drop down into the hold to put fish away in clean boxes, which Bluey had newly washed and passed below as they became empty. With less than an hour to go I called the lighthouse on the radio, asking 'Jacka', the officer on watch, if he'd ring Dad to come down to help us and to try to get a couple of other hands to assist. I asked if he could also arrange for some extra ice to be left for us in boxes. We would exhaust the supply of ice on board before we got home.

It wasn't unusual to ask for extra labour ashore. Skippers would frequently call in for assistance if they had good catches. Some men were regular 'lumpers' on the pier, turning out each evening for anyone who required help. They'd be paid for their trouble in fish if the catch was moderate, plus cash too if the work warranted it.

The *Courage* was deep in the water and felt sluggish to handle. I'd never seen her so full of fish. It was with a feeling of euphoria that I guided her through the harbour entrance in the early evening. A couple of haddocks were thrown to 'Jacka' as we passed the lighthouse. These watch-keepers were always willing to assist with ship to shore messages and phone calls for the boats. I'd be sure to buy him a couple of pints when we next met.

Dad and his brother George were quickly on board as we tied up to the pier. Another willing hand began lowering boxes down. Several other vessels came in to land good hauls during the evening while we were gutting our catch, but none had more than a quarter of what we'd caught. The work was much easier with twice the manpower and our helpers worked with a will, but even so, it was after midnight when we finally finished landing and were able to leave the pier. The stack of fish on the market looked spectacular as we sheeted it down. I thanked our helpers and would show more than gratitude at the weekend. We'd be sailing again at five in morning, to see if any fish remained in our bonanza location. The herring would have gone but if they'd spawned, there would be fish feeding on the eggs. The location wouldn't be exclusive though. Half the fleet would be keeping a look out for the *Courage*.

Some plans are doomed to failure and ours fell into this category. During the night the wind had freshened from the north and was blowing strongly. The boats that had remained at sea overnight were now back in port. We wouldn't be going anywhere. It was early on Thursday morning before we were able to sail again. The wind had fallen away but there was still a northerly swell in the water. We made directly for our lucrative grounds, accompanied by several other vessels. It was impossible to keep the secret of our bumper catch, so I'd told any skippers who'd asked, the general area, though not the precise reading. I wanted to be the first across that position again before it was depleted.

It was still dark when we trawled over the ground and a grey cloud two or three fathoms high was evident on the seabed for several minutes duration. This would be fish, feeding on the herring spawn. The other skippers would also see this evidence, though the sign would disappear again with daylight. Our first haul was a good one, about two hundred stone, though consisting mostly of haddock and whiting. The cod, which we'd caught earlier in the week had been feeding on the herring as they spawned. The herring and most of the cod had now gone, leaving billions of eggs scattered across a wide area of the seabed, which the smaller fish were now gorging on.

Other boats were hauling with similar success, but as the day wore on catches were getting smaller and masses of immature fish were being killed for little financial gain. Our final haul of the day was a mixture of immature species with only two or three boxes for the market. We all looked in disappointment and sadness at the waste, as the thousands of little fish lay dead on the deck. There was nothing of value to merit the slaughter. Looking at the wasted fish, I said, "t' ragman wouldn't give yer a blow on 'is bugle fo' that lot."

My crew stopped in their tracks and Bill said, "yer what?" They all looked at me quizzically.

I repeated the expression.

Bill was the first to ask, "what's that mean?"

It wasn't a saying I'd used much, it just came into my head. I explained it was a term Sid, my former deck hand from Hull, used. He said it was a popular expression in the days of his youth. When the rag and bone man came round on his horse and cart, he carried a bugle on a short length of light chain, which he would blow to attract attention. He would encourage the youngsters who gathered round his vehicle, summoned by the clarion call, to gather rags or woollens for his trade, by offering them a blow on his bugle, hence the saying.

I thought this was a lovely, descriptive saying, appropriate on this occasion and said I wasn't intending to shoot the trawl back again on this ground and repeated, "t' ragman wouldn't give us a blow on 'is bugle fo' what we've jus' caught."

Blank looks and "oh" was all I got in return for my explanation.

We landed a good catch that evening and the following morning, to our astonishment, received over a thousand pounds each in our pay packets. This was an unheard of amount and gave my confidence to pay for a new boat, a massive boost.

Strangely, John left our crew soon after, leaving us short-handed.

CHAPTER 16

VISIT TO THE SHIPYARD

The skeleton of my new vessel was formed. A phone call from Jimmy Noble informed me all her frames were now in place. She was taking shape on the paint slipway under a scaffold structure with canvas sheeting attached for protection from the elements. He asked, "are ye nae gang to come an' see herrr? Ye'll need tae watch hoow we're putting herrr together," in his distinctive north-east burr.

I would have loved to see the progress of my baby, but it was an eight-hundred-mile round trip and though after four attempts I'd finally passed a driving test and acquired an old Ford banger, I didn't relish the return journey in the brief shore time available to me. Jimmy said that if I flew into Aberdeen, he'd pick me up at the airport and drive me the fifty miles to Fraserburgh.

This mode of transport hadn't even crossed my mind. I'd only been on an aeroplane once before on a cheap package holiday to Malta. This was 'jet setting'. I booked a flight from Humberside, not far from the new bridge, for the following Friday, then bought an instamatic camera to record the occasion.

We were in port early on Friday and I spent hardly any time with my family before I was on my way to the airport. A severe, south-westerly gale was blowing, which had caused us to work in the lee of the land during the previous twenty-four hours. I was quite apprehensive as I drove south. I didn't mind being at sea in a gale but didn't much relish the thought of flying in one. My fears were not allayed when informed that the flight I was due to take was delayed by an hour coming from Schipol, due to the adverse weather. The wind was still blowing at gale force plus.

There were no catering facilities established yet at this little airport but I was told I could use the bar in the adjacent flying club. I was desperately in need of a beer to calm my nerves and took no second urging to visit this building. It was like stepping back in time when I entered the doors of the clubhouse. The inhabitants were mostly dressed like 'Biggles' from the books of my school days. Brown flying jackets with fur collars were de rigueur. Leather helmets with raised goggles were common. Even silk scarves were plentiful. I ordered a beer and sandwich and sat at the bar, killing time and making a mental note of the time warp I'd found myself in. A tall, ginger-haired man with a handlebar moustache, flying helmet in hand, was standing close by. I couldn't believe it when he said, "what ho, too jolly fresh for flying today old chap. I've just been up there and my old girl was really performing. Very lively what! I've just tethered her down while this little lot blows over."

I could have been in a wartime film set. I looked round for other members of the cast. Almost everyone in the room could be playing a part. Were they filming, or was I on the television programme, 'Candid Camera'? Neither, it was just a different world to anything I'd ever seen before.

My plane eventually arrived, but not before I'd managed another couple of beers. The aircraft, a twin engine 'Fokker Friendship', was bigger than I'd expected, but looked quite elderly. Most of the passengers joining me on the flight appeared to be rig workers or divers, making their way to the growing oil base at Aberdeen. The obvious exception, in the seat across the aisle from me, was a young mother with a tiny baby, who seemed only a few weeks old. We had a very bumpy taxi and take off from the runway and the plane was shaking dramatically as we began to ascend. I was pleased to note I wasn't the only person feeling apprehensive. Most of my fellow travellers were looking wild-eyed and worried, though the plane did settle down a little as we gained height and rose above the cloud level.

All was now calm on board the plane, except for the baby, who was demanding a feed. The hostess had delivered pre-packed food and beverages to the passengers and was in the process of warming a bottle of milk for the child at the mother's request. I was tucking into the light meal, trying not to think about the forthcoming landing, when without warning, the pink clad infant was thrust into my arms. The mother, hand over mouth, dashed to the toilet at the rear of the cabin. The crowd of macho riggers found this highly amusing. I'd been left holding the baby, literally.

Once I'd grasped the situation I was unfazed and took the warm bottle from the concerned crewmember, inserting the teat into the squawking mouth. The noise stopped immediately as the little girl began to feed. Everyone close by seemed relieved now the yowling had stopped and impressed with my handling of the situation, but it wasn't difficult. It was only a few years ago that Paula and Danny were this age and I'd often given them bottles.

The sheepish, apologetic mother returned to find everything under control and I insisted on finishing the task, then winding the child who was now almost asleep. She slept in my arms for the remainder of the flight and helped me to take my mind off the landing, which turned out to be equally as hairy as the take off. I assisted the young mum and her charge from the plane towards the terminal building. She carried the empty carrycot and all the necessities required for transporting an infant, while I gently walked with the babe in arms; the little lady nestled cosily into the warmth of my jacket, sheltered from the cold wind.

"Well done matey, nice one," and "I couldn't 'ave managed that," were two of the several friendly comments from the smiling, macho men as they walked with us towards the arrivals lounge.

I could see Jimmy Noble and Madge scanning the passengers as we made our way from the secure section of the airport. They looked in my direction then away to the people following. The pair were looking for a solitary traveller, not a couple with child and were surprised when I approached them with my new family. Luckily, close by was the young lady's husband who, after getting over the shock of seeing his wife in the company of a stranger, was pleased to unburden me of my beautiful, little companion.

A large basking shark caught by Courage. *Circa 1975.*
Photo by Dennis Dobson

Arthur Godfrey on board Mekong.
Courtesy of Arthur Godfrey

Paul Gridley, hotelier with Noel White, bank manager.
Photo by F.G. Normandale

Harry 'Whisper' Cammish with his pal 'Sparky'.
Photo by Ken Wigg

It was an hour's drive to Fraserburgh, but as it was lunchtime, we stopped en route in Ellen, a little town mid-journey, for a drink and a bar lunch. I was amazed when Madge asked for a brandy and Babycham. "What a lethal combination," I thought, but then Jimmy took a half of beer with a large whisky chaser. This was heavy stuff at lunchtime. I settled for half a beer. My next surprise was when the boat builder ordered Cullen skink and stovies for three. I still struggled occasionally with the dialect in this part of the country, even though I'd been to the Broch several times, but to be faced with a foreign menu was a little disconcerting. It transpired that I was to have smoked haddock soup and a sort of meat and potato fry up. Both were delicious.

Soon it was time to visit my own new baby, which we found, still taking shape on the edge of the wide concrete slipway. She was hemmed in by three large Scottish vessels, propped on blocks, awaiting painting and underwater repairs. My new craft, though still skeletal, looked fantastic. The smell of new wood in the air, even in the makeshift tent was overpowering and gave me goose-pimples.

The keel and stem-post, which were scarfed together, were of oak, from a massive tree. The towering frames, also of oak, looked immense, reaching high above me. Larch planking had commenced at both deck and keel levels, putting flesh on the bones and these would eventually meet in the middle. Much activity was in evidence from the workforce and all seemed intent on playing a part in bringing life to my dream.

The experience of seeing my very own, new boat under construction, of watching these superb craftsmen working on my behalf was so emotional; it would have taken little more to draw tears. I found it difficult to speak when Jimmy asked what I thought of her. I continually walked round the oak structure, trying to take in every aspect, totally forgetting the camera sitting in my jacket pocket, so would return home with no record of my visit. I would later ask Jimmy to arrange shots of her development for my album.

Eventually we drove to Noble's boatyard, at the other side of the harbour. Here in the huge green hangar, were all the component parts of my boat, stored in readiness for installation.

The large, olive-green engine with eight chrome cylinder head covers, looked powerful. Two immense, fuel tanks, painted in maroon primer, each capable of holding fourteen hundred gallons of diesel, looked too big to fit in the engine space available. This was a massive contrast to the *Courage*, whose mere four hundred gallons a side, was more than ample for her needs. This was a measure of the step up I was taking.

The winch, hydraulic pump and auxiliary engine all seemed outsized but everything I could see was dwarfed by the towering, combined wheelhouse and galley in the next workshop. This construction looked as if it should be on a vessel twice the size of mine. Jimmy saw the horror on my face and assured me it was fine and wouldn't look out of place. I went inside and up the stairs onto the bridge. "We could 'old a dance in 'ere," I said, looking at the space within. Even with the specified array of electronic equipment, and comfortable seat I'd ordered, there would be lots of room to spare. The *Courage's* wheelhouse was full with two occupants. I felt like pinching myself. Could all this be happening to me?

Leaving the boatyard, I arranged to meet Jimmy in an hour, when he'd drive me back to the airport. I spent the time clearing my swimming head as I wandered round the piers. There were so many details involved in the construction. Was there a major flaw in my planning? I'd specified tried and tested equipment, not wanting to be a guinea pig for any new product that could go wrong.

My flying visit was soon over. The journey back was uneventful and early evening found me back at home, attempting to tell Dotty all that I'd seen during my day. She was particularly amused when I told her I'd been left holding the baby.

Little Danny, now spending his Saturday mornings at the harbour with me on the *Courage* was already interested and excited at the prospect of our new vessel and asked obvious questions. "Was it big Dad? Has it got a flat back like t' *Our Heritage*? Is t' wheelhouse big?" He didn't have to ask the colour. She would be blue, as the two previous vessels I'd skippered had been. Blue had been a lucky colour for me so far and I wasn't about to change it.

There was good news and bad news the following morning when I walked on the pier. A prospective buyer from Bridlington was interested in the *Courage* and was waiting to look round her. He was delighted with what he saw in the old vessel. She wasn't a new boat, but was in very good condition for her age and had the latest electronics and new machinery. We shook on my asking price of thirty thousand pounds, on the understanding that she wouldn't be available until April of the following year. I couldn't afford to be idle until the time my new craft was ready.

Elated at having found a buyer, I climbed the ladders to meet Bill and received the bad news; he was leaving. It wasn't a rash decision he'd made and we wouldn't fall out. He didn't want to sail in a bigger boat, with the inevitable, additional sea time, so he'd made his own arrangements and was going to buy the *Success II*. I was very disappointed, but pleased for him and respected his decision. He would do well; he had the drive and determination required. I was aware of this, first hand. Apart from Dotty, it had been mainly Bill who'd kept me going through the difficult times.

Good news followed the bad. Rusty would be pleased to come back in the *Courage* and then in the new boat. He'd also been in touch with Sid, and he too was keen to rejoin, though he wouldn't be available for several weeks, as he'd signed on for a six-week voyage on a freezer trawler, bound for Greenland. Walt Sheader joined our crew temporarily while Sid was unavailable, so we were four-handed again. Bluey was still in situ, and would remain so for the foreseeable future.

Dotty and I were in a dilemma. What were we to call our new vessel? She was coming together quickly and the builder wanted her name. I'd been to Fraserburgh again and the planking was almost in place and her hull formed. It was traditional to name vessels after female members of the family, but Dotty ruled herself out of this option. There was the choice of calling her *Paula*, or *Doris*, the name of both our mothers. These names didn't really seem to have the right ring for a boat.

After lots of deliberation we decided on *Independence*. Paula was born on July 4th and also, we were independent. We'd gone it alone, with no outside assistance or influence, other than the bank. There were a few venture capitalists around, investing in skippers with potential. The trawler owners from Hull, looking to diversify into inshore waters were very shrewd and backed the best men available. Some, who thought they only had to buy a boat and appoint a skipper to make a fortune, would get their fingers burnt. No qualifications of any kind were required to skipper vessels under twenty-five tons, but experience was essential.

Had I taken a step too far by going it alone? Would my independence pay off? Time would tell, but I was optimistic. Fishing was a lucrative business at present. Almost anyone with the desire and a half decent boat could make a reasonable living. People who'd never been to sea before were wanting to be fishermen. Fish were plentiful and prices on the market buoyant.

Things went terribly wrong at home on the following Thursday night. We'd landed our catch in the morning and Dotty and I had been to the 'Leeds Arms' for a few drinks and to meet up with friends. On the way home a discussion we were having developed into an argument, which became heated. I didn't want to argue. I was very tired and only wanted to go to bed, but Dotty was determined to continue the vocal duel to 'clear the air' before going to bed. My wife was insistent that we should never sleep on an argument. After further heated exchanges and with no sign of a sensible conclusion in sight, I decided I needed sleep. "I'm going t' sleep on me boat," I shouted, as I made for the door. For some reason it had always been a constant source of irritation to Dotty that I had an alternative bed, even though my bunk was far less comfortable and never used in port.

This made her even angrier and she put her shoulder to the door, attempting to prevent me from leaving. With some difficulty I was still able to open the door and stepped out into the street.

"Well if you're going, take this with you," she shouted, reaching inside the door for a large transistor radio, standing on the window ledge, which I'd bought earlier in the year for her birthday. She raised the radio above her head and hurled it in my direction. Fortunately the heavy instrument missed the chosen target, landing instead with a crash in the road. "You might as well take these too." The next projectile was a box of ceramic tiles, the remnants of some work I'd done in the bathroom the previous weekend. A sound very much like the shattering of glass, but much louder, rent the still of the night as I hot-footed it down the hill to the harbour.

It was quite pleasant on the harbour side and I no longer felt sleepy. There wasn't a breath of wind and the air was warm. The reflection of hundreds of seafront lights, strung between the lamp standards, shimmered in the harbour water as I sat on a mooring bollard, watching the crew of *Pathfinder* landing a huge catch of cod. I enjoyed talking to the lads as they efficiently went about their work and was pleased to accept their invitation to " 'ave a beer" from the remains of a case of 'Longlife', close to hand. A couple of cans of beer later, after discussing a range of fishing subjects and fielding some good humoured enquiries as to why I wasn't at home in bed, I thought it was probably safe to return.

Making my way back up the hill, I quietly approached number nineteen, which was in darkness. I was soon to discover the doors were locked and I had no key. Fortunately, walking to the back of the house, I noticed Danny's bedroom window was ajar and I was easily able to climb through the aperture via the flat roof of the kitchen. It didn't seem wise attempting to sleep in my half of our bed, so I got in bed with Danny. I didn't wake him and though I had a restless night, he slept soundly.

Next morning at breakfast the atmosphere was calmer. The heat had gone from our conflict of opinions and we had a truce without pursuing the debate, though I don't think either of us could remember what we'd been arguing about. Paula and Danny were soon dressed and ready for school and we accompanied them to the door. School for them was 'Friarage', about a five-minute walk.

Mrs Wilkinson, a delightful, elderly neighbour, whose late husband Bill had been a former Mayor, was standing at her gate as we stepped onto the pavement to wave our bairns off. I wished her good morning and she responded then said, "did you here that car crash in the hill last night? It was ever so loud. It woke me up."

Dotty and I looked at each other, then at Mrs Wilkinson. Straight-faced and almost in unison we replied, "we didn't 'ear anything, we must 'ave slept through it."

CHAPTER 17

AN UNWANTED CATCH

Fishing continued to be good throughout the next few weeks and there was much good humour and a pleasant atmosphere on board the boat, though I missed Bill's encouraging influence. We were hauling the trawl one morning during our second day at sea and the catch was unusually heavy. We began steadily pulling the load to the surface and though weighty, it was manageable with assistance from the roll of the boat. Something dense within the net was preventing the catch floating. We seesawed the sleeve up the *Courage's* side slowly but before we arrived at the codend, a huge fish's tail emerged from the water inside the net. There was a large, strange creature in our trawl. The weight of the catch now became unmanageable, as most fish are semi-buoyant in water.

We secured the unknown catch alongside then Walt managed to pass a rope strop around the tight netting. I passed him the cargo hook and nodded to Rusty, now in position at the winch. Hauling on the wire, he began to draw the bag steadily from the sea. As the strange catch came up the boat's side, Walt and I craned our necks to identify the mysterious fish. It was huge but wasn't threshing wildly or even wriggling. The bag swung inboard and the codend was released, allowing the contents to spill into the fish pound.

A massive basking shark dropped from the net with a thud, dwarfing the dozen or so large cod surrounding it. A gaping mouth sagged open, lifelessly. Sadly the poor monster was dead, having drowned in the net. This harmless creature, which lived entirely on a diet of plankton, had to keep swimming, its huge mouth constantly sieving water through a myriad of filters, to obtain oxygen and food. We'd interrupted its passage then probably towed it through the sea for hours in the trawl. This was a sadness to us all, especially to Rusty, a keen lover of nature. The shark had no value, posed no danger to man and we'd killed it, though accidentally, for no purpose.

I don't know what we'd have done if the lovely creature had been alive. We would have had a struggle to get the thrashing fish back overboard. We had to use a block and tackle to get the dead weight over to the port side, clear of our working area. When the fish was stretched out, Rusty measured its length with the 'two-foot stick'. "Fifteen foot," he announced, "an' it mus' weigh a couple o' ton." No wonder the *Courage* was listing to port.

The remainder of our trip was uneventful and we returned to port in the evening, where our unwanted catch created great interest. The only way we could discharge the poor thing was by crane. We used the static crane at the pier end, near the entrance. This machine, provided by the harbour authorities, cost a pound for each lift. We lowered the shark onto a handcart, wheeled it to the fishmarket, then tipped the lifeless leviathan off the barrow, alongside our catch. We were interested to see what the merchants would pay for the huge fish. Our curiosity was satisfied next morning, when a single bid of two pounds, with no opposition, took the fish. The poor thing would be chopped up for pet food. What an ignominious ending for such a majestic creature.

* * * * * *

Arthur, my friend from the diving club had acquired a sailing vessel, which he renamed *Mekong*. Being an adventurer, he was keen to be off on his travels. After a little boat handling practice locally, he decided to cross the North Sea, sailing to Holland and invited a few friends to join him. I respectfully declined the invitation, as I didn't think I'd have the time to spare for what was a voyage of unspecified duration. Also, I was used to getting from the harbour to the fishing grounds and back as quickly as possible. I was sure I'd be unhappy on a meandering course at uncertain speed.

Undeterred, Arthur enlisted three other friends for the voyage to Amsterdam. Unfortunately, on the day of sailing, on his way to the little ketch armed with stores and supplies, he dropped the boat's compass on the road. There appeared to be no damage, so he retrieved the instrument and thought nothing further of the matter. What Arthur didn't realise, was the impact of the fall had disturbed the polarity of the sensitive piece and the compass was now at least thirty degrees out of true. There were no other means of navigation aboard the vessel, only his charts of the Southern North Sea and a small depth sounder, so this was to be more than an interesting voyage of discovery.

The intrepid mariners set a course for Ijmuiden, situated at the western entrance of the North Sea Canal. From here it would be a twenty-mile cruise to the bustling Dutch city. There was much excitement and good-humoured interaction as the motley crew made their way in a south-easterly direction.

Strangely, the compass error remained undetected as the little craft sailed towards Flamborough Head, so when the land was lost from view astern, it was impossible to assess any course error. Next morning, doubt was raised in Arthur's mind as to the accuracy of his course line when a massive gas rig stood in his path. According to his chart there were no gas fields within miles of his position. Unfazed, the skipper sailed his craft close enough to read the name on the side of the towering structure, then called the rig on his radio.

"This is the ketch *Mekong,* calling the gas rig on my starboard bow. Are you receiving, over?"

Immediately a reply came back over the airwaves. "This is the gas rig. Yes we are receiving you sir. Go ahead, over."

Arthur was the model of politeness as he attempted to obtain his position from the rig's radio officer. "Good morning sir. I didn't expect to see a rig on my present course. Could you give me your position please, over?"

"Yes sir, stand by." The officer then gave out the coordinates of the platform, not only in degrees and minutes but also in seconds and decimals of the same. This position was accurate to within metres on the earth's surface.

Arthur's reply left the rig's communicators totally lost for words. "No I'm sorry, I don't make you there."

The little craft and its crew sailed ever south-eastwards hoping to arrive at Ijmuiden, but only sure they were heading in the general direction of Holland. Early next morning, as the water grew shallower and their destination remained uncertain, Arthur and his now doubtful team of volunteers began to worry. When eventually, land in the form of sand dunes was spied, the relief on board was tangible. The skipper took the little ketch inshore as close as he dared, scanning the coast for habitation. A small, isolated wooden building on the beach was the only sign of civilisation.

Arthur decided to use his VHF radio once more to seek advice, calling the coast station at his required destination. "Ijmuiden Radio, this is the sailing vessel *Mekong*. We are close inshore on your coast but cannot see the entrance to the sea lock. Can you give me any assistance?"

The English-speaking operator came back loud and clear, asking Arthur to describe what he could see on shore.

The description of a single beach hut with sand and grass left the operator perplexed for quite some time, but he was eventually able to plot the *Mekong's* position, thirty miles north of the required location. It took most of the third day to make up the leeway and it was late afternoon when the little craft finally arrived at the entrance to the North Sea Canal. A further twenty-mile cruise lay ahead once through the lock, before their destination, a marina close to the magnificent Central Station was reached. Arthur was unperturbed by his experience, but his shipmates, pleased to be onshore and now a little doubtful of their skipper's navigational skills, ironically named him Vasco, before heading for the nearest bar.

Their stay in the wonderful Dutch city, though exciting, was for three of the group, slightly marred by the thought of sailing home again. Arthur however, was totally satisfied that this wouldn't be a problem. Setting sail on the homeward leg, with compass re-adjusted, the skipper was able to prove his navigation was accurate when, shortly after sunset on the second day, Flamborough Light was sighted ahead. Apologetic for their doubting of his ability and happy at this familiar signal, the three went below to wash and prepare to go ashore for a much welcomed celebration. Unfortunately, unlike the skipper, they hadn't taken into consideration the wind and tidal directions. Much to their dismay, they arrived back in their home port in time for breakfast.

Not long after, Arthur was to prove his navigational skills by completing a single-handed, transatlantic crossing, though a sceptic suggested anyone sailing west would find it difficult to miss land.

CHAPTER 18

A FAMILY HOLIDAY

The herring had gone, moving south in their endless migration and I thought it time to give the *Courage* a coat of paint before the weather became too unsettled. Rusty and I took her to Grimsby, where she was hauled onto the giant slipway, dwarfed between two arctic trawlers, to be washed off and bottom scrubbed before getting her new coat.

With the prospect of reasonable weather, Dotty and I decided to take our first family holiday and would drive to the south coast in our old jalopy, an Austin A40. I wanted to visit Devon and Cornwall, which as I'd tried to convince Dotty, had spectacular scenery, as well as fishing ports like Brixham and Newlyn. This excursion was a little adventurous, maybe even foolhardy, considering the condition of our vehicle with its leaking radiator. My brother-in-law Jonty, a car fanatic, supplied me with some 'Radweld' solution to slow the leak but underlined the fact that the mixture would not build me a new radiator. Other people had previously suggested porridge and even raw egg as potential cures to the problem. These remedies hadn't worked either but I would take plenty of water for the journey.

We loaded up the car with lots of toys, crayons, books and a few drinks and sandwiches for the journey, which for the first couple of hours was uneventful. The inevitable, "are we nearly there yet?" questions from the back were fended off wonderfully by a very patient Mum and the, "I want a wee," calls were answered with "soon" by a frustrated Dad, who was keen to press on and cover some miles. The pee stop came sooner than expected when white vapour began billowing out from under the bonnet as we careered down a major motorway.

I pulled onto the hard shoulder and while the little ones emptied bilges between the car and the embankment assisted by Dotty, I decanted a gallon of water into the steam-belching radiator, taking care not to scald myself while removing the top. Unperturbed, we were soon on our way again, though for the little ones, the journey was beginning to drag and they were becoming restless. Not being used to close confinement with our small children for any length of time, I was finding this difficult to cope with and was becoming short tempered, until it was explained to me in no uncertain terms, that this was natural behaviour for youngsters and there was no excuse for mine. Ouch!

Following a couple more stops for the bairns to stretch their legs and to answer further calls of nature, as well as topping the engine up with coolant, we eventually reached Exeter. "Were on t' south coast now, it won't be long," I explained, not realising there was still more than a hundred miles to Newlyn, till I saw a signpost indicating the distance to Penzance, the adjacent town. "We'll go t' Brixham first," I hastily suggested. "It'll give us more time t' find somewhere t' stay." This was another aspect I'd not considered, but was sure we'd sort out. Dotty rolled her eyes then looked skywards to the heavens, as if for some divine assistance.

It was six o'clock, following the third radiator top up, when we finally arrived in the picturesque, historic, little port. Dotty's prayers were answered when we found a little B & B overlooking the harbour, run by a pleasant couple with three school-aged daughters. These friendly girls immediately offered babysitting services to allow us some free time in the evening.

Our hosts were wonderful and we decided to stay in Brixham for the duration of our holiday, occasionally travelling short distances in the car. The weather remained fine and warm, so for the next few days we were tourists, doing the things I'd only seen others do when visiting Scarborough. It seemed really strange having time to wander around sightseeing and relaxing, though Dotty said I took more looking after than the kids. It took us a whole day to get to Land's End and back from our base, though we did go via Newlyn, where there were plenty of boats to inspect. I silently thanked fate that I hadn't attempted to reach West Cornwall as part of our journey down, inwardly cringing at the scenario of arriving late with two small bairns then looking for accommodation. While at Land's End, we had our family group photo taken alongside a sign saying, 448 miles to Scarborough.

Our holiday flew by and in no time we were heading north again. Apart from a few stops to fill the radiator, empty the kids and take on food, a puncture in the outside lane of the motorway was the only incident in an otherwise, uneventful journey home. It had been a very pleasant break and great to spend some time with my lovely family, but I was desperate to get back to sea and with a new vessel on the stocks, the next and only family holiday for some time, would be to Scotland.

When Sid had completed his Arctic voyage, Walt left to team up with some former deep sea shipmates on the *Alida T*, also sailing from Scarborough. Sid was pleased to be back and thought the easy atmosphere and humour on the inshore boats much better than the harsh life of the deep sea trawlers. It was no laughing matter for Sid one day soon after making his return. Bluey and Rusty were heaving on the quarter ropes while hauling the trawl, when a shackle on the aft gallow gave way under the strain. The heavy pulley block, which the shackle was retaining, catapulted across the deck, hitting Sid with full force on the buttocks. He dropped to the deck in agony and for several minutes lay prone, while we assessed his injury. Fortunately, he'd been hit on a fleshy part of his body, so there were no bones broken and eventually we were able to help him to his feet. The atmosphere on board was lightened when Rusty said, "it's a good job yer weren't facin' t' other way Sid, or you'd 'ave been singin' in an 'igh-pitched voice now."

I offered to take Sid ashore for treatment but he steadfastly refused. Though only small in stature, he was as hard as nails and had seen far worse injuries during his days in the northern seas. For weeks following the mishap, Sid found sitting down uncomfortable and on the occasion when he insisted on showing us his injury, we were horrified to see his rump was purple and so swollen he appeared to have three buttocks, which must have been tremendously painful.

* * * * * *

It was the BBC's 'Children in Need' night. A few weeks earlier, Paul Gridley, the genial owner of the 'Crescent Hotel', a family run establishment in the centre of town, had asked if I could gather a team of fishermen to enter a Yorkshire pudding eating competition. We were to compete against several other groups, including police and students, for a trophy which Paul had offered to donate.

The 'Crescent' was famous for its Yorkshire puddings, which were not of traditional size, but were made in bread tins and were the size of small loaves. The delicious puddings usually arrived filled with a choice of onion gravy, mince and mushrooms or a creamy, seafood mixture.

Paul had devised this challenge as a means of raising money for the popular children's charity, as well as advertising his own establishment's catering excellence and filling his bar. The teams would each pay an entrance fee and would be sponsored by friends and relatives. Paul would also make a donation to the cause.

I'd chosen the best three eaters I knew from among the fishing fleet to join me. Mick, Rory and Phil were renowned as trenchermen in a world of big eaters. These hard working guys could eat for England.

It was almost time to commence battle and I was in a state of anxiety. One of our team hadn't turned up. The bar was packed with spectators and a reporter from Radio York was on hand as adjudicator and to report on the event, but there was no sign of Mick. I was about to ask Neil, one of our supporters, to sit in as substitute when a breathless Mick burst through the doors. "Sorry I'm late," he puffed.

"Where 'ave yer been?" I asked, concerned. "We thought yer weren't comin'."

This huge mountain of a man suddenly looked very sheepish. "It was me Missus, she wouldn't let me out o' 'ouse till I'd 'ad me tea."

We all laughed at the scenario of this big fellow, browbeaten by his little wife, but then I said, "If you've 'ad yer tea yer won't be 'ungry now."

"I didn't eat it all," he said defensively.

Before the conversation could be continued there was a call from the hotel owner, introducing the master of ceremonies for the evening and asking the competitors to take their places. Along with the other teams, we were given plastic aprons and were sat at tables for four, where a large pudding, filled with onion gravy, was placed before each contestant.

The compère standing in the centre of the room, now holding a microphone in one hand and a free pint of beer in the other, cleared his throat into the instrument, which being on full volume, startled everyone in the room. The master of ceremonies must have taken note of his briefing from the owner, as he gave a long and very big thank you to the host for his valuable fund-raising. For a few seconds Paul stopped his head count and mental calculation of hourly takings, to acknowledge the applause. The spokesman continued, praising the good work of the 'Children in Need' fund-raisers present, then addressed the evening's business. "Gentlemen, the time allowed for eating tonight is thirty minutes, may the best team win. On your marks, get set, go!" He dropped his arm dramatically.

We grabbed our cutlery and began hacking into the huge puddings, tearing them apart and stuffing large pieces into our mouths. At first we were also consuming a large amount of gravy, but then realised the police on the next table were leaving theirs. "It's only a puddin' eatin' contest mate. It doesn't say gravy," spluttered the copper sitting next to me, through a mouthful of dough.

As we each emptied a plate, another full one was placed on top. In this manner, the judge would only need to count the empties to find the total number of puddings consumed and thus, the winning team. Our group were doing well, troughing heartily, but realised the policemen were ahead. They were now tearing their puddings apart with their bare hands. It was horrible to watch, but effective.

"I can do better than that," Phil said, picking up a whole portion and crushing it between his hands to remove the air, reducing the food to the size of a tennis ball, which he quickly devoured. This messy technique was disgusting, but worked well and we all adopted the method. It was such a good idea that our rivals also used the tactic and from then it was a two horse race.

Though we started the competition as favourites, it was becoming clear that the police were going to win. My stomach was feeling bloated and though there were still several minutes left, I couldn't eat another mouthful. My team-mates were also at a near standstill. The plods, with more empty plates than us already, were still very slowly picking at their food and were deemed worthy winners at the final whistle, which I was very relieved to hear. The dough in my gut felt the size of a football, and the pint of beer I was handed to wash it down was sticking in my gullet as I attempted to swallow. I felt simply dreadful and couldn't get involved with the remaining proceedings at all.

"You look bloody awful," said Neil, at my side.

"I feel bloody awful. I've got a solid lump o' puddin' in me gut that feels like lead an' aches like 'ell," I replied.

"Go in t' toilet an' mek yerself sick; that'll get rid of it," he suggested.

"I wish I could," I said. "I've never been able t' do that. I just can't. A big meal usually teks hours t' wear off an' work through." The discussion about my digestive system seemed quite normal under the circumstances.

"Come on in t' toilet, I'll 'elp yer," Neil said sympathetically and I followed him in silent discomfort. He led me into a cubicle rather than expose my potential vomiting to anyone simply needing a pee. "Now then, all you 'ave t' do is put yer two forefingers in yer mouth an' you'll get rid of it. Come on, do it. Get it up."

I could hear men entering and leaving the room while we were behind the locked door and the enormity of how this situation might appear to anyone passing through, hit me like a hammer. I was in a locked toilet cubicle with another man, who was saying, "come on, do it, get it up." Putting a finger to my lips, I said a gentle, "shhh."

The potential scenario obviously hadn't occurred to Neil either, but it quickly dawned on him. "Fuckin' 'ell, Nommy, keep quiet. We'll sneak out as soon as t' place is empty," he whispered, his face red and eyes bulging. The thought of the embarrassment we'd suffer trying to explain the circumstances kept us silent. Though everyone would know there was no other motive in this friendly gesture, there would be heaps of good-humoured innuendo directed at us.

My stomach-ache hadn't gone away, but it had been superseded by a bigger worry, which luckily went immediately after I left the toilet, on my own. I never was sick that night and slept very fitfully, with the dough ball still rolling around in my stomach.

* * * * * *

Autumn was turning to winter and the working conditions were unsettled. We seemed to be in a continuous stream of low-pressure weather systems. These 'lows', coming from the Atlantic were disruptive to our fishing, though each was short-lived. We seemed to be forever sailing, getting a few hauls in, then retreating till the latest gale had blown through. We could occasionally fish close inshore in the lee of the land, but this wasn't always productive.

Letting go of the ropes late one afternoon, impatient for the south-westerly wind to abate, we rounded the pier end to head north-east. The sun had gone and it would soon be dark. Half a mile offshore and still assessing the weather, wondering if I'd sailed too soon, I heard banging on the side of the wheelhouse. It was Rusty, attracting my attention and pointing abeam. I dropped the window. "There's summat strange an' coloured in t' water out t' starboard. Yer can just mek it out in t' gloom. It looks like somebody wavin'."

Whatever the object was, it wasn't visible on the radar, though the centre of the screen was filled with clutter due to the weather, making viewing difficult. Maybe the target was just too small to detect. I put the wheel to starboard and eased back the engine. A few minutes later we were alongside a very distressed and exhausted windsurfer. The man, clad in a black wetsuit was extremely relieved to see us. He eventually managed to separate sail from board, passing both up to my crew, who were hanging over the side to help. Next, with some assistance and aided by our old, tyre fenders, the casualty was able to climb on board.

Though cold and tired, he was otherwise in good health and quickly told his story. It transpired that the man, who was a local dentist, had recently taken to the new water sport and was enjoying the exhilaration of flying through the water across the strong, offshore wind. Using his strength to hold the sail against the strong wind and frequently falling off, he'd quickly tired. As his stamina waned, he found it more and more difficult to get back on the board, which was quickly being blown away from the land. As the board drifted further offshore, the waves grew bigger. When he did manage to get back up, he wasn't able to hold the sail or keep his balance for long, before falling off again. The surfer was trapped in a vicious circle and the elements were against him. The strong south-westerly wind continued to blow his board out to sea and darkness was quickly approaching.

It was totally dark by the time we returned man and board to the harbour. Had Rusty not spotted him, there was every chance he wouldn't have been found in time. Even if the lifeboat had been summoned when he was reported missing, the man would have been some distance offshore and the search crew would have had difficulty locating such a small object in the dark, in an expanding search area. The R.A.F. rescue helicopter based at nearby Leconfield, could only be used for operations during daylight hours, so wouldn't have been able to give assistance. Rusty's alertness had possibly saved the man's life but this was never said. A large bottle of gin, delivered to my house was sufficient reward.

Strangely, two weeks later, in early December a similar circumstance arose. Sailing again just before dark in fresh weather, we noticed a small boat, this time anchored about half a mile offshore from the headland. It was showing no lights and there were no signs of activity on board. There was no reason for this craft to be where it was. The weather was too poor for a boat of this size to be trawling and there was no potting ground where she was brought up at anchor. No one would be hauling pots at this time of day anyway, so I decided to investigate.

We quickly identified the little craft as the *Gina Sue*. She was about twenty-five feet in length, double ended, with a small cockpit cabin for'ard. Her skipper and sole operator, Fred 'Frankeye' Sheader appeared from inside the little cabin as we drew close.

"By 'ell I'm glad t' see you lads. I've been 'ere for 'ours," he called when we stopped, close to the anchored boat. "Me engine's packed up an' t' battery's flat. I couldn't call anyone for 'elp. Can yer gimme a pull in t' 'arbour." Five minutes later Fred had hauled up his cable, recovering his anchor. Fifteen minutes later, *Gina Sue* was alongside the quay.

The man in the lighthouse looked quite perplexed as we towed the little boat past his office. He explained later that there was no record of the *Gina Sue* sailing, so his predecessor on watch had missed the craft exiting the harbour.

"Thanks lads, I'm in yer debt, I owe yer one. I'll get yers a beer at t' weekend," he called with a cheery wave as we left him berthing his little command.

This small diversion hadn't been a problem for us and we'd been pleased to assist the lone mariner. I'd been on the wrong end of a towrope enough times to know how this felt. Everyone at sea needs help occasionally and no one had ever refused me. It was an unwritten rule that everyone helped each other at sea. Fred had assisted plenty of people in the past. He was a member of the lifeboat crew.

For several years following this incident, whenever 'Frankeye' saw little Danny, he'd say to him, "your Dad saved my life," and Danny's chest would fill out with pride. I hadn't of course. Fred lived alone, so wouldn't have been missed at home, but even then, at worst I'd saved him from a cold, unpleasant night in his little cabin. He was wearing suitable clothing, oilskins and sea boots so wouldn't be hypothermic. *Gina Sue* was safely anchored and was in little danger. Fred would have been picked up eventually by a passing fishing vessel at daylight had I not spotted him. He would have been cold and miserable but otherwise unharmed. Danny didn't know that.

* * * * * *

Rusty arrived on board for our final voyage before the Christmas holiday and couldn't wait to tell us of his latest prank. His mother 'Dolly' had recently had a phone installed and he'd dialled her number, speaking in a disguised, official sounding voice. "Hello, is that Mrs Drydale?"

Dolly confirmed it was.

"I understand you've recently taken delivery of a new telephone."

This too was confirmed.

"We'd like you to do a line test for us please Mrs Drydale, to make sure the equipment is working properly. Could you please, in your best voice say, "I cannot hold the hot potato in my hand."

His mother dutifully repeated these words down the line.

"Well stick it up yer jumper," he replied, then put the phone down to wait for her return call and a telling off.

CHAPTER 19

THE FESTIVE SEASON

We tied up about a week before Christmas and I was delivering some vouchers to the elderly fisher folk near the harbour for the Fishermen and Firemen's Charity Fund. The old people would be able to redeem these tokens for coal, meat, groceries or fruit from various local traders. The funds to finance these vouchers came from a collection taken on Boxing Day, during the comic football match, played on the beach. Following this debacle, collecting tins were taken round the pubs by willing volunteers. Boxing Day was a very special day in the 'Bottom End' calendar.

Originally played between fishermen and firemen, this match had been held annually for more than eighty years. The fishermen had been deck hands, working on the old steam-driven trawlers and the firemen, stokers from the engine-rooms of these vessels. Now the teams were mostly crewmen from the local boats. The first match was played to raise money for the dependants of a sailing smack, the *Evelyn and Maud*, lost with all hands in 1893. This tradition had been kept going since and the proceeds distributed to the needy.

I knocked on the door of a cottage, to be greeted by Annie, a small, grey-haired, bespectacled, old lady, recently widowed. Recognising me, she invited me into the quaint house, where a roaring fire burned in the hearth, radiating heat into the tidy little parlour. I put her voucher on the table and her gratitude was quite humbling, as the value of the token wasn't great. "It's not t' money love," she said, as if reading my mind. "It's nice t' know I 'aven't been forgotten. I've just made a pot o' tea, d' yer want a cup?" It was difficult to say no and I sat in a comfortable, cushioned chair near the hearth for a while, listening to her chatting as she pottered and fussed around the oilcloth-covered table.

I looked round the neat little room, which contained a lifetime of possessions and memories. On the sideboard was a photo of her late husband, proudly wearing a naval uniform. Catching my gaze, she said, "that was Bob durin' t' first war. 'E was in t' minesweepers an' went all over t' world. 'E was at t' Dardanelles an' Galipoli." There was another picture of the couple's wedding and though I'd known them since I was a boy, I found it hard to recognise the young, handsome pair in the picture. The little old lady I was listening to, was a beautiful, striking woman in the photograph.

Annie told me of her childhood days, when she was one of a family of eight children. She said the family's house had three bedrooms, but all the children slept in one room, because her father kept his pigeons in the third one.

I had to laugh, though was shocked when she said, "nex' door neighbour's cat got in t' room one day an' killed 'em all." She went on to relate how the neighbour, who was quite unpleasant, had found it difficult to apologise to her Dad for his loss without sniggering.

"It doesn't matter," her Dad had replied, "I've already 'ung yer cat."

Finishing my cup of tea, I left Annie still chuckling at her Dad's treatment of the poor creature and stooping, passed through the low doorway, out into the street. My next call was only a few doors away. There was more than a hundred recipients on my list. I was quite perplexed at one house, when an old fisherman was explaining to me about a friend who'd recently died, leaving no family. He said, "t' poor ol' bloke, 'e 'ad to 'ave one o' them porpoise funerals."

I'd never heard of a porpoise funeral. It sounded very peculiar, then I realised he meant a pauper's funeral. The old man had died leaving no family and no wealth, so had been buried by the local authority.

172

It was always a busy time in the pubs round the harbour in the days leading up to Christmas. Fishermen had money in their pockets and time on their hands and their custom was keenly sought by the many hostelries, though the landlord of the 'Leeds Arms' was no more welcoming. I entered the already crowded little pub early in the afternoon of the next day with half a dozen friends. It was my turn to buy the beers and my pals were standing close behind. Recently Les had taken on a new assistant and protégé, Bill, to help when he was busy. Some evenings he would also have an attractive, young girl behind the bar. Helen, Bridget or Catherine would take turns to work and attracted extra trade. Today Les was on his own, attempting to cope with the pressure and was clearly not at his best. Never a tolerant person, now he was struggling to keep his composure. Cyril, formerly a pub landlord and member of our group, observing his plight, offered to help him behind the bar.

"No thank you, I've been on my own all day so far and I'll manage now," came back the rude, abrupt reply.

All along the bar, numerous people were trying to attract Les's attention, but Alan, a red-faced chap with glasses, standing directly in front of him and waving a ten pound note calling, "whisky and Highland Spring water please landlord," couldn't fail to be noticed.

Steadfastly refusing to even look in his direction, Les called out loudly, "does anyone want serving before Alan Buchanan?" The poor man would wait patiently until he was finally attended to. I briefly wondered why Alan kept coming to the pub, and didn't frequent another, more friendly establishment, then realised it was for the same reason we all continued to patronise the place. There was no jukebox, no pool-table, no one-armed bandit and not even a cigarette machine. The place had low ceilings, a good atmosphere and Les, despite his many failings, behind the façade was good hearted and also kept excellent beer. When strangers asked for cigarettes, he'd say, "I'm sorry we don't sell them, but do you know, people are starting to bring their own in the place now." The visitor would walk away baffled.

Les next chose to serve Stan, a painter and decorating contractor, a man who thought he was an attraction to the opposite sex. While trying to catch the barman's eye, Stan was also attempting to charm two attractive, well-dressed, young women at his side. Les approached, also drawn by the pretty girls and his foul mood briefly lightened. He said, "yes Mr Bradley, what can I do for you?"

"I'd like a large brandy and soda please Leslie and these two lovely ladies would like large gin and tonics with ice. Thank you kindly."

"Would that be fresh ice or frozen sir?" Les asked formally, looking at the ladies for some reaction to his humour.

He was rewarded when they both giggled, but Stan, briefly lost for words muttered, "frozen." The drinks were prepared and placed on the bar before the trio, but Stan failed to notice their arrival. He was too busy with his charm offensive. Les stood quietly for a few seconds, ignoring other waiting clientele, including me, listening to the sweet talk then produced an aerosol spray from under the bar, spraying Stan liberally.

The poor man immediately began to cough and splutter. "What the hell's that stuff?" yelled the poor chap, as he attempted to regain his breath and composure. Wordlessly, Les put the canister on the bar, took the cash from Stan's hand, then turned to his cash register. Emblazoned in bold, red letters on a white background, were the words, 'Bullshit Repellent'. It was a product from the nearby joke shop.

Les returned with change for the dumbstruck man and was about to tackle his next customer when Stan regained his voice and tried his charm once more. "Would you have a drink with me please Leslie?"

"No thank you," came back the equally polite reply, though with a grimace. "I've just refused one with a friend."

No one was immune to the barman's barbs or occasional tantrum. Weeks earlier, a famous playwright, living not too far away and who often visited the pub with his acolytes, had left the place and gone into self imposed exile when asked by the host, "what do you want fatty?" as he approached the bar.

Les turned to me next and his frown had returned. Others were trying to attract his attention on both sides of me and I was immediately flustered. My pals behind, unaware of the entertainment I'd just witnessed, were becoming impatient.

Someone behind me said, " 'urry up Nommy."

"Three pints o' bitter, two whiskies an' a lager fo' Cyril, please Les," I spluttered.

"I don't need to know who they're for," replied the landlord curtly, as he moved to address my order. He returned shortly after with my drinks, and I handed him a banknote.

Noticing the small, plump newspaper-seller at my side, dressed in his best attire, attempting to get served, I said, " it's Christmas Benny, what can I get yer?"

Usually Benny, an elderly Irishman, who'd left his homeland many years before, would drink halves of bitter, but today he thanked me politely and said, "ass it's Christmas, coould I haave a little whuskey."

"Will yer tek for another whisky Les?" I called to the landlord, addressing his back at the till, only a few feet away. He chose not to hear me and returned with my change. "Sorry Les, can I 'ave another whisky fo' Benny?"

"I've told you, I don't need to know who the drinks are for. I wish you people would make your minds up," he hissed through clenched teeth. "I've got others waiting to be served y' know." He went off in a huff.

I began to pass the drinks to our group behind me and realised I'd got the order wrong. I needed an extra beer and had a whisky too many. I gave the spare dram to Benny, who accepted it with good grace and, "God bless ya sur," but I had a problem and the landlord wasn't going to like it.

He returned with the additional glass of spirit I'd ordered and I softly said, "sorry Les, I've got it wrong. I don't really need that one, but I'll pay for it, an' give it t' Benny. Can I 'ave another pint o' beer as well?"

He reacted as if I'd lit a fuse. Even his false posh voice disappeared. His Teesside twang came to the fore. "Now look 'ere, if yous lot can't decide what y' wantin' t' drink, yous can go somewhere else. I'm too busy t' be messed about by yers." The irate landlord attempted to grab my pint from the counter, but I grabbed it first.

"I've paid for it, an' I'm gonna drink it," I said sharply, reacting to his attitude. "What's matter wi' yer, yer miserable sod?"

"Yer barred. Finish it an' ger out," he yelled at me, "an' "urry up."

I was devastated. This was my favourite pub. It wasn't my fault he was having a bad day. Cyril, standing close behind me, catching the landlord's angry words, attempted to intercede. "What's the matter with you Les, calm down. I offered to help you."

"You're barred as well. Yer can all ger out."

Cyril was speechless. In fact the whole pub went deathly quiet. Everyone was observing the boss's tantrum, but no one dare speak for fear of banishment. I very slowly finished my beer, while the hovering barman waited for the empty glass. It was already clear he was regretting his outburst, but he'd never admit to being wrong, or apologise. It wasn't in his nature. Neither Cyril nor I would attempt to return in the near future, though we'd been regulars in his pub for years and we also met lots of other friends there. It didn't matter much to the rest of our group. Most of these lads usually frequented the 'Newcastle Packet', 'Dolphin' or 'Lord Nelson' on the seafront.

Boxing Day of that year again saw the usual antics on the beach, but in addition, a raft race took place round the harbour, organised by the diving club. Later in the day and on the wrong side of several beers, having taken part in and survived the football match, I found myself in the Sub Aqua Club. A trophy was being presented to the race winners. The place was packed to the doors with revellers but I managed to squeeze my way to the bar. Attempting to pass through the narrow room with glass in hand, I accidentally spilled some beer on the Club Chairman's wife.

Christine was wearing a new woollen sweater and was very upset at my clumsiness, insisting I pay for the cost of the garment, seven pounds. I put my beer on a nearby ledge and gave her the money, which mollified her. She was immediately upset again when I quickly whipped the jumper up over her head, insisting that as I'd paid for it, the top was now mine. Chris was left standing in the crowded room, revealing a very attractive low-cut bra and contents. This action seemed to find approval with every male in the place, though definitely not with the lovely lady, who, with arms folded before me, was open-mouthed and speechless. I did return the sweater a few minutes later, having discovered it was too small for me.

Feeling quite pleased with my mischief, I pushed through the throng to the far end of the bar, where some of my diving mates were gathered in the corner. In front of my pals, a middle-aged female, who I didn't recognise, was leaning against the counter, a glass of spirit before her. The woman immediately began talking to me, and it was obvious by her tone, she was going to be unpleasant.

"I know who you are. I remember you when you were a kid. You weren't very nice. I remember yer Mam and Dad as well." She continued with her insulting diatribe, though not making any specific points. It was clear the old biddy was worse for drink and was maudlin.

I wasn't interested in this conversation at all and attempted to speak to my mates but I couldn't escape from this woman's attentions without being extremely unpleasant. Noticing her glass was getting low I said, "can I get yer a drink missus?" She seemed surprised at my offer, but accepted a whisky and water.

At the earliest opportunity, I caught the barmaid's eye and whispered, "put me three whiskies in there, with just a bit o' water." Handing the glass back to the harridan, I attempted to extricate myself from her company, but still found it difficult as she rambled on in her unpleasant manner, now maligning other people from my youth. Keeping an eye on her glass, I was soon able to get the dragon another, as her spirit level had quickly dropped. "Put four in this time," I whispered to the girl behind the bar. A few minutes later, my unwelcome companion made a forced dash through the crowd, heading for the door. I had escaped her clutches.

Everyone looked forward to the Christmas and Boxing Day celebrations, but most were equally pleased when these revelries were finally over. It would be great to be back at sea for a few days; to dry out before the New Year and more partying. No one could face sailing on the morning after the football match and it wasn't only heads that ached. Most had bruises and stiff limbs from playing ninety minutes on a pitch of sand. A few of the lads played football regularly and were reasonably fit, but for some participants in this annual act of lunacy, this was their only exercise.

Several vessels, including the *Courage* could be seen leaving harbour in the early hours of the 28th. Almost everyone was feeling delicate and food wasn't high on anyone's agenda. Not all the crewmen had taken part in the sporting activities, but most had been boozing. No one on our boat could face breakfast, so Sid decided to leave a dish of boiled eggs on the cabin table. Unknown to anyone, Rusty slipped a couple of raw eggs on top of the pile. Bluey was the innocent victim and after cracking the shell on his plate, releasing the gooey innards, he dashed to the deck and spent ten minutes hanging over the side, spewing and cursing.

The three days we spent at sea, though cold and uncomfortable, were welcomed by all, at least days two and three were, when we'd recovered from the excesses. The *Courage* returned to port in the early hours of New Year's Eve but her catch would be retained on board, to be landed in early January when the first market of the year would be held.

New Year's Eve brought another lively party at home and this year I had a special culinary treat for any guests caring to try the delicacy. A few days before Christmas, while putting some home-made wine on a shelf in the shed at the back of our house, I'd found a discoloured, plastic bag containing a brown liquid. At first I thought this was perhaps putty or some cleaning product, but on closer examination, discovered the contents were mostly solids in a fluid, and were shiny. I realised this was a bag of herring, preserved in salt, which had turned to brine. I racked my brains, but couldn't recall putting the fish in the shed. The herring season was August and September and I was sure I hadn't stored the fish then.

In the recesses of my mind I recalled how Bill, my old shipmate, had often packed herring in salt like this, to store and pickle later. These must be some he'd done, but they were definitely not from this year. I realised these herring must have been lying on the shelf in the shed for about fifteen months.

Very cautiously, I split the bag with my knife, expecting to quickly dump the smelly contents into the bin, but this wasn't necessary. There was a strong smell of salt and fish, but it wasn't unpleasant. I was delighted with my discovery and took the find into the kitchen, where I decanted the contents into the sink, rinsing the hard, brown-coloured fish under cold, running water, much to Dotty's disgust. I then left the twenty or more fillets to soak, frequently replacing the water.

This process took most of the afternoon and many changes of water before I was satisfied with the product. The flesh had lost most of its discoloration and was now softer. I rolled each piece of fish in chopped onion, stacking them in a large screw-topped jar, which was then filled to the brim with vinegar. I couldn't wait to try one and intended serving them up on New Year's Eve, though Dotty said they'd poison anyone who ate them.

My lovely wife, as always, spent most of this day preparing food for the evening, assisted by a couple of her friends. The day passed quickly and by ten o' clock that evening, the house was full of guests, some of whom we only seemed to meet on this one day of the year. The party was swinging and everyone dancing, drinking or talking, when Dotty announced that food was served in the back room.

At the end of the groaning table was the plate of herring, which I was convinced were edible, having tried one earlier in the evening. The brown-tinged fish, though not looking too appetising, tasted delicious. I was able to persuade several of the men and one or two women to try the delicacy, not revealing its history. Everyone seemed to enjoy my special dish and requested seconds, so the plate was soon empty. The only negative effect of this speciality was that everyone who had eaten the herring had a raging thirst, which couldn't be slaked for the rest of the night. So much drink was consumed during the evening, that for the first time ever, our stock began to run low in the early hours.

Dotty reminded me we had the home-made, red wine in the shed, though this brew hadn't been bottled long. This dubious stock was the result of a wine making kit that had been bought as a birthday present by one of my sisters. On the day I'd bottled the produce, I couldn't find the purifying tablets for cleaning the bottles, but Dotty assured me bleach was equally as good, and I'd taken her advice.

I retrieved this emergency supply, and my brother-in-law Roland, a keen wine buff, insisted on sampling the first of the batch. He decanted a small amount of the doubtful plonk into a glass, sniffed the contents, swirled it around quite professionally then tasted the red liquid. Dotty and I looked at each other, anticipating the worst. "Very palatable," was his judgement and the remainder of the bottle was quickly dispensed into waiting glasses.

I sidled up to Dotty and whispered, "bloody 'ell, Roland must be pissed."

She replied, "just as well Nommy. You've managed not to poison anyone with the fish, lets hope the wine doesn't kill 'em off."

The last of the partygoers retreated sometime between four and five in the morning, with no obvious signs of distress and my special dish was deemed a huge success.

New Year's Day brought the usual frivolity, though we celebrated the arrival of January in the 'Newcastle Packet', due to my exile from the 'Leeds Arms'. Early next morning and all feeling groggy, we turned out to land the fish we'd caught the previous year. We also took ice and stores, preparing the *Courage* for sailing; to begin another year; one that would see me leave her.

The New Year was only a few weeks old when the Grimsby 'lumpers', the dockers who discharged fish from the trawlers, pair teams and seine-netters in the port, unilaterally declared the right to land all boats, except 'inshore' fishing vessels. We in Scarborough classed our boats as inshore vessels. This claim was disputed by the lumpers. Occasionally, when landing into this huge port with good catches, we were pleased to engage one or two helpers and pay for their assistance, but the lumpers would only work in gangs of eleven men. Furthermore they were not prepared to allow nonunion members to participate in the landing. According to their demands, if we wished to continue landing our fish into Grimsby, we either had to accept an expensive gang of eleven lumpers while we sat watching them work, or fight the case. We collectively chose to fight.

The case was to be taken before an 'Industrial Tribunal'. All the skippers from Scarborough who'd landed fish into Grimsby and wished to continue this practice, attended the hearing, held in Lincoln and we were not on our own. Many of the smaller Grimsby boat skippers were also challenging this imposition. Both fishermen's groups were represented by the experienced marine solicitors, 'Andrew M. Jackson' of Hull. The Lumpers' Union's interests were handled by a high-powered practice from 'the city'. The losers would pick up the costs for both parties, so it would be a costly affair if we lost. It was for the presiding judge to define an 'inshore fishing vessel'.

Each of us in turn had to take the stand and be cross-examined by the barrister as to our modus operandi and had to describe our boat, its age, length and tonnage. The proceedings continued for a full day. The judge was very attentive and listened to all the evidence, occasionally asking searching questions to help him grasp the situation. He then retired to consider his judgement.

His Lordship spent some time deliberating the case, but finally returned to give judgement. He found in our favour and awarded our costs to the Lumpers' Union. There were deep frowns on the faces of their representatives, but we didn't care. We had won our case. There was much jubilation in our group and of course it was necessary to find the nearest pub, to celebrate with our Grimsby colleagues.

The judge, in his wisdom, had decreed that the definition of an inshore fishing vessel was a boat that was under sixty feet in length and was at sea for no more than eleven tides, or approximately six days. Exceptional circumstances could extend this period. We were never at sea for more than three days usually. Even the bigger boats stayed at sea for no more than four days. All our vessels were shorter than sixty feet. This was a wise decision as the major port handled large quantities of inshore fish throughout the year. This trade for the port's merchants would certainly have been lost, as no one was prepared to pay these exorbitant charges. The judgement was a major victory, not only for us but for common sense. Next day we were all back at sea, the radio airwaves buzzing as we relived our dramatic day in court.

In mid February, with snow on the ground, we landed a catch on a very frosty, windless evening. Even the water in the harbour near Sandgate slipway had a thin film of ice on its surface. A couple of coblemen were on the quayside as we left the boat and Rusty said, "d' you lads need any pot bait? We've a few boxes under t' cover with our fish."

"Naw, not while this crab food's on t' ground," came back the cynical reply. "We won't be goin' to our pots 'til it's melted."

We understood what he meant. It was an amazing phenomenon that even the slightest snow shower stopped the crabs from feeding. Very few crustaceans would enter crab pots when it snowed. Catches would fall to a quarter or less than usual. How could these creature, sixty to a hundred feet below the waves, know it was snowing on the surface, but this strange occurrence always happened.

The snow was frozen solid, making the route dreadfully slippery underfoot as Rusty and I crossed the road to make our way home. We reached the bottom of 'Pump Hill', the steep, curved, cobblestoned lane, without too much difficulty. We were then compelled to hold on to the iron handrail to prevent ourselves from falling, as we began our ascent.

The path had been turned to glass by dozens of youngsters who'd been sliding down the hill earlier, holding on to the rail. We hauled ourselves hand over hand round the blind corner with trepidation and were stunned to see a very large, round-faced, portly, old gentleman hurtling down the hill in our direction, seemingly out of control. It was 'Whisper' Cammish. "Aye up you pair o' buggers, ah can't stop, ger out o' me way," bawled the old man, his voice like the foghorn. Anyone who'd heard Harry Cammish speak would instantly know how he'd acquired his nickname.

We pushed ourselves away from the handrail, almost losing our balance as the big man shot past. "Steady now 'Arry. Mind yer don't fall," Rusty called out to the rotund figure's back.

Amazingly for such a large man, he slowed himself down with his hands as he neared the bottom of the hill, then gingerly manoeuvred his way to the flatter part of the road. "It teks more than a bit o' snow t' stop Whisper," his booming voice echoed back up the hill.

The old boy was dressed, as always in a baggy, black, pinstriped, three-piece suit, with double gold fob chains to waistcoat pockets. His grey, flat cap was low over his eyes. 'Whisper' was a well-known character in the town. In his younger days, when trawlers were driven by steam, he'd been one of the most successful skippers in the port. For many years now, following his retirement from the sea, 'Whisper' had operated a highly illegal, bookmaking business. He would collect racing bets from most of the pubs in the 'Bottom End' each lunchtime, select the wagers he wanted to keep, laying the remainder off at the official betting shop further up town. Each night 'Whisper' would visit the same pubs, leaving any winnings for successful punters. Harry was notorious for not paying out the correct amount, always getting the calculations wrong, in his favour of course. We'd just encountered him on his way to the 'Dolphin'.

It was still extremely slippery as I turned right to make my way along Princess Street, having bid Rusty good night near the top of Pump Hill. It was only a short walk home now but potentially hazardous and I stepped warily. I couldn't afford an injury with a new vessel on the way and realised at that point that I'd soon have to give up my weekend football for the same reason, but I'd see the season out.

My thoughts turned to the new vessel. She was coming along steadily and I was receiving frequent reports from her builder, though hadn't had an opportunity to inspect her recently. As she was being constructed on the paint slipway and not indoors, there were no confining height restrictions. Not only could the hull be constructed, the machinery, wheelhouse and even masts could be fitted in situ. The *Independence* would not only look like a working boat when she took to the water, she would be almost ready for sea, though there were a few months' labour involved yet.

Nearing the end of the street, I passed Alfie Hopkin's grocers shop on the left. Alfie 'Hop' was a lovely, kind man who always had time to talk, not only to his customers but to passers-by, as he sat outside his premises when the weather was fine. Like most men from the 'Bottom End', Alf had been in the Naval Patrol Service during the war. He'd never married but was friendly with all the youngsters in the area. When business was slack, as it often was, Alf would encourage the kids in the street to race around the block, giving prizes from his 'penny counter' for the winners.

I turned the corner at the end of Princess Street into Castlegate. There would be no chance of slipping on ice here. Michael 'Snotty' Evans, in total contrast to the kindness of Alfie, had been out with ashes from his fire. He didn't only melt the ice on the path near his house, which was laudable, he also spread the ash liberally on the road. This was a calculated act of meanness to prevent kids from sledging down the hill. I could remember him doing the same when I was a youngster, when dozens of tobogganists were playing on the street. It must have been a family trait, as his father, also known as 'Snotty', had spread ashes in the road when my Mum was young.

The Evans's were continually at war with the youth of the area. In return for ruining the sledge track, the kids would pelt snowballs at the door and windows of their enemy. This in turn would cause Michael to chase them, which turned out to be better fun for the young ones, than sledging. This was a constant neighbourhood battle that had gone on for many years. Kids would frequently knock on Snotty's door then run away. I'd done this myself as a youngster, along with pals. Michael even bought a pair of plimsolls so he could run faster, though he still didn't catch anyone. If he'd ignored the knocks it would have been no fun and the pests would have stopped bothering him.

CHAPTER 20

SPRATTING

The hard frosts had brought huge shoals of sprats further south than usual and close inshore. Even the harbour was full of these little fish. This fishery had been pursued around the River Tyne each winter for many years. We'd often seen Grimsby vessels sailing for home at this time of year, almost sinking with the weight of fish. Their holds were full of bulked sprats and the boats also carried a deck cargo. Caught by the million in small mesh trawls, these small, herring-like creatures were rendered down for fish-meal and oil. At fifty pounds a ton, this was lucrative fishing and now these unpredictable little fish were on our doorstep.

Alan Morse, an enterprising North Shields skipper, observing a massive shoal of sprats in the River Tyne, close to where his vessel was berthed, cast off his boat's ropes, took the vessel to the middle of the river, shot his net against the incoming tide and was back alongside within an hour, his boat full of fish. Needless to say the river authorities took a dim view of this practice.

Several Scarborough skippers opted to change over to this method of fishing, which was very economical. Once the initial outlay for gear had been made, there was little wear on the equipment. The net was a mid-water trawl, so no contact was made with the seabed at all, in theory. No ice and very little fuel were required. There was no fish to gut, no boxes to rent and the catch was pumped from the hold of the boat into waiting trucks.

Deciding to have a go at this new fishing, I was able to acquire a second-hand trawl and we would use our existing boards, so the set up costs were minimal. Trawling for sprats did indeed prove to be an easy way to catch tons of fish. Our first landing was eight tons, caught in two short hauls. The harbour was congested as boats lined up to be emptied. Some vessels were so deep in the water they could only get to the pump, located at the shallow end of the pier, at high water and skippers dared not let their vessels ground in this berth with full cargoes, for fear of damage. This difficult situation created friction between skippers, as those who commanded bigger, deeper-drafted craft, insisted on jumping the queue. As soon as their vessels were empty they were back out fishing again while the smaller boats still queued.

The market was glutted to such an extent that the rendering factories couldn't cope with the supply. The fish-meal factory in Hull had mountains of the stuff, stacked in huge heaps outside in the open, waiting to be processed. The situation was becoming a health hazard. Seagulls from miles around were so full of fish they couldn't fly.

Our next landing was sixteen tons and my little *Courage* was down in the water like a loaded barge. This was a major concern to me, as she now had planks below the surface that had never been totally immersed in water since she was built. All wooden craft leak until their seams take up as the wet wood swells, but these submerged, four-inch strips had been exposed to the elements for twenty-five years. I was compelled to run the boat's bilge pump continuously to check the ingress and monitored the water level in her bilges every few minutes.

We arrived back in port within a few hours of sailing, but then waited two days to discharge our cargo. When we did finally unload our catch, the market for sprats had dropped from fifty pounds to thirty pounds a ton. It was the end of our sprat fishing experience and I wasn't sorry. Some boats, the ones that could carry huge amounts, continued the practice, but we converted back to bottom trawling, once more chasing whiting and cod.

Following another, much less stressful flight to Aberdeen and drive to Fraserburgh, I discovered my new baby was developing rapidly. Her engine was already sitting on its beds and the wheelhouse was ready for mounting into position. The first of many coats of paint was adorning her sides and she was wearing her new, personal identification number, FR 196.

Jimmy informed me that unless I had any objections, the launch date and naming ceremony for my *Independence*, was to be May 17th. I was pleased to have a date to work to and be able to inform people. For several weekends prior to this visit, Dotty and I had been compiling a guest list of family, friends and business acquaintances who we hoped would be prepared to travel this great distance for a two-night stay and party.

I handed Jimmy my guest list, expressing concern at the large number. I enquired what the likely cost of the launching party would be, including transport and accommodation for seventy-plus travelling guests, as I wasn't sure we were going to be able to afford it.

The builder was totally unconcerned. "Dinna fash yer sel', it's nae problem. It's ah' takken care o'."

Apparently there was a sum taken up within the cost of building the vessel for the launching celebrations, though I never actually saw this sum written anywhere. I was delighted with this news, as I had been dreading the bill. Subsequently, the invitations to the launch were sent out by Bessie and pleasingly, with the exception of our bank manager, Mr White, who nominated his deputy, everyone accepted.

There was still time for several more weeks fishing before I relinquished the *Courage*, though I was being pressured by her prospective buyer to let her go early. I'd become very attached to the old lady and would miss her. There was never a day, when in harbour, that I didn't check to see if she was in good order, her bilges dry and ropes secure. It became a regular complaint from Dotty that every pair of trousers I owned were streaked where I'd come into contact with a greasy or oily surface while on board. She even offered to stain my new trousers, to save me the trouble. Dotty often said I thought more of my boat than of her, which wasn't at all true. Much to my wife's delight, a cartoon appeared in a national newspaper, showing an old Viking, lovingly painting his longboat on the beach. The Norseman's wife, Helga, was looking on as her husband fussed over his ship and her comment was, "she get two coats a year!"

My wife said, "I know just how she feels."

Dotty had recently passed her driving test and we decided to trade in the old banger, as I wasn't at all happy at the thought of her driving our clapped out wreck, even though it now had a new radiator. We made an appointment to see Mr White, with a view to buying a new car. Together we sat in his office, chatting amiably. I'd explained to him how the present car was dangerous, relating our experience of driving to Land's End with the bairns. His eyebrows rose subconsciously. "We don't want a new un, jus' summat newer, that'll be safe fo' Dotty t' drive."

He listened attentively then said, "my advice to you both, is to go to a reputable dealer and get a good one, with a warranty. I know people in the motor trade and it's my opinion that bladdy car dealers used to be bladdy horse traders. Now what sort of car do you have in mind Dorothy? You'll be the one who drives this vehicle the most."

Our poor bank manager almost fell off his chair when Dotty quickly replied, "a Jensen Interceptor." She'd recently seen this wonderful, new sports car on television and had fallen in love with the name. We settled for a two-year-old 1750cc Austin Maxi.

A drive in the new car proved eventful shortly afterwards, when we made a family visit to Dotty's parents in Hull. On our return the road was covered with hard packed snow in places, and as usual I was driving too fast. Putting my foot on the brake on one slippery section, I was horrified when I lost control of the car. The wheels locked and the vehicle spun 180 degrees, finally stopping in the centre of the road, heading in the direction we'd just come from. Luckily there was no other traffic on the road in either direction. A look from my wife was all that was required in the way of chastisement, but this was more than cancelled out when two little voices from the back chirped, "that was good Dad, can we do it again?" and "are we going back to Grandma's?"

The poor weather persisted throughout the week and our fishing pattern was severely disrupted. Despite the adverse elements, on the following Friday, Kurt Christiansen and his brother Olaf arrived in Scarborough by train from Grimsby. The pair had been invited to attend an 'Auction of Promises' evening, which was being held by the Scarborough Fishermen's Wives Group. This enthusiastic group of ladies were fantastic fund-raisers and put huge efforts into their projects. At a 'Summer Fair' the previous year, the wives had taken over the entire West Pier, organising lots of interesting stalls and displays, including a 'kipper-eating competition'. The winner of this challenge set a world record, which appeared in the Guinness Book of Records. Through the leadership of their Chairwoman, Maggie Mainprize, this body had to date, supported the local hospital with more than £300,000 in cash, for the purchase of life-saving equipment.

I knew the Christiansen brothers well. I'd known Kurt from my earliest visit to Grimsby, when he'd been our agent's representative on the dock and had greeted us on arrival. I'd subsequently met both brothers, whose parents had emigrated from Denmark after the war, at fishermen's meetings and on my occasional visits to Grimsby. Kurt, a smartly dressed, tall, thin, bearded blond, had offered his services as auctioneer for the evening's entertainment. This would be a different platform for his auctioneering skills. Kurt, a great raconteur and an extremely amusing person, now sold fish to belligerent merchants in the Humber port. I was sure he'd play a leading part in the coming proceedings, to be held in the 'Golden Ball', a seafront pub overlooking the harbour. The 'promises' pledged were many and varied; anything from a holiday in a local hotel to a box of kippers or a babysitter for a night. These lots were all donated freely and would raise further funds for the worthy cause.

If Kurt appeared to have lived through a famine, his brother Olaf looked to have caused it. I could imagine Olaf as a Viking warrior. His huge, portly frame, bushy beard, red face and semi-permanent grin were everything a film producer could desire for an epic Norsemen film. Though the quieter of the brothers, Olaf also had a great sense of humour and was good company. Following in his father's footsteps, he too was a skipper and was in command of the *White Bank*, a sixty-foot vessel, pursuing a new type of fishing with tangle nets, catching cod on shipwrecks and offshore reefs. Olaf had been at the Industrial Tribunal I'd attended in Lincoln.

The brothers were staying at the 'Crescent Hotel' overnight, where Dotty and I met them early in the evening. The official start to the proceedings was not until nine o'clock and there were lots of hostelries between the two establishments to visit before then. Despite the frequent snow showers, we enjoyed the tour of pubs, encouraging friends we met along the way to attend the fun auction. The brothers renewed many acquaintances en route, and were in fine form when we arrived at the venue. The 'Golden Ball', with only a small road between it and the water, had a commanding view of the busy harbour. My Dad had been born in the adjacent house where his Aunt Ann had lived. Some of my earliest memories are of standing in her window, gazing through the small panes at steam trawlers, keelboats and cobles, as they passed through the narrow harbour entrance to ply their trade in the sea beyond. I'd also watch boats returning to land their catches on the clearly visible fish market.

The 'Golden Ball' was packed to the doors as the important business of the evening began. Rachel, at the front of the room, needlessly bawled into the microphone, quickly bringing order to the waiting crowd. Holding aloft a stack of labelled envelopes containing pledges of varying values, the enthusiastic lady thanked the donors for the myriad of gifts then introduced Kurt, handing him the mike. The salesman was soon in his stride, entertaining all present with his wit, while taking bids for the various items from enthusiastic participants in his slow, Lincolnshire drawl. Most of those actively participating didn't really want the goods on offer, so didn't want to get caught holding the bid, but were keen to see the prices increase in a form of Russian roulette. When interest in an item seemed slow, the auctioneer slickly plucked bids from thin air, as he probably did occasionally on the fish market, attributing the nods to anonymous faces at the back. I was caught with several unwanted 'bargains', though these were not too costly and I thoroughly enjoyed the involvement.

When all the envelopes had gone, Kurt said, 'OK everyone, there's nothing left to sell, so I'm going to auction a jowk."

I could hear people around me saying, "what's 'e sellin' now?" There was confusion in the room.

"What are yer sellin'?" Someone near the front asked, perplexed.

"A jowk," came back the reply.

There was still an air of bafflement among the audience. "What's one o' them?" came a call from the back

"A jowk, a funny story."

Enlightenment filled the bar. Almost in unison, the audience said, " 'e means a joke." Kurt's different emphasis on the same word had completely thrown the whole crowd.

" 'Ow are yer gonna do that?" Another question was directed at the smiling salesman at the front.

"Well", he said, already drawing out the proceedings, "I know a very funny story. It's one none of you will have heard before and I'm going to sell it to the highest bidder."

The interest in this final, unusual piece of merchandise was extremely brisk. Rachel was bidding so furiously, that on occasions she was raising the ante against herself. People who knew her were also aware that when she set her mind at something, she invariably achieved her goal, so felt safe bidding against her. Finally, the 'jowk' was knocked down at twenty pounds, to Rachel. On receipt of her cash, Kurt said, "It's yours, but this is such a good story, it seems a shame not to share it with everyone else."

Before Rachel could speak or even think, he set off on a long, convoluted story about Quasimodo in his bell tower, being visited by an American tourist, who wanted to ring the bell. Kurt had everyone in stitches, managing to extend the story considerably by gesticulating, changing voices and acting. The punch-line of the convoluted tale came when the tourist was knocked from the tower by the bell and was lying in Notre-Dame Square. Quasi hurried from his domain to the casualty, acted brilliantly by Kurt, who, with hunched back, was turning in circles, pretending to rush down a spiral staircase. When a gendarme asks Quasi if he knows this person, Quasi replies with the corny line, "I don't know his name, but his face rings a bell." This anticlimax brought a huge collective groan, which quickly changed to applause and the star of the show headed for the bar to rapturous cheers.

Next morning I was due to attend a fishermen's meeting in Grimsby and as prearranged, collected the brothers from their hotel. Snow was still on the roads and was piled high in the hedgerows as we drove south to the Humber ferry. We were reviewing the previous evening's proceedings and laughing at the various memories when fresh snow began to fall, reducing visibility. Soon red tail-lights appeared as we caught up with traffic ahead, compelling us to slow down. It was soon clear that we'd become part of a small, crawling convoy. The snow shower continued unabated and our speed remained at snail's pace until, frustrated, on a straight piece of road, when a line of vehicles had just passed in the opposite direction, I pulled out to overtake the three of the cars ahead of me. I couldn't have timed the manoeuvre worse. A police motorcyclist came out of the gloom, trailing the opposing cars and witnessing my folly. My chatting passengers were suddenly dumbstruck, firstly at my overtaking, then at the perceived near miss. The lack of words didn't last long. Abuse in stereo quickly followed.

Looking in my rear view mirror, there was no sign of the officer and I fervently hoped he'd kept going in the same direction, though I doubted it. In an attempt to escape the scene of my crime, I put my foot down, thinking that if the speed cop did turn to follow me when the situation allowed, he might not catch me on a motorbike in the poor conditions. I was to have no such luck. Five minutes later, the reflection of a blue flashing light appeared in my mirror and my fears came true. Not wanting to make matters worse I slowed down before pulling into the roadside. I didn't wait for the policeman to alight from his bike, but immediately left the car and though wearing no outdoor clothes, went to meet my fate. I could only attempt to mitigate my problems by cooperating now.

Already shivering from the cold, I approached the policeman, who had rested his machine on its stand and was removing his helmet. Static crackled from the radio on his pannier. Unexpectedly, he turned out to be a young man with a pleasant, non-aggressive countenance. "That wasn't a very smart manoeuvre, sir. You very nearly knocked me off my motor cycle."

Despite my careless driving, the policeman seemed very reasonable and I wasn't going to argue. "I'm really sorry sir, it was a stupid thing t' do. I realised as soon as I'd pulled out that it was, but it was too late by then. I am sorry officer."

The policeman took his notebook from his top pocket and my heart sank. He was going to book me. "You really must take more care in these difficult conditions sir," he said politely. "We've had two accidents this morning already."

Though freezing cold now and with snow collecting on my head and shoulders, I continued to grovel my apologies.

The officer politely took note of my name and address, make and model of car, the time of the incident then gave me a ticket. "This requires you to present your insurance details and driving licence to your nearest police station within five days. In normal circumstances I'd charge you with driving without due care and attention, but there are so many traffic problems at present, I simply don't have time. Please be more careful in future."

He wasn't going to book me. I assured him I'd take more care, while offering a mental prayer to my guardian angel. Official procedure over, the constable now began a normal conversation, asking where I was bound and what was my business. My teeth chattered as I replied and the officer, who was now smiling at my discomfort, prolonged the dialogue until, prompted by his radio, decided to continue his patrol.

The grinning brothers asked what I was being charged with, but their smirks changed to looks of disbelief when, still shivering I said, "I'm not being charged. I just 'ave t' produce me documents."

"I don't believe yer," said Olaf.

"You jammy bastard," from Kurt

I did go steady for the remainder of the journey and encountered less snow on the other side of the ferry in Lincolnshire.

* * * * * *

Winter was hanging on, though March had arrived. With the new month came frequent, mad, March gales. There was still good fishing at Flamborough, where we regularly trawled, along with many other boats. In the hours before daylight, the line fishers, mostly cobles, but a couple of small keelboats, shot their lines off from close inshore, out into the sea. This activity forced the trawlers further offshore away from the best grounds. The trawlers would gradually work their way closer in again as the liners hauled back their gear. These line boats would be heading home to Bridlington and Flamborough's North Landing around midday. There was quite a lot of interactive radio traffic between both types of fishers, with a view to avoiding conflict, though there was often unpleasantness too. The trawlers were aggrieved at being pushed out from their desired location. The line fishers thought the trawlers were taking all the fish by fishing round the clock. Mostly the two parties managed to work together, though lines were occasionally towed away.

An earlier appeal to the district 'Sea Fisheries Committee' by some of the coblemen, for the introduction of a bye-law keeping all trawlers beyond the three-mile limit was vociferous, though unsuccessful. Vessels over sixty feet in length were already excluded from this area. The irony of this failed appeal was that the leading exponent of the move had previously been a successful trawler skipper who had been in frequent conflict with the cobles.

A midnight shipping forecast predicting south-easterly winds, reaching gale force eight to storm force ten, failed to deter the line fishers one morning and though there wasn't a breath of wind when they sailed, with the coming of daylight this savage weather burst, catching these little craft at sea. Both the Flamborough and Bridlington lifeboats were launched to escort the small craft back, but unlike the trawlers who had scrambled their nets on board and were already heading for home, these boats still had their lines in the sea. The crews continued to recover their gear as long as they could until, reluctantly, putting buoys on their gear, they left their remaining lines until the weather abated.

We were well on our way home, travelling at speed with wind and growing swell at our stern, when the skipper of the coble the *Peggy K* was heard on the radio. He informed the Coastguard that they were too far off to make their way across the wind and waves to Bridlington, and were going to head for Scarborough. The lifeboats were busy escorting other vessels, nearer to port and this lone coble, with three men on board was in trouble. I called to her skipper, asking his position, which he reported, giving radar distances from two points of land. I plotted his location, which was approximately five miles astern of us. Slowing the *Courage* down, I turned her head into the wind. A face appeared at the cabin hatch, asking what the problem was.

"Were gonna escort a Brid coble t' Scarborough. 'E's too far off t' get 'ome." I yelled. The lads put on their oilskins and came on deck to the wheelhouse, where they stood holding on to the handrail, looking into the wind as we steamed as fast as the weather would allow. Spray was flying full length, and I constantly used the throttle, easing her down as she plunged into troughs then setting her on again when possible.

The little boat was impossible to detect on the radar, with spindrift filling the air and the *Courage* constantly lifting her head and plunging. There would have been no comfort in our cabin on this course. Rusty was the first to spot the little vessel and tapped on the window, pointing two compass points to starboard. I nodded in acknowledgement, looking along the line of his arm. The coble, riding the surf, was surging downwind, her skipper, standing aft, was fighting the tiller to stop her broaching. She was spooning water as the waves passed on ahead of her. Her electric bilge pump was spewing a constant flow from her side. I gave her skipper a reassuring wave as I passed, then turned hard to starboard, crossing her stern.

With the *Peggy K* located, my crew, their faces caked in salt and wet through despite their oilskins, were pleased to get back to the warmth of our cabin. They could quickly be back on deck if required. A welcome pot of coffee soon appeared at the wheelhouse, delivered by Sid, who, now we were going down hill again, had discarded his waterproofs. "I know which boat I'd rather be on," was his wry comment.

I didn't argue. There was no comfort whatever in these little open boats. I'd worked with my Dad in a coble for a while when I was a teenager, and could vividly remember some very cold, wet days. Even in storm conditions, my *Courage* was relatively comfortable and dependable. I told Sid I'd ease the engine down when we had three miles to go and that we were going to spread some oil on the sea, prior to the coble entering the harbour. As the water shoaled, the swell would grow and the waves would become breakers. The little boat would have to turn broadside to these waves to enter the harbour. The term 'oil on troubled waters' was no hollow saying.

At three miles from home and now a half mile ahead of the coble, Rusty passed two five-gallon drums of hydraulic oil from the engine-room to Bluey and Sid on deck. At a mile from the entrance, the drums were taken for'ard and punctured several times with a spike. Both tins were hung over our bows on light ropes and the oil began to flow, slowly. We were going dead slow now and the oil was washing ahead of us on the rolling seas. Its effect was amazing. Though the waves were still big, the lubricant had a wonderful calming effect and took the sting out of the breakers. The coble moved ahead of us, entering the harbour on the big seas without too much trouble. We followed her in with equal ease.

With both boats tied up at the quayside, I climbed the ladders to the pier, intending to talk with the coble skipper, who had started to land the fish from the lines recovered. "Are yers alright?" I enquired.

The man was quite abrupt in his reply, saying, "thanks fo' that, lad. If I can do owt fo' you anytime, let me know," before turning his back on me to continue his work.

He could have offered to replace the oil we'd used, but didn't. He might have paid for the caulking that had been knocked from between our planks with the pounding, but I wouldn't ask him. This was the man who wanted a three-mile, exclusive limit for cobles.

* * * * * *

A few weeks fishing was followed by my final trip to Scotland before the launching. I arrived at a bright, cool Aberdeen Station for a final visit to see my new baby, meeting Jimmy in the entrance hall. He was clearly shocked when he saw me approaching, as in addition to a small overnight bag, I was also struggling with a large, flat, chart table. This beautiful piece of polished furniture, four feet by three feet had been made for me by a skilled cabinet-maker in Scarborough. Not only would I be able to put full-sized, navigation charts on top, there was also space for dozens of charts within the piano-hinged cabinet, though the total depth was only three inches.

Before Jimmy could utter a word I said, "Ah thought with all that room in me new wheel'ouse, I'd 'ave a proper chart table. Can yer get yer men to fix this at t' back, in t' corner." I could see he wasn't too pleased, but I knew he'd have either persuaded me to change my mind, or charged me a large amount to construct and install a chart table, as this wasn't part of the specification.

Making our way to the car park, I was greeted by Madge, sitting in the car. She too raised her eyebrows when she saw my luggage. With some difficulty the piece of furniture was manoeuvred into the back of Jimmy's car, leaving just enough room for me to sit. I'd had difficulty finding somewhere to stow the case on the train from Scarborough to York and had exchanged words with a guard on the mainline route, who suggested I should have paid to stow my table in the guard's van. "T' train isn't full," I pointed out. "Ah'm not deprivin' anyone of a seat." The man had reluctantly relented, allowing me to keep the unique piece in my possession.

We stopped en route at our usual calling place in Ellen for refreshments, solid and liquid, so Jimmy was quite mellow when we arrived at his yard. He called his foreman over as we pulled up outside the big green doors and on the man's approach said, "hey mon, will ye tak this piece o' junk frae ma car an' throw it oot the back somewhere?" then grinned in my direction.

The foreman carefully withdrew the table from his boss's vehicle then gave the piece a critical inspection. I registered his unspoken approval of the workmanship as he nodded in my direction. He'd make sure my new table was looked after and installed to its best advantage. Later, when visitors entered my wheelhouse, I'd say, "I took this chart table t' Noble's boatyard and said, "build me a boat round this."

Next, having dropped Madge off at her nearby home, Jimmy took me to see my new baby being fitted out at the other end of the harbour. I could see her cream-coloured masts towering above the slipway, long before we got near and couldn't wait to inspect her. I was out of the car before the engine was turned off. My 'dream come true' was gleaming with a new coat of blue paint, hardly dry on her sides. A deep, plum red antifouling paint covered her bottom. The huge, four-bladed propeller of manganese bronze, shrouded by a tapered nozzle to give extra thrust, was gleaming in the spring sun.

The *Independence* had changed dramatically in the short time since I'd seen her last and I wanted to examine every part of her exterior, but also couldn't wait to get on board to see how she'd progressed. There would be many developments for me to inspect and absorb.

I examined all round her exterior above and below the water line and was pleased to see that the inlets to the sea-cocks, where the cooling water for the engine and pumps would be drawn, were screened with perforated copper plates. These hundreds of small holes would only allow minute particles through the systems. I'd had trouble in the past when plastic bags, weed and even small fish had been drawn in through the inlets, causing pump blockages and rises in engine temperature.

The hull on each side, close to the keel, was fitted with an echo sounder transducer. These would electronically create the noise that would rebound off the seabed, to be marked on the pair of sounders in the wheelhouse. This data would indicate depth of water, hard and soft ground discrimination and would denote any fish in the water table. One of these sounders, a 'Kelvin Hughes' Mk 44 was identical to my set in the *Courage*. I'd had a lot of experience with that machine and felt I could read its signals minutely. The other instrument specified was from a rival company 'Simrad', which also had a good reputation for electronic equipment. The pair would operate on different frequencies, allowing them to work simultaneously without their signals becoming confused.

At the forward end of the hull on the portside, above the keel, was a new piece of gear, housed inside an eight-inch diameter, vertical tube. This was the sonar transducer, which would be lowered mechanically from the housing when required. This sophisticated kit was the equivalent of a forward scanning echo sounder, which step-scanned ahead in an arc to a distance of 1500 metres. Its audible ping, amplified through a speaker, was the sound everyone heard when watching exciting submarine films. There was no need to look at the recording paper on this machine. The returning echo was clearly audible and I would soon learn to distinguish between the noise of hard ground, wrecks and large shoals of fish.

It was time to climb the precarious, almost vertical ladder to the deck now and I wondered what I'd find there. My curiosity was soon satisfied and I looked in awe at my new possession. Her wheelhouse towered above the deck and the winch, for'ard under the whaleback shelter, looked far away; such was the deck space available. The gallows, one on each quarter and one forward on the starboard side, meant we would be able to work a trawl over the stern or the side. These gallows were probably twice the size of those on the little *Courage*, as were her bulwarks. There was no danger of falling overboard, as her sides were almost waist high. I couldn't help comparing my new craft with the first boat I'd sailed on as a teenager. The *Whitby Rose's* bulwarks were only about ten inches high. It was amazing how quickly I'd found my sea legs on this lively little vessel.

On entering the wheelhouse, immediately inside the door, I noted a grey electrical switchboard with fifty circuit-breaker switches, which looked impressive. When I looked at the array of electronic equipment installed, I was once more lost for words and swallowed hard. The two sounder cabinets were in the forward corners. Two Mk 21 Decca Navigators with a plotting machine between them, held centre stage. Two VHF radios were conveniently handy for easy access. I'd specified two of each of these essentials so I'd never have to return to port if any component failed. The luxury I'd allowed myself was a very comfortable chair with shock absorbers to deaden the impact of the swell. This was a far cry from my first fish box seat. The chair was already mounted in position, though shrouded in heavy polythene to protect the covering from unintentional damage. I couldn't resist sitting in my chair for a test drive, though the view from the window spoiled any illusion of being at sea.

Another non-essential was an automatic pilot, which would take the tedium out of steering, allowing me to concentrate on navigating and fish finding. It was at this point I noticed there was no steering wheel. A pedestal for a wheel was inconveniently placed at the rear of the wheelhouse so I'd have to stand in front of the helm and would only be able to use one hand. When asked, Jimmy said I'd never use a wheel ever again and the six-inch, electronically operated tiller levers, situated on both sides close to the windows were all I'd ever need. He was subsequently proved right, but it was a weird thought, not having a steering wheel on a boat. A medium frequency radio for long-range communications was fitted at the rear of the wheelhouse.

With head spinning, I left my *Independence* and departed for the 'Alexandra Hotel', where Jimmy had already deposited my bag. A quick bath, followed by a light meal and a phone call to Dotty, giving her an update on the progress of the vessel and I was ready for a night on the town.

It was still early in the evening and I had time on my hands so I wandered along the seafront looking at the dozens of boats in port. Next I called into some of the harbourside watering holes and it was no real surprise when I met a group of fishermen who I knew. These were former drifter-men, not much older than me, who'd fished from Scarborough in the days of my youth. These men were now working on highly profitable, purse seining vessels, which caught hundreds of tons of herring and mackerel each voyage using gigantic nets.

It was very pleasant reminiscing about the days of the drifters, which had now sadly been consigned to history. I'd had some wonderful times with these men, occasionally sailing with them to pursue the vast shoals of herring on overnight trips, but more so, spending Saturday and Sunday nights out in Scarborough, attending discos and pubs that provided live music. None of the drifter skippers would ever fish on the Sabbath day. I could recall going to school with a hangover on more than one Monday morning.

Along with James, Alec and Robert, I frequented several more bars along the waterfront before closing time, at which point the lads suggested we continue our session in the lounge bar of the 'Royal Hotel', where it was possible to drink after time. Though quite fuddled by this time, I was certainly in favour of this extension. Several drinks later, and making little sense, I vaguely remember informing the landlord I was building the new boat at Noble's Yard. He could expect about twenty guests to bide at his hotel, booked via the shipyard, sometime in May. At this point he began treating me like a brother, insisting on plying me with even more strong drink and I quickly departed, looking for the gent's toilet. I remember little else except saying in my best Scots accent, "ahm awa t' ma baed," as I staggered through the front door en route to my accommodation.

I awoke next morning, still dressed, lying on top of the bed with head thumping. Unable to face breakfast, which though I was late was still available, I settled for three cups of black coffee. There was little sympathy from the waitress, who having seen it all before, enjoyed clearing the cutlery and crockery from my table with a clatter. "Ye dinna look too well jus' noo," she said grinning. "Yer eyes are awfa red."

"Yer should see 'em from where I'm lookin'," I replied, feeling slightly better as the coffee kicked in.

It was mid-morning before I got to the slipway, once more boarding my vessel. I felt extremely uneasy mounting the sheer ladder and didn't look down. Craftsmen were working in all sections of the vessel as I roamed round, mostly getting in the way and stopping progress. Below, in the engine-room, two boiler-suited men were fitting belting to the auxiliary engine. Another was working on a very complicated, electrical junction box, from which dozens of wires were leading. I didn't ask what this was, as I didn't think I'd be able to cope with the answer, so instead, climbed the stairs to the wheelhouse. I was delighted to see my new chart table already in place and it looked terrific. The shipwright fitting the unit gave me a huge smile and a witty comment on my unkempt appearance. Proudly he showed me how the piece was mounted, adjacent to the steering pedestal, but was hinged and could be lowered, allowing me to use the wheel, should I ever need it. He'd also fitted a sheet of clear plastic on top, under which the current chart could be viewed and protected.

Leaving my new boat, I wandered round the harbour back to the boatyard and was grateful to accept a cup of coffee from Bessie, who also commented on my appearance, though I was now feeling almost human. Jimmy took me to the 'Alex' for my bag, then back to Aberdeen Station in near silence and I slept for most of the journey south, arriving home very late. I was back at sea early the next morning.

CHAPTER 21

BIRTH OF AN ORGANISATION

A meeting was called at a large hotel in Whitby by some of the senior skippers on the coast. Fishing was on the political agenda and these men, who up until now had only been involved in their local organisations, realized we should all be speaking with one voice. It was time for English fishermen, as the Scots had done before them, to form a National Federation, a body that could present a united voice to government. A sham organisation the F.O.S. was already in existence, but this was a government quango, financially supported by the government and was effectively allowing the government to hold talks with itself.

Fishermen from every port on the east and west coasts were invited to attend and they did so in large numbers. The main thinker behind this plan was again George Crawford, the seine net skipper from North Shields. George had an ability to motivate people, to see the greater picture and was aware of political events unfolding. He could also drink copious amounts of whisky, which he usually managed after his meetings.

The gathering was to take place on Saturday, shortly after noon, when most men would be available. I left home with three other skippers at about eleven in the morning, telling Dotty I wouldn't be late, that it shouldn't take too long. I'd been offered a lift to the meeting and would return as soon as the proceedings were over. The bar was already open when we arrived and there were several familiar faces, already socializing. It was only polite to join them, before the meeting started. There was time for a couple of drinks before everyone was summoned into the main hall for the start of the proceedings. Drinks were of course taken into the conference and tables were put together to accommodate our extended group.

The Chairman opened the proceedings with a welcome to all present and immediately asked if we wanted a national organization, which would be representative of our views. He paused for effect then said slowly, "if not bonnie lads, we can aall haway back t' the bar noo." Everyone in the room was adamant it was necessary to have better representation to government.

The meeting began but the bar remained open and most of those attending, who were not part of the organizing group at the front, continued to use this facility. Our table now had a large ashtray, full of cash in the centre: the kitty. I thought it prudent at this point to find a phone, to let Dotty know I may be a little later than originally planned. Her response was characteristic; a little disappointed but understanding.

It was already early afternoon. The meeting had been late starting and there were many questions being asked from the floor about the form the new organization would take. How much would it cost to run? Was it to have permanent staff? If so where would the headquarters be? Who would be the Executive Officer? What form would the Management Committee take? Who would be the Chairman? How frequently were meetings to be held? The meeting was going well, but so was our party near the back of the room.

Mid-afternoon came with more questions from the floor and more drink from the bar. I again rang my wife, saying I was still stuck in Whitby and that the thing was going on a bit. This time she was less charitable. "How much longer is it going to go on? You said you wouldn't be late."

I apologized, saying they must be nearly finished now and the meeting couldn't go on much longer, but it did.

There was still a final debate as to what the new body was to be called. The name had to incorporate the word national and as the body was a group of federations, this word was also desirable. In a rare, lucid moment, I shouted, "what about t' National Federation o' Fishermen's Organisations? N.F.F.O." The room went quiet. For most of the proceedings there had been considerable debate about the various topics, but there was no dissent or counter proposal to my suggestion. Maybe no one was bothered too much what the body was called, or perhaps the debate had run its course and all present had had enough discussion. Someone seconded my proposal and the name was adopted and carried unanimously. The NFFO was born. This was probably my only input into the day's proceedings.

Now it was time to retire to the bar. The elders were already there, having consumed nothing but water during the afternoon so far. George was downing the first of what would be many whiskies, having won the day and given birth to his brainchild.

Andy, one of our group said he was going to ring his wife Christine, to say he was going to be late. In a rash moment I said, "ask Chris t' give Dotty a ring an' say t' same for me." On reflection, I realised this wasn't wise, but he'd already gone, so the decision was irreversible and things were starting to get a little muddled in my head. By five o'clock I knew I was in bother and started to worry, sobering slightly. "Come on lads its time we were off. Ahm gonna be in big trouble."

"Me an all." slurred Andy. "Lets get goin'."

Our driver, Kenny became belligerent at being rushed and said, "just a minute, it's my bloody car an' we'll go when ahm ready. We'll 'ave another beer first."

Now I knew I was in deep, deep mire. I wandered back once more to the telephone. Yet another mistake. When Dotty answered I said, "Ahm sorry love, I am tryin' t' get 'ome. It's Kenny, 'e's supposed t' be ...."

My words were cut short as my wife loudly interrupted my feeble excuses and I quickly held the earpiece at arm's length from my spinning head. I could still hear every word. "Don't bloody bother. Me and the kids have waited in all day for you and how dare you tell Christine to pass your messages on, second-hand. Don't bother coming home at all. Stay where you are if it means that much to you."

I only managed "but," before the phone was slammed down at the other end.

I considered ringing for a taxi but luckily, when I got back to our dwindling group, Kenny had been persuaded to leave. "Yer can allus get a pint in t' 'Dolphin' when we get back," Andy had reasoned. He too was in trouble.

The trip home couldn't go fast enough, though with Kenny driving, I occasionally thought I wouldn't get there at all. There was a definite frosty atmosphere when I arrived home, but Paula and Danny were pleased to see me and I was at least able to tuck them into bed. I probably wouldn't see them awake again for a few days, as I'd be sailing the following morning.

I did manage to persuade Dotty that it had been a very important day for the fishing industry and that I'd played a part in it. She was slightly mollified at this, though didn't know how small my input had been. No doubt by the state of me, she suspected it was minor and that I'd been off on a jolly, but to her eternal credit, she never stayed mad for long and would never sleep on an argument.

Chapter 22

Independence at last

When I relinquished my *Courage* in late April, I felt I was deserting her. I knew every working part of this vessel and all her little idiosyncrasies. It was as if a part of my life had gone. My crew had no problem getting temporary berths, while I stayed ashore compiling lists of fishing gear, spare parts and pored over the guest list in case of omissions. I spent hours tracing plastic plotting sheets of fishing information, loaned to me by skippers who already had Decca plotting machines.

After what seemed an eternity, the big day was almost upon us. I decided to go to Fraserburgh a day early to ensure the arrangements were in hand, but would be certain to stay sober. I didn't want a repeat of my last visit.

My *Independence* looked immaculate and ready for sea at first glance, though there were lots of small, technical aspects yet to be completed, much like building a house. It would be sometime yet before she'd be finished.

"There's nay problems wi' ony 'o the accommodation," Bessie assured me in Noble's office, passing a list with up to date arrangements of who was staying where. Most of this had been confirmed and the guests informed previously. Bessie also told me that a flat backed lorry, loaded with fishing gear had arrived from home and she'd found a corner in the yard for me to store the nets, doors, chains, wires and bobbins. She'd efficiently organised a fork-lift truck to unload this equipment. My crew and

I would assemble this assortment into working order, ready for deployment on the boat, before the *Independence* was ready for sea. Most skippers prepared their gear in their home port, taking it on board on arrival, but I wanted to test the boat and gear together. It was a twenty-four hour passage from Scarborough to Fraserburgh and I didn't want to return if any winch or hydraulic problems appeared subsequently.

Two luxury coaches for guests had been arranged and names given to the various hotels in Fraserburgh. Some guests decided to travel north by car. I was surprised when Dotty decided on this option. It was only a few months since she'd passed her driving test, but at least we now had a newer, safer car for her to travel in. She thought this would be an easier journey for the little ones and less disruptive for coach travellers. Her intention was to make the trip with her sister Margaret and her two children. With the four youngsters in the rear and the back seats laid flat, providing a greater space, the bairns could play together on their journey north. The sisters planned to stop off somewhere near Edinburgh to break their journey. Margaret, who lived in Hull, had recently had an unsettling experience when she thought she was receiving a 'heavy breathing' obscene phone call. She put the receiver down abruptly. Very sadly, her neighbour was found dead next morning. She'd died of an asthma attack.

* * * * * *

I met up with Dennis, my old school pal, in Rosehearty three miles along the coast early that evening. He'd offered me accommodation for the night, prior to the arrival of the guests. While still at school, Dennis and I had sailed to North Shields on two Scottish vessels, then travelled north to Fraserburgh with the crews, by coach. Later Dennis had shipped up in a drifter, moving to Scotland, where he'd met and married Vera. He spoke the local dialect like a native and was now a shareholder in a new seventy-five-foot vessel, *Kimara*, built at the nearby 'Forbes Yard' in Sandhaven.

Though I'd had good intentions, it was impossible not to have a few drinks in such good company. We enjoyed a meal at the 'Cliff

View Restaurant' in the village, chatting about school days, then moved to the popular 'Masons Arms' for the remainder of the night. Vera must have felt quite left out as we relived our youth; making shrimp nets to catch brown shrimp at low water on the beach and selling them for a shilling a pint. He reminded me of the little sailing boats we made from fish box wood, using candyfloss sticks for masts and discarded drinks cartons, which were waterproof, for sails.

I did imbibe more than intended during the pleasant evening and also took a wee nip back at the house, so I was pleased to hit the pillow. I woke to the realisation that today was the day when the guests would arrive for the launching. Family and friends were already well on their way north. In a few hours time, I'd be greeting them and directing them to one of the three hotels which Bessie had arranged.

By the time the first coach pulled up outside the 'Alexandra Hotel' late in the afternoon, I was up to speed with the accommodation arrangements and greeted everyone as they alighted. First from the coach were my Mum and Dad, followed by sisters and brothers-in-law. Dotty's parents came next. Old Mrs Wilkinson, our friendly neighbour, though not good on her legs, was keen to be off the bus. Many other familiar faces followed. As each gathered their luggage, they made their way into the hotel lobby, where I joined them to reel off room numbers to those in doubt. Minutes later the second coach arrived. Some in this group would stay on the bus to be taken to the Sultoun and Royal Hotels, a short distance down the road.

To make up the party, a fairly relaxed Dotty and Margaret arrived in the car. Having followed the route map, apart from taking a wrong turn near Whitby and finding themselves in Sandsend, they'd completed the journey without event. Considering Dotty had not been driving long, this was a major achievement. Some people would never undertake a trip like this in a lifetime of driving.

I assisted with the bags and while Dotty was unpacking, joined the majority of the men, who having deposited their suitcases, had headed for the bar. Little Jeannie was as usual behind the counter. She said, "yous Scarborough folk canna stay awa frae the Broch. It's good tae see yous a' agin."

We all looked at each other confused, then at Jeannie. Everyone nodded and smiled. My brother-in-law Ian standing next to me said, "what's she say?"

"Dunno, I missed it by that much," I said, spreading my hands wide, though I'd got the gist of her greeting. The glass of beer in my hand seemed to take forever to force down and I was saying to myself, "'ere I go again."

It was a warm sunny evening and all the guests were keen to see the *Independence*. I was equally keen to show her off, so a couple of beers later, before the dinner, when we'd been joined by wives and families, we set off on the ten minute walk to the slipway. Mrs Wilkinson declined, saying she would wait until the following day, when transport would be available.

Had the new vessel been in the boatyard, the premises would now have been locked up, but here on the slipway she was exposed in all her glory. The giant ladder had been removed by the last of the retiring yard workers so there was no access to the deck. Towering above her visitors, the spring sun reflecting on her deep blue hull, my *Independence* looked magnificent. Even now I still found it difficult to believe this fantastic vessel was mine. She more than passed initial scrutiny and tomorrow the visitors would be able to look on board.

An hour later and back in the hotel, all our guests were seated in the banqueting hall for a welcome meal. There were no speeches, just a brief greeting from Jimmy Noble, welcoming everyone to Fraserburgh and hoping that everyone would enjoy themselves.

Ian, sitting opposite, looked at me uncomprehending. "What's 'e say?"

"Dunno," I said grinning, though I'd understood most of what Jimmy had said. "Summat about 'avin' a good time,"

"As if we need tellin' to 'ave a good time," he replied, laughing.

Following an excellent meal, we retired to the bar where everyone was in holiday mood and the party atmosphere continued. Jeannie was going to be very busy. Rusty in particular was in great form and I listened from the side as he regaled a group of giggling ladies with a story about the late Jimmy Ritchie. Jimmy, was reputed to have been very generously endowed in the manhood department and Rusty was saying Jimmy was able to balance twelve, old pre-decimal pennies on this member.

" 'Ow do ya know?" squealed one woman, clearly fascinated, while the others, all wanting to ask the same question, hung on his every word.

"Everybody knows," came back the stock answer. Undeterred by the disappointment his answer had brought, he went on to relate how Jimmy had a collection of old ladies around South Cliff who paid him to visit. This was the classy end of town, where many old properties were divided into up-market flats, with sea views. It was clear that his audience wanted to believe him, and there were several rude innuendos.

I could remember Jimmy as a white-coated doorman at the front of the 'Pier Café'. All the restaurants along the seafront employed touts, encouraging visitors to eat in their establishments. It was talk of the harbour that Jimmy's spiel was worth hearing so one day I went along to listen.

Undistinguished in appearance, the red-faced, stocky man with furrowed brow and thinning, dark hair, combed back, winked as he noticed me hovering close by.

It was true what I'd been told. Jimmy's chant, which he reeled off quickly and which was almost undecipherable, began normally. "Roast beef, roast pork, roast lamb, plenty o' seating upstairs," but then he added, "get your knob in here, no waiting."

He winked at me again, as he knew I was paying attention, but crowds of people walking past within earshot, didn't get the message.

The entire evening was one of wonderful interaction, jokes and frivolity that continued long into the night. Jeannie behind the bar dashed back and forth non-stop, supplying the revellers with their requirements. Eventually, well after midnight, when most of the group had drifted off to bed, having had a long day and with another in prospect, Jeannie seized her opportunity to close the bar, without too much opposition. She bawled, "should ye nae be takin' tae yer beds ma loons an' quains. T' morn's a beeg day fo' ye' all."

Ian looked in my direction with a daft expression on his face and said, "what's she say?"

I scratched my head, gave him a similar grin back and replied, "dunno" again, "I think she mean's t' bar's closin'. But," I said, pausing for effect and tapping my nose knowledgeably, "I know where we can get another beer." We both looked round to see if anyone wanted to join us, but it seemed not. Dotty had retired a short while earlier, having seen the bairns safely to bed. My weary wife, having had a long, tiring day, wanted to be fresh and ready for the special occasion, tomorrow. I wasn't ready for bed yet and neither it seemed was Ian, so together we headed for the Royal.

A few of our guests, resident in the hotel, were still in the bar along with many locals, enjoying the flexible opening hours and we joined in the company. The landlord was again most welcoming and immediately provided our drinks, chatting amicably. In his thick brogue he said I looked much better than the previous time he'd seen me, though Ian hadn't a clue what was said and just gave me another blank look. Another couple of strong drinks and I was again heading for the gent's room. I wandered around in the passage beyond the lounge bar, where I'd staggered a few weeks earlier, but could only find the ladies room. Baffled, I returned to the bar. "'Ave yer moved t' toilet signs around landlord? It says 'Ladies' now, on t' door I was usin' las' time."

"Och no siirr, I've nae touched 'em. 'T was the quain's room ye was usin' las' time you were here."

There was a snort and a cough at my side, as Ian choked on his drink, then he spluttered, " 'e said you were usin' ladies toilets las' time."

I blushed and squirmed as Ian milked my embarrassment. How he'd understood the dialect when the barman had used the word 'quains', a localised word for females, was a mystery. He was still laughing when we decided to leave the bar half an hour later. The landlord wished me well for my big day, as we made for the door. Ian looked at me perplexed and said, "what's 'e say?"

I swore at him in reply.

At last the launch day had arrived. The morning was fine and there were no problems. It seemed an eternity since I'd spoken to Jimmy Noble then ordered the boat to be built at his yard. I took Danny down to see the new craft while Dotty was at the hairdressers. My Mum was taking care of Paula and had gone to visit the local shops along with my sisters. The men from the yard were putting the last remaining section of bunting between the masts as we arrived and the *Independence*, decked out with flags, looked spectacular. Boats didn't usually have masts in place when they were launched.

As usual, most of the menfolk had gravitated to the harbour and slipway. Several of our guests, including my Dad and brothers-in-law were already on board when we arrived. I was pleased to see Ian was looking a little delicate while he listened to one of the workers explaining some detail on deck.

"What's 'e say?" I whispered as I passed.

Danny was so excited that immediately he was on board, he was dashing to and fro, wanting to see every part at once, then reporting his findings back to me as if I'd never been on the boat before. It was almost midday before we finally left my dream boat to return to the hotel and prepare for the launching ceremony. Dotty looked terrific in her new, brown, suede outfit and would grace the occasion when she blessed the boat and broke the bottle on her stem iron. There was no danger of the champagne bottle not breaking. I'd insisted on the glass being thoroughly scored with a glasscutter, to weaken it. I was taking no chances on bringing bad luck to my new boat.

At two o'clock we were gathered at the bows of the *Independence*, waiting for the 'go' from the builder. A nervous Dotty was at my side, waiting to perform her official duty. I looked around at the dozens of people who'd travelled hundreds of miles to be with us on this day to help us celebrate our good fortune. Standing here on the slipway, surrounded by family and friends, holding Dotty's hand with our two lovely bairns already on the boat waiting to be launched down the track, I felt an immense surge of pride and happiness. Could there be anyone in the world more fortunate than me? I was sure there couldn't be.

At a nod from Jimmy, Dotty cleared her throat and clearly, for all to hear, spoke the traditional words, "I name this ship, *Independence*. God bless her, and all who sail in her." She then released the bottle, which gave a pleasing crash as it shattered, throwing champagne into the air, dampening those close by. Dotty then turned to me with a wonderful smile and said, "was that alright?"

I couldn't speak for a while. I just hugged her close with tears in my eyes, then whispered, "thank you," and kissed her.

Totally oblivious to the initial movement of our new craft as she commenced her first journey to the sea, we were brought back to earth by the cheering all around us. The *Independence* was moving sedately and in a controlled manner, supported by permanent blocks under her bilge, down the track-way, held back by a huge wire hawser. Had she been launched from the boatyard, she would have been set free to run down the 'slip', supported by blocks, which would break apart on impact with the water. Though we couldn't see them, Paula, Danny and their cousins were on board the boat at the stern, along with other youngsters related to the yard staff.

We hurried along the side of the slipway to the harbour, where my dream was now floating high in the water. She was gently hauled alongside the quay by willing hands, so the guests who'd been unable to climb the big ladder, could now clamber aboard. Every part of the vessel was filled with people wanting to see her.

With curiosity satisfied, we returned to the 'Alex' where the splendid official dinner was about to take place. The large room was decorated with more bunting and even the tables were decked out in red white and blue. The table napkins, also in the three colours, were printed, 'Launch of the Independence, FR 196, 17th May 1977, in gold lettering. These serviettes were so attractive I thought it a shame to use them for their correct purpose.

*Christening of Independence. Left to right: Sid Withers,
Frank 'Rusty' Drydale, Barry Bryan, Fred Normandale,
Dorothy Normandale, James Noble.
Courtesy of North Eastern press*

*Independence takes to the water.
Courtesy of North Eastern Press*

Launch of Independence, May 1977.
Courtesy of North Eastern Press

Jeannie was once more inundated in her little bar before the guests took their places in the main hall. The top table was set for me, Dotty and our bairns, plus Jimmy Noble and Jimmy McDonald and wives. Both men were directors of the shipyard. Our parents, brothers, sisters and their spouses were close to the front.

Jimmy Noble stood up, microphone in hand, best wig neatly in place and once more welcomed everyone, then asked our office agent to say grace. The meal was swiftly served and was piping hot. The 'Alexander Hotel' was 'the' place in Fraserburgh for functions and ours would be small in comparison with some of their bookings. A drinks waitress was kept busy throughout the meal, then orders were taken for liqueurs for 'the toast'. Dotty asked for her usual, dry Martini and tonic. I requested a glass of rum.

Jimmy Noble rose to his feet again, tapping on the table with his spoon for order. The room hushed. First, Jimmy presented Dotty with an expensive, gold watch to mark the occasion and for fulfilling her important role of naming and christening the new vessel. Next there were 'good luck' cards and greetings telegrams to be read, just like at a wedding. A 'wire' from our wonderful, bank manager, Mr White read, "Good luck and every success, don't forget who paid for her."

There was a thoughtful card from Mum and Dad saying, "it took *Courage* to gain your *Independence*," and a very silly cable from Kurt which read, "ignore last telegram."

Jimmy then commenced the main part of his speech and I quickly realised it was virtually the same as he'd done for the launching of *Our Heritage,* except the name of the boat was different, but I wasn't bothered in the least. This one was special, because it was ours. The James Noble boatyard had built scores of fishing vessels. He couldn't write a different script for them all.

At this juncture Jimmy looked to me for a response and for a moment I was lost for words. I'd known I was expected to speak and I knew what I wanted to say, but was tongue-tied. I wasn't used to speaking in public.

Turning crimson, I managed to thank the yard for their fantastic vessel and for making my dream come true. I then thanked the various tradesmen who'd put their personal skills into the project. Last but most importantly, I thanked my dear wife Dotty for launching and naming my *Independence* and for breaking the bottle first time, at which she rolled her eyes. I then spoke of her unfailing support through some difficult times, when I'd struggled to keep going. It was short and hurried but I meant every word of it. I sat down sweaty, trembling and in a daze while people around me were applauding. I vaguely heard my Mum say, "well done."

Out of the spotlight I quickly cooled down again. Next Jimmy called on Joe Taylor, the Kelvin agent, whose Company had installed the main engine, to propose a toast to the new vessel. This stocky, grey-suited, chain-smoking man with thinning hair, stood up and in his archetypal north-east Scots voice said, "will ye a' stand an raise yourr glasses to the fine vessel, *Independence*. He could have been saying, "ah'll come doon frae the hills wi' ma claymore an' hack ye down," by the tone of his voice, though this wasn't how Joe was at all. He was a very obliging, professional man but his voice was deep and gruff.

Immediately after the formalities were over the band struck up with a Scottish reel, which Dotty and I were expected to lead off. I didn't have a clue what to do, so after a few seconds of fumbling and hobbling, I grabbed Dotty and began shuffling around in my interpretation of a waltz. Several others joined in and there was total confusion on the floor as Scots attempted to hurl themselves across the floor in their traditional manner, with the English constantly in the way.

The versatile band played a variety of music to suit most tastes and a disco churned out the latest hits between the group's sessions, so we danced for most of the early evening. It was with great pleasure that we watched our two bairns enjoying the occasion and being fussed over by the many relatives present. In the manner of all launchings we'd attended, the lights came up halfway through the night and tea and sandwiches were served. These were devoured as if the crowd hadn't eaten for days, then the dancing and revelling continued.

In what seemed no time at all, it was one o'clock in the morning and the band struck up 'Auld Lang Syne'. Everyone in the room was persuaded to join in and form a giant circle, including Mrs Wilkinson, who I gently and protectively led to and fro, while others surged back and forth like lunatics as the music speeded up. Then all went quiet and the lights came up. The party was over. At least the party in the 'Alexandra Hotel' was over. There were lots of people, including Dotty and some of our immediate family, still in the mood for revelry, so at least twenty of the group again relocated to the Royal for another extension.

For the next few hours there was even more partying and jokes before we decided to return to our accommodation. Most of these guests were leaving at ten o'clock in the morning to return home. I didn't envy them. It was daylight and a pleasantly, mild morning as the remaining half dozen of us stepped outside, making our unsteady way back to the 'Alex'. I felt weary after several consecutive late nights, so was really disappointed to discover the hotel door was locked. Furthermore, there was no response to our constant ringing of the doorbell or banging. Did all the hotels in the area lock the doors at night?

"What are we going to do?" Dotty asked.

I hadn't a sensible answer, so shrugged my shoulders and said, "I don't know, maybe ring the hotel from a phone box?" I wasn't optimistic.

The door of a baker's shop opposite the hotel was already open for trade from the boats due to sail, and from it emanated the wonderful smell of fresh bread. Dotty said, "I quite fancy a hotcake." This idea found favour with everyone and we trooped into the shop en masse.

If the proprietor was surprised to see us he showed no visible sign. Did he regularly serve customers dressed in suits and evening dresses at five o'clock in the morning? Dotty requested a hotcake with a butter and jam filling and again we concurred. Maybe it was a Scottish tradition to breakfast in this manner. Without turning a hair, the man took a jar of strawberry jam and a pack of butter from the shop shelves and proceeded to slice and butter the piping hot rolls.

"We'll have ten please," I chipped in, feeling hungry and less tired. I received a nod of acknowledgement.

His mouth-watering produce, in two white, paper bags were placed on the counter. The unshockable gentleman then surprised us by asking a trivial amount for his service. He smiled for the first time when I gave him a pound extra. "Enjoy yourrr breakfast," he said, thoughtfully handing us a small packet of tissues, as we left his premises. He clearly knew we'd make a mess of our finery without his napkins. Melting butter had already stained the wrapper as the excess oozed from the hot bread.

We sat in a line at the kerbside in front of the shop and passed the still hot buns along the row. Nothing ever tasted as good as these delicious rolls and we munched contentedly in the early sun. Margaret, looking up at the locked building opposite, pointed and said, "there's a window open up there at the side of the hotel on the third floor. You could get through there, couldn't you Barry?"

Her husband, who was going to be the fifth member of our crew, choked on the piece of bread in his throat, coughing the dough into the road and rolled his eyes. He looked up at the drainpipe and the small, landing window he was expected to climb through. "But I can't cli..."

"Of course you can. It doesn't look too difficult," Margaret interrupted. "You can't expect us to sit here half the morning, waiting for someone to open the place."

Knowing he had no further say in the matter, Barry reluctantly rose to his feet and slowly crossed the road, to whatever fate had in store for him. The light, pleasant, carefree feeling had gone from his life. I was pleased Margaret hadn't instructed me to attempt the task. Under normal circumstances it wouldn't have been a problem, but after a long night of celebration, I didn't fancy the challenge. To his credit Barry reached his goal unscathed and apart from a slight hitch with the window, was soon inside. Two minutes later he opened the front door to a round of applause.

Five minutes later Dotty and I were in bed and though brilliant sunshine was streaming through the thin curtains, we were soon in a deep sleep. At eight o'clock Danny and Paula came into the room from next door, bright as buttons. They'd had a very late night too, but were fresh and ready for the day. I couldn't say the same, as I was feeling quite groggy. What a contrast in only a few hours. "Mebbe it's sleep that meks me feel bad," I suggested to Dotty. "I felt alright when I went t' bed." I was pleased to see it wasn't only me that was green around the gills, when we joined the throng for breakfast. There were several pale faces and few eaters.

An hour later with Dotty, the bairns and Mrs Wilkinson, who had opted for a scary ride back in the car, I watched our family and friends board the coach. I was pleased we weren't joining them and were driving home, while Margaret and family were returning by bus. As they boarded, I pointed out the drainpipe to Barry reminding him of his epic assault on the north face of the hotel, which he could only vaguely recall. I left him standing, gawping at the wall. His only words were, "fuckin' 'ell, did I do that?"

We had, what was for me, a leisurely drive home, including a couple of short stops, though our lovely neighbour seemed a little stunned when we arrived back in the street. I carried her bag into the house next door and she thanked us for a very enjoyable time. I'm sure it had been a memorable experience for her and Mrs Wilkinson was too much of a lady to mention my atrocious driving.

I now had a period of two weeks to kill while my boat was fine-tuned and ready for service.

CHAPTER 23

HOMEWARD BOUND

Along with Rusty, Bluey, Barry and Sid, I boarded the train. Loaded with sea bags, we were on our way to join our new ship. The *Independence* was finally ready for sea. It was a strange journey north. The lads were their usual, joking selves but I was full of apprehension and had butterflies in my stomach. The waiting, build up and launching were now all in the past and my head was buzzing with the thousand and one things I needed to remember. A car and works van picked us up in Aberdeen and soon we were on board the new vessel in Fraserburgh Harbour. There were still a couple of white boiler-suited technicians in the wheelhouse, but she did look finished. There was a scramble to select the choicest bunks in the cabin, but I insisted on the berth at the bottom of the ladder, so I could easily be called when required.

We were not allowed to start the boat's engine, or use any of the equipment on board, other than the lighting and cooking appliances, as officially the vessel still belonged to James Noble & Co. If tomorrow's sea trials were successful, I'd sign to accept her, then she'd be mine.

It was already late afternoon but there was plenty to be done and I was keen to make a start assembling the gear. I'd received permission from the Harbour Master to assemble our bobbin rig on the harbour's outer wall, the port's breakwater. The equipment was transported to this nearby location from the yard by fork-lift. We managed about three hour's work constructing the ground gear, running wires and chains out along the quay and shackling them together. At about seven o'clock we called a halt, returning to our new home, where we found Sid had prepared a hearty steak meal, which wasn't wasted. Following the feast, we went ashore for couple of pints, but were back on board in good time and turned in, ready for an early start.

Though lying in my bunk, sleep wouldn't come. My head was whirling with thoughts of fishing gear, electrical stuff, engineering spares, navigation charts, fuel, oil, gas. Was there anything vital I'd forgotten?

After breakfast we again spent time on the breakwater among the gear, before being summoned at midday to go on the sea trials. This was the acid test. I was in the wheelhouse with the builder as we let go our ropes, but only as an observer. I wasn't allowed to handle the vessel. A retired Fraserburgh fisherman took control of her under Jimmy's supervision. Though I knew this was the correct protocol, I couldn't help feeling a little resentful. She was my boat and this person was an intruder. I was feeling protective of my new baby.

Peter Bruce, a surveyor from the White Fish Authority was also present in the wheelhouse. Peter had watched the development of my new boat from her early stages on my behalf, authorising each stage payment as she grew through her gestation period, ensuring the yard kept to the Authority's required standards.

There were lots of tradesmen on board, representing all the various component parts of the vessel. Peter, notebook in hand, would talk to each of them in turn during the trials, testing the performance of their equipment. I would also spend time with each of these men during the afternoon, gaining as much information as possible to assist me in the future, though I was well aware it would be a steep learning curve for many months to come.

There were two Kelvin representatives on board, Dougie and Joe, men who I'd already come to know as friends. These people had worked for the company all their lives and were superb engineers. Joe, wearing a pair of ear defenders, was below in the engine-room, monitoring the machinery for the slightest problem, though the motor had already clocked up many hours on the test bed in the Glasgow factory.

I watched the temporary skipper manoeuvring my boat, gently using the tillers and engine controls and I warmed to him. He was treating her very tenderly, to the extent that she wasn't manoeuvring too well. I would have used more power from the engine to assist each turn. As my new craft cruised slowly through the harbour entrance, Jimmy reached for the throttle and before anyone could stop him, put the lever down hard, saying, "wee'll see whaat she'll dae."

I cringed and Dougie, who was monitoring the engine panel, swore loudly. Dougie had built this engine personally, took a pride in his work and didn't want his machinery abused. The control lever should have been eased down, allowing the speed to grow slowly. Jimmy said nothing but his expression went from anger at being shouted at by one of the workforce, to one of regret when he realised his mistake. There didn't seem to be any repercussions from this malpractice, as his mate Joe, who'd dashed into the wheelhouse at the sudden increase in revolutions confirmed, but we didn't seem to be going very fast.

"She seems a bit slow," I commented to the engineer as I looked through the window at the water passing by.

Dougie didn't agree. "Yourr a lot higher up, an' yerr boat's bigger than yerr used tae. She's jus' fine."

If Dougie was happy, so was I. He'd commissioned plenty of vessels in his time and I would soon know for sure. We were heading east from the harbour towards Cairnbulg point, to the measured mile, where the boat's speed would be assessed.

We were to run at top speed along this course at slack water, passing across the two sets of transits. These took the form of pairs of poles, sited ashore among the tufts of long grass, beyond the sand dunes. First we would steam in a south-easterly then north-westerly direction across the course. Peter Bruce, in possession of the stopwatch, would add the resulting times together then divide by two to derive the mean time across the mile.

The average of 6.59 minutes for the course, resulted in a calculated speed of slightly less than 9.1 knots. This information was also recorded in the surveyor's notebook though strangely, the *Independence* would never again achieve this speed, unaided by outside elements.

Following a searching examination of her capabilities and Peter Bruce's expression of satisfaction, we headed back to the Broch. "Can I 'ave a go at steerin' 'er now?" I asked Jimmy. We were still about ten minutes away from the harbour so he could hardly refuse. I stood by the port tiller, nudging it slightly, first to port then starboard. The glowing rudder indicator, showing green and red sectors, high above the front windows, moved slightly, responding electronically to each gentle touch. The tiller was extremely sensitive and would take some getting used to, but was clearly very effective and faster than the manual operation. It seemed really strange not using a steering wheel, though the helm was fixed on the pedestal at the back of the wheelhouse, for test purposes only. I looked at the comfortable chair, out of reach from my steering position, then at Jimmy, raising my eyebrows.

He read my thoughts instantly and laughed. "Ye'll nae be usin' they tillers at sea at aall, yerr autopilot'll tak aah the worrk." He flicked a switch on the panel, then another on a small control board in front of the chair. My levers were now inert. A steady click, click of electrical relays and minute alterations on the rudder indicator were the only movements. This was miraculous. I sat in the chair, which was still covered in polythene and it sagged lightly, absorbing my weight. Leaning back, my elbows resting on the chair arms, I felt extremely comfortable: a far cry from my polished plank on the *Courage*.

Reaching for the dial on the varnished console before me, I altered a point to starboard, away from the land. The clicking increased, the indicator went to ten degrees on the green side and the boat turned easily. The needle corrected to midships and she straightened on the new course. Now steady in this direction, I looked astern through the back window. Our wake was dead straight. There was no deviation in our course at all. This was amazing and so simple. Even the best helmsman had lapses of concentration and wandered off course. My new autopilot wouldn't err from her required direction. This piece of kit was not a luxury at all; it was an essential wheelhouse item. How had I managed before without this wizardry?

Jimmy beamed and winked, knowing I was delighted with this special toy, in what was a whole new box of goodies and they were all mine.

He switched off the automatic steering and I reluctantly relinquished my charge back to the temporary skipper. At my request we berthed on the outer wall, close to where our fishing gear was spread out. The lads could be putting the final stages of the gear together while I went with the builder and 'White Fish' man to the shipyard office for the final acceptance and hand over.

This was the moment I'd been waiting for, but it was such an anticlimax. "Is she OK?" Jimmy asked when we'd closed the door.

"Yeh, she's great. I'm really pleased with 'er," I enthused.

"Ye jus' need tae sign a paper tae accept herr then." He took a silver pen from his jacket, indicating the document on his desk, which Bessie had prepared.

I fumbled my signature without smudging the ink. I hated using fountain pens. Being left-handed, I usually moved my hand through the still wet ink as I wrote. My schoolbooks were always a mess. Peter Bruce signed on behalf of the lending authority and the deed was done, clearing the way for the final payment to the builders. The beautiful *Independence* was now mine, but it hadn't sunk in. Nothing seemed to have changed. "Arr ye's forr a dram?" Jimmy asked, shaking our hands on completion of the deal.

Peter said a swift "no," waving the palm of his hand vigorously. I'd only ever seen him drink a half of beer and that was at the launch party. I also declined the offer. I enjoyed a drink or two, but it didn't mix with work and I never touched whisky ever, so that was that. There was really nothing left to discuss. "She's a goood ship, ye'll do jus' fine in herr," the builder said, not quite ushering us through the door, but intimating that we should leave.

Out in the yard, the shipwrights were working on the new vessel. Her keel was laid and stem-post erected. Some other fortunate person was to be blessed with the fruits of these men's labour. By the time this hull was constructed, the harbour development would be finished and she would have a conventional launching. I thanked Peter for his involvement, shaking his hand, then headed for the breakwater to 'my' boat. The lads had completed their work when I arrived and the gear was ready for taking aboard. We were all unsure of what power and speed our winches were capable of, so it was a useful exercise handling the machinery in the calm of the harbour. It took two more hours to haul warps and bridles onto the winch, then the trawl and doors onto the deck. There was lots of other equipment to take on board from the yard and we also required more provisions. This would occupy a full morning tomorrow.

Shortly after midday, with engine running, all the electronics in the wheelhouse working and my mental tick list exhausted, we were prepared for sailing. I was about to step aboard, after ringing Dotty to say we were ready to leave, when a man in a suit carrying a briefcase approached and I sensed trouble. Men in suits are very conspicuous in fishing ports, especially when armed with document cases. "Are you the skipper?" he enquired in a typically, formal manner.

"I am."

"Do you know the number of your radio certificate, skipper?"

"Er, no I don't."

"Have you got it with you?"

"No, I 'aven't."

"You do have a radio certificate skipper?" he asked, raising his eyebrows and sounding even more official.

"Er, no, I 'aven't, but I 'ave a skipper's ticket. It's at 'ome."

He wasn't impressed. "I'm afraid this boat isn't going anywhere till you get a radio certificate," he said sternly.

"Well you'd better give me one then, 'cos she's goin' in 'alf an hour," I snapped back at him. "I've been 'angin' about 'ere too long already." I wasn't going to be detained for an undetermined period chasing a bit of paper. I'd spent three months at the Hull Nautical College five years earlier, gaining my fishing skipper's permit. I'd learned correct radio procedure, but hadn't been required to take an operator's exam.

Mr Suit couldn't have been expecting my outburst. He rocked back on his heels and spluttered, "I can give you the exam now, but it costs eight pounds."

"Righto let's do it then," I said, less aggressively, mollified a little now I wasn't to be prevented from sailing.

He asked me three questions. "What is a Mayday?" "What is a Pan message?" and "What is a Security message?"

I had no difficulty giving him the answers. The first is a distress call, to be answered and acted upon if possible, by anyone receiving it. The second is an emergency message, transmitted by person or persons in a dangerous circumstance, which could possibly escalate and the last, a navigation warning. These may not have been the definitive answers, but they were my interpretation.

He nodded and said, "that's fine, skipper."

Putting my hand in my pocket, I was dismayed to find only a crumpled fiver, but noticing Rusty working on the foredeck, I called out, "Rust, can yer lend me three quid?"

I was relieved when he produced three, Scottish pound notes. He handed the money ashore, grinned and mischievously asked, "is this t' last payment on t' boat? Can we go 'ome now?"

My examiner didn't get the joke. He was busy writing on an official looking pad. When he finally took the cash and my details, he said I'd receive my certificate by post and I was now free to carry on. Mr Suit left the pier satisfied and I felt greatly relieved as I watched him go. Three weeks later, through the post, I received a very smart, dark green, passport style certificate, embossed with gold.

A small group of Scottish friends and personnel from the yard had gathered to wave us off, including Jimmy and Madge Noble, George and Hazel McLean, who I'd first sailed to Scotland with and Dennis and Vera. I said my goodbyes to them all, thanking them for all they'd done, but I was keen to get away, before any other problems appeared.

I stepped aboard, climbing the steps to the wheelhouse. Rusty and Bluey were for'ard, Sid and Barry aft, ready to handle our ropes. I had to get this manoeuvre right. I didn't want to look as if I didn't know what I was doing with these spectators gathered. "Leggo for'ard, and can yer give us a spring on t' stern rope, please?" I requested through the open window to the workman in attendance. With the head rope free, I engaged the engine in reverse, putting the tiller to port, first making sure there was a fender between boat and quay at the after end, to absorb the impact. Her head slowly angled away from the pier. Putting the engine to neutral then into forward gear with rudder amidships, I called "leggo aft," to the hovering attendant. Sid slacked his rope from the cleat, allowing the man to release the stern line.

The *Independence* gracefully left the quay and I eased the tiller to port again, pointing her towards the wide entrance. She behaved perfectly. I leaned out of the window and looked back, waving an arm and shouting, "thanks for everything," to the waving group.

They too were waving and I heard calls of, "safe journey," and "good luck," as we moved away from the pier.

I was concentrating on steering with the tiller as we cruised down the harbour. The *Independence* was responding eagerly to each little touch, as if she too was keen to get to sea. The celebrations were over. We'd played hard and soon it would be time to work hard. Once clear of the harbour and incoming traffic, I began to relax. Setting the autopilot to north-east, I sat in my chair. It felt good to get clear of the land and its complications.

We steamed for about an hour in this direction, to a clear piece of ground marked on a plotting chart, given to me by George. Here we stopped to have a practice shoot with the trawl to test the winch and hydraulics properly. Getting the fishing gear over the side was a different experience from on board the *Courage*, where, with her low bulwarks, we were able to throw the ground gear over by hand. Now we had to use the boat's various lifting wires and ropes to get the heavy bobbins over the side. There was no rushing to get the net shot, this was only a dummy run. This new trawl, stretched out in the water alongside, looked huge.

The lads had already worked out for themselves who was to take up the various positions on deck. Rusty and Bluey became winch operators, Sid dealt with the after trawl door and Barry, the least experienced crewmember, handled the for'ard door. In this position he was visible to the winchmen and to me from the wheelhouse, in case he should make any mistakes.

There was little difference now in despatching the trawl to the seabed, as the winch did the work so the net was soon on the bottom. I wasn't intending to trawl for long, but even in the time it took to get a pot of tea and a sandwich, it became evident how useful the autopilot was when fishing. I was able to monitor the plotter and then if required, adjust the boat's heading at the touch of a dial.

We retrieved the gear without a hitch and were rewarded with half a basket of fish for our trouble. "That's tomorrow's breakfast taken care of," observed Sid, who was keen to test his new, prototype fish pan and had already mentally filleted the haddock, plaice and cod.

Now satisfied that the hydraulic system would operate under normal working conditions, I was content to set a course for home. It was late afternoon and we had about two hundred miles to steam. At a little over eight knots, this would be a twenty-four hour passage. The first of the Admiralty charts, 'Buckie to Arbroath', with Decca lines overlaid, was already on the chart table. We would steam south by east, plotting our position regularly to be sure we didn't veer too far off course.

Everyone was keen to take a watch; to sit in the comfortable chair and just press the watch-alarm button every four minutes. A low beeping noise was regularly emitted to ensure the person in the wheelhouse stayed awake. If the button wasn't pressed within a minute of this sound, a loud Claxton made sure everyone woke up. I was to set this off during the night, while making a cup of coffee in the galley.

We were making good time, steaming at slightly less than full speed, both for economy of fuel and ease on the engine. Rattray Head, then Buchan Ness were passed close to starboard, then the *Independence* headed for open sea as the land slipped away to the south-west. She had a good feel about her as she rolled gently in the lazy swell.

Sid, with his galley spotless, came into the wheelhouse to take the watch while I went below for the evening meal. He'd prepared home-made soup, followed by a roast beef and Yorkshire pudding dinner with trimmings, then steamed pudding and custard, which was superb. The gulls hovering at our stern would be disappointed if they were expecting leftovers. Sid had been an officers' cook in the army and certainly knew his stuff.

Two-hour watches continued through the night, though no one was very sleepy with the anticipation of our arrival home. Somewhere east of Arbroath, though well offshore, we changed charts to the 'Montrose to Berwick' copy, then before daylight, 'St Abbs to the River Tyne'. In the early morning twilight, as we drew closer to land again after crossing the Firth of Forth, the reassuring blink of the Longstone Light, of Grace Darling fame, showed in the far distance. There was less than a hundred miles to run.

Soon after sunrise, Sid, using both hands, lifted his new pan onto the stove. This piece of kit had been designed and commissioned by our cook, for frying food in bad weather. The oven top was fitted with moveable fiddles to prevent pans moving when the boat rolled. Sid's huge construction was the exact size to span two of the four oven rings and also fit within the fiddle frame. Fabricated by the port blacksmith from stainless steel, rectangular, high sided with an internal splash lip, this was the ultimate piece of galley hardware. Rusty suggested we have a launching and naming ceremony for this vessel too. Though at first we thought this monster was a little over engineered, the beast was to prove its worth, over and over again. A fine layer of cooking oil in the bottom would form a wave, running to and fro across the pan as the boat rolled. The ripple of oil would wash over fish, chips or whatever food was cooking, but would never spill from the receptacle, even in the heaviest weather, thanks to the lip. I never discovered what this construction cost, but whatever the price, it was good value.

Breakfast was a mountain of various types of fried fish, in golden, crispy batter, accompanied by mushy peas, with tea, bread and butter. There were several pieces of fish left over from breakfast, such was the quantity, but this wasn't wasted either. Cold, fried fish sandwiches with vinegar and salt were one of our favourite snacks. The hungry gulls had long since departed, seeking better pickings.

The excitement grew throughout the morning, and was further added to when the remaining chart, 'River Tyne to Flamborough Head' was produced. We could now see our destination marked and could measure the remaining distance with dividers.

The lads took care not to foul the revolving radar scanner when decking the vessel out with the flags and bunting ready for our arrival, as we drew closer. Now we could see the old ruined abbey at Whitby to the south-west and the white, chunky lighthouse nestling into the cliffs. It was here the *Van Tromp* had been tragically lost. There was no sign at all of her now. The sea had swallowed her up.

The radar was marking the distinctive Bay Wyke on our starboard bow. I'd spent many nights trawling in the bay for Dover sole as a teenage deck hand on the *Whitby Rose*. It seemed now as if the clock had stopped as the *Independence* crawled along this familiar coastline. The beautiful bay, with the old smugglers' village clinging to the cliffs at the northern end and the towering heights of Ravenscar Cliffs to the south looked spectacular in the afternoon sunshine, but the magnificence was lost on us. We just wanted to get home.

With an hour to go and Scarborough Castle headland in sight on our stem, I called the agent's office on the radio, asking them to notify Dotty, who had a list of phone numbers to ring, to report our imminent arrival. There was also a consignment of drink to come on board for anyone wishing to 'wet the baby's head'.

We passed slowly by the waterfall, known to coblemen and anglers as 'Watta Slash', probably meaning, 'Water Splash'. This fall was fed by a hidden lake, high up on an inaccessible, overgrown plateau, within the cliffs. The cataract, splashing white in its almost vertical drop, had never been known to dry up, even in the hottest of summers, though it did reduce to a trickle.

Uneven layers of the earth's strata, clearly visible in the cliff face, moved down to the sea as we cruised south, to the aptly named, Littlecliff. I'd caught crab and lobster here with Dad, in the coble *Alison* in my youth. I used to imagine dinosaurs and other prehistoric creatures roaming the shore along the coast, as we hauled our pots close to shore. This wasn't difficult to visualise; there was no sign here at all of man's influence on the planet.

Slowly we crept past the pretty coves of Hayburn Wyke and Cloughton Wyke to reach Creek Point, the only remaining promontory on our passage. This headland was marked as Long Nab on the chart. Now only fifteen minutes from home and drawing towards Scalby Ness, we could see 'ant like' cars in the distance on the Marine Drive. This road, passing round the Castle Headland, linking Scarborough's two bays, was a marvellous Victorian structure, which had stood for more than seventy years, battered by the worst the North Sea had to offer.

Almost at the end of our journey, time seemed to speed up again and soon we were crossing the North Bay. Rusty pointed out a couple of people waving from the promenade. These two sentries, whoever they were, were seen climbing into a car and heading towards the harbour, to announce our approach.

The flowing tide had half covered, 'Coffee Pot Rock' on the north-east corner of the headland where, as a boy I'd gathered limpets; bait for the long-line fishers in winter months. Even then I'd wanted to be a fisherman and dreamt of being a skipper.

Through the opened windows, above the noise of our machinery, I could now hear the incessant noise of thousands of kittiwakes, nesting on the cliffs beyond the road. I eased the engine down and switched to manual steering with lots of time to spare. I was still unsure of my new command. The crew were already preparing mooring ropes, though they'd not be needed for long. Our welcoming party would be expecting a trip around the bay to experience the new vessel first hand. I gently turned the *Independence* to starboard, lining her up for the harbour mouth. A little crowd of family and friends began waving and cheering on the West Pier of the entrance as we hove into view. At the front of the group, I could see Dotty with our two excited bairns; both with little flags, which they were shaking furiously. We were home.

I could feel my heart pounding as I tried to concentrate on steering and waving to the reception party as we slowly sailed past them, heading for an empty berth at the fish market. I spied Mum and Dad, my sisters and their spouses and Dotty's folks, directing my waving at them in acknowledgement.

I felt quite light-headed, as if I was floating on air. Was this really happening to me? Not even in my wildest imagination could I have dreamt of a moment like this. I was entering my home port, in this superb new vessel, with a huge family welcome.

A sudden shiver ran through me, briefly spoiling the moment. This was only the start of this new venture. Suppose things didn't work out and I couldn't make the boat pay? The monthly repayments to the bank were going to be massive. Had I taken on more than I could manage?

What did the future hold? Only time would tell.

The End

The 'Bottom End'

The 'Bottom End'of Scarborough, like all towns and villages on the coast has changed dramatically over recent years. The inhabitants who lived in the area have mostly passed on. The way of life and the fishing industry they knew, to which this book relates, has gone forever.

I hope that by recording the characters who feature in these pages and the life that they led, their memory will live on.

'Bottom Enders' recently departed

Jack 'Bulla' Bullamore
Jack 'Bludge' Blades
Ben 'Benjy' Colling
Eileen Crawford
Marcel Eade
Walter 'Pellet' Eves Jnr.
Richard 'Foxy' Fox
Billy 'Sausage' Haylett
John Howard
Dorothy Kirkpatrick
Charlie 'Cutsy' Leader
William 'Billy Boono' Mainprize
Jack 'Bosun' Mann
George 'Nowty' Normandale
Fred 'Skelly' Skelton

In writing this book the author intended to give his readers an insight into the way of life in the 1970s as seen through his eyes. It is clearly acknowledged that certain events are not in chronological order. The tales have been telescoped for reasons of brevity and so the volume doesn't read as a diary. There were many, long, cold winter nights spent rolling about at sea, going through the motions and catching little.

Some characters depicted are fictitious.

A FRIARAGE INFANTS SCHOOL HYMN

When lamps are lighted in the town
The boats set out to sea
The fishers watch when night comes down
They work for you and me

We little children go to bed
Before we sleep we pray
That God watch o'er the fishermen
And bring them back by day

The boats come in at early dawn
Before we wake in bed
Upon the beach their boats are drawn
And all their nets are spread

God has watched o'er the fishermen
Upon the deep dark sea
And brought them safely home again
Where they are glad to be

With grateful thanks for the reminder to the Holgate sisters, Pamela, Barbara and Brenda.